CW01333422

BEHIND THE FORBIDDEN CORNER

BEHIND THE
FORBIDDEN CORNER

COLIN ARMSTRONG

FORBIDDEN CORNER
2001

First published 2001 by
THE FORBIDDEN CORNER
Tupgill Park
Middleham

© Colin Armstrong 2001

All rights reserved. No part of this book may be reproduced, stored or introduced into a retrieval system, or transmitted in any form or by any means (electronic, mechanical, photocopying, recording or otherwise) without the prior permission of the author.

The right of Colin Armstrong to be identified as the author of this work has been asserted by him in accordance with the Copyright, Designs and Patents Act 1988.

ISBN 0 9541047 0 6 hardback
0 9541047 1 4 paperback

Designed, printed and bound by
SMITH SETTLE
Ilkley Road, Otley, West Yorkshire LS21 3JP

To Cecilia, Nick, Diana and Alex
the most important people in my life

CONTENTS

The Armstrongs	1
The Racing Armstrongs	16
1945 Onwards — Colin	27
Mevagissy	34
Flinton	36
Harper Adams	38
Swaziland	42
Writtle	48
USA	51
ICI	55
Malaysia	58
Mexico	69
Ecuador	75
Bolivia	107
Mapan	116
British Caledonian	125
Ecuador 1980	135
The Niño	153
Tupgill 1980–85	156
Holidays	175
Schooldays	179
Ecuador 1986–90	185
Mapan 1991 todate	204
Agripac: Recent Times	214
The Forbidden Corner	235
Court and Social	271
Epilogue	284

LIST OF ILLUSTRATIONS

Johnnie Armstrong returning to Gilnochie Tower	5
Bill of Sale for the George Hotel	9
Bob on his horse	10
Lamplough family at Manor House Hotel	11
Clifton Hill House	12
Clifton Hill Hotel	13
Gerald in uniform	13
Middleham Village about 1800	14
Middleham 1908	14
Capt. J. Fielden, Bob and Lord Lonsdale	15
Gerald and Bob	18
Bob by his car	19
Gerald riding H.M. horse 'Whitehead'	20
'Tiggy' Wilson with her sisters Diana and Kathleen	21
Do, 1960	22
Kate, Colin and Jane with Nanny Bobby Reynolds	23
Jane, Kate and Colin, 1949	24
Kate, Colin and Jane, 1998	25
Margaret and Doug Weatherill with Florrie Hammond	32
Colin on Swaziland residence permit	43
Colin, 1968	49
Colin and Elaine in front of the Tupgill gates	93
The Agripac staff	100
The Mapan house	120
Colin and Ceci, 1982	137
The oldest cowboy on Mapan	137
Mapan's Brahman cattle	138
The 2000 Q.B.P.	149
H.M.A. Richard Lavers, Brigitte Lavers, Ceci and Colin	151
Aerial photo of Tupgill Stables	157
Building of the Fishing Temple	158
Removing the plaster	159
In its undress state	160
The new look	160
The renewed entrance to Tupgill stables	164
The building of the clock tower	165
The digging of the lake	165
The finished clock tower	166
Ferngill House	168

Aerial photo showing new farm buildings	169
Statue showing the Armstrong crest	171
Racehorses passing the lake	173
Alex, Diana and Nick with Charlie	182
H.M.S. *Montrose* visit	192
Colin greeting H.R.H. The Princess Royal	201
Anthony Rosen's tour visit	211
The Agripac sales force	213
The Zeneca Partnership Club	216
Agripac shops	220
The Agripac truck	220
Tomas Guerrero, Chris Richards, John Greaves, Chris Bailey and Colin	222
The 25 year celebrations	227
Agripac head office	228
The wind howled down the yard	235
Malcolm generally took an idea and magnified it	237
A large 25 foot hole had been dug	238
Denis Fawcett	239
The dairy cottages	241
The new Tupgill gates	242
Detail of the Tupgill gates	242
The main chamber	244
The boulder canyon	246
The Temple	247
The glass pyramid	248
The thatched bridge	250
The castle	251
The stepping stones	252
The eye of the needle	253
Denis building the face tower	254
The peeing boy	256
The green man	258
Two ladies had jumped from the tower	259
Closed by the planners	262
Newspaper cuttings	266, 267
Follies magazine	269
Gilnochie tower	272
Coat of arms	273
The Armstrong family	274
Garden party at Buckingham Palace	278
Ceci presenting the Armstrong Cup, 1986	282
Diana, Nick and Alex with Sushi	285
Colin and Ceci, 2000	286

ACKNOWLEDGEMENTS

The following people have been of significant help in my writing of this book; Malcolm Tempest for his suggestions and cartoons, Rocio Torres (who has recently been appointed British Vice Consul in Guayaquil) for her careful typing of the manuscript and Elaine Lister for helping me put it all together.

Colin Armstrong
Tupgill, April 2001

THE ARMSTRONGS

THE ROOTS OF MY FAMILY go back for ever or at least for, say, 100,000 years in our present form. But we must pick a moment in time to start our story. The Americans as often as not take the *Mayflower* as their starting point. Some British families can date their origins to the Norman invasion of 1066: others are content to remember their grandparents and leave it at that.

In the case of the Armstrongs, our exact origins are obscure but it is a fair assumption that we are descended from Norwegian Vikings who arrived in the Solway Firth in the tenth century AD. The surname Armstarker, meaning Armstrong, still exists in Scandinavia today and the Vikings were well known for using physical descriptions as names, such as 'Blood-axe', 'Blue tooth' and 'Fork beard'.

So let's take a date at random and start the Armstrong story in AD 904, the year in which Eric called the strong-arm rowed up the Solway Firth to join his cousins who had left Norway the year before.

For generations, the family had lived at the top of a fjord near where Bergen is today, but the last years had been dreadful. Feuding between local warlords had reduced the time and manpower available to harvest the land. The winters were hard, the people weak, famine caused deaths and finally the pirate raid by people from further North had destroyed everything. His parents dead, his sisters taken by the pirates, and only surviving because he had been hunting away from home when they struck, Eric was alone in the world.

He had heard of the colonies being set up overseas. The Vikings had begun raiding the prosperous lands of Britain years ago. Then they had over-wintered there and finally they had stayed to colonise, taking their women with them. It was easy to join an expedition. There was always a need for sturdy young men to row the difficult waters of the North Sea around the top of Scotland. Eric was certainly sturdy: though only of average height, he had always been strong and even as a young boy took his turn with his father at the plough. So the rowing was not difficult for him. It had been an easy trip, anyway. The summer was well advanced but the strong autumn winds had not yet appeared. Still, he looked forward to getting ashore. They had been rowing up the Solway Firth for some hours now and the land was getting closer on each side — flat, marshy land, quite thick with vegetation and trees. He could see a settlement ahead where he hoped he could get news of his cousins. They must have settled in by now, he thought. He had not heard anything from them for few ships made the trip back to Norway, and it was a one-way flow. He wondered if they had acquired land and wives, had started families in this rich promised land that his people had taken by the sword. The fighting was over now, his people and the native people had mixed, married and intermingled for some years. This was the place for him, a future beckoned, all would be well here, and the past of death and despair was behind him. He just knew it.

1069

Alfredin saw the rabbit fall and went to pick it up and remove his arrow, which had pierced its neck, with a shout of triumph. He enjoyed hunting and was good at it, which was why he was spared the farm work more often than his brothers were. He inevitably brought back something for the pot and it was more than welcome, as the family was large and the farm small.

Eight generations had passed since Eric first landed. He had been successful in finding his cousins but less so in getting land. The cousins had arrived penniless and had enlisted in a band of mercenaries, a footloose and poorly paid profession, particularly in times of peace. But these were mercifully short as the local landowners were more often at each other's throats, or rather land, than not.

Eric was a useful man with a sword and was welcomed by them. For his part, he was less enthusiastic. He had seen all the fighting he wanted to see in his young life; his ambition was to farm the land and raise a family. But necessity is a hard master and Eric joined the mercenary band of good-natured, if somewhat, rough fellows. This employment was short-lived, however, as his group was ambushed on only his second raid. Most of them were killed and Eric was wounded in the leg by an arrow, taken prisoner and thrown into a prison hut belonging to his employer's adversary. Settlement between the principals in the conflict involved the delivery of prisoners to work as slaves in the victor's fields.

Not what Eric had dreamed of, but at least he was out of the dangerous trade of soldiering and into farming. His master was a fair man and noticed that Eric worked with a will and put his considerable strength to good, productive use. He was made foreman of a group of workers and allowed to marry, but remained a slave. Towards the end of his life, he was given a small plot of ground to work for himself.

Between the time of Eric and that of Alfredin, the family had been released from slavery and become free men but were still poor. The little plot of land which Eric had been allowed to farm had eventually been acquired together with several more fields but it was still only just enough to keep them all alive. So today Alfredin was hunting to complete the family dinner.

As he bent to pick up the rabbit, he glimpsed something blue among the bushes. It moved and he reached for his bow and slotted an arrow. Rabbits did not come dressed in blue but perhaps outlaws did. The countryside was generally peaceful here but occasionally thieves and broken men were to be found in this heath on the run from who knows where. Peaceful folk did not travel without their lord's permission in Norman times.

She got up suddenly from the bush and he was struck by her youth, yellow hair and pleading look. He put his bow down, then raised it again quickly as a second figure stood up. 'Peace', she said, 'this is my grandfather.'

They were travel-stained and hungry so, on an impulse, he held up the rabbit and saw hope light up their faces. Well, he would just have to get another for the family lunch. The rabbit was soon skinned and prepared and after they had eaten, he heard their story.

They were fugitives from Coverdale, twelve days' journey away towards the south-east. The Saxons of the north of England had rebelled against their hated Norman overlords and William the Conqueror had ordered that the land be harried in reprisal. Harried it had been, indeed. Whole villages had been destroyed, thousands of people killed, women raped and those people who survived thrown off their land.

Mary, the maid of Coverdale, lived with her family on a little farm called Tupgill towards the eastern end of the dale where her father and three brothers raised cattle and sheep, grazing the fells all summer and making hay on the lower fields to feed the stock in winter. They also traded livestock, buying it from the Scottish stock masters who would come this far south and selling it in the towns of York and Ripon, so the family was relatively prosperous among their people. Mary and her grandfather were away from home, collecting berries in the woods when the Norman soldiers arrived. Her brothers could not stand by and see everything taken from them so they fought, but there were only four of them against twenty men. They had no hope of success and were cut down, as was her mother who ran from the house to try to plead for them. Then the house and buildings were set on fire and the soldiers rounded up the livestock and took it to their master, Bertrand Le Scrope, who had been rewarded with the title to all the land that he harried.

When it was safe, Mary and her grandfather approached the house and over the next two days buried their dead. Then, as they could not stay there any longer, they headed north because they had heard that Scotland had been spared this punishment. But before they left, her grandfather got up sadly from where he had been resting and walked into the still smouldering remains of the cottage and motioned her to help him to lift the debris from one corner of the room. She worked with a will as she knew what he was looking for. Eventually they unearthed the iron box which had lain under the floor, opened it and took out a large leather bag of coins. The Norman troops had been too quick to kill and destroy. If he had been there, her grandfather could have bought them all protection.

Cumberland was spared the vengeance of the Normans so Mary and her grandfather found sanctuary there. In due course, the old man spent his money buying a good farm and Alfredin became his son-in-law.

1530

Will Armstrong was prosperous, middle-aged and worried. He sat around the table with the other Armstrong chiefs waiting for Johnnie to speak. They had been summoned to Gilnockie Tower at Hollows a week ago and all the important ones were present.

Much had changed on the English-Scottish border since Alfredin had become a husband to the maid of Coverdale and, in due course, the owner of a good farm. The border folk had formed clans: Maxwells, Johnsons, Kerrs, Elliots, Nixons, Crosers, Grahams, Scotts and many more, but the greatest of all were the Armstrongs. The chief of the clan, Thomas Armstrong, had his towerhouse at Mangerton but he was old. The clan was run by his younger brother Johnnie from Gilnockie Tower on the River Esk, just five miles on the Scottish side of the present-day border. At that time, this area was called the Debatable Land, claimed by both England and Scotland but in fact held by the reiver clans, whose allegiance was to neither and only to themselves. The border area was in constant turbulence with clan raiding clan, burning, killing and stealing cattle, sheep, horses or whatever else came to hand.

Both governments had appointed forces for law and order — the Wardens of the Marches. The English West March was based on Carlisle Castle whose warden at this time was Lord Dacre, and his counterpart in Scotland was Lord Maxwell. But neither held sway over the Debatable Land, an area of marsh and forest difficult for troops to penetrate but known to the reivers. In addition, because England and Scotland were perpetually at war, the reivers played both sides off against each other, the Scots reivers raiding into England with the tacit support of Maxwell, while the English reivers raided Scotland with Dacre's support.

Two years earlier, Dacre, provoked beyond measure by Johnnie Armstrong, had invaded in force and burnt Gilnockie Tower but, on returning home, had found that the Armstrongs had been visiting and had burnt his house of Netherby.

But today the clan had heard of a new development. The young Scottish King James V had had enough of the anarchy along his border, which made peaceful travel impossible, and had raised an army of 10,000 men to pacify them. He was camped at Carlenrig some distance away and had summoned the chiefs of the border clans to meet him there. The men in the room argued hotly for some hours. Most did not want to obey the king and said that he could not be trusted. Others, including Johnnie, were for making their peace and ratifying the lands which they held. 'Make peace now', said Johnnie, 'while we are at the height of our power. Even the king would not dare cross us: we, who can raise 3,000 men, who can keep the Scottish border safe for him although he cannot do it for himself. We will go and show him the Armstrongs. Fifty of our best will come with me, decked out in our finest. We will show this king who is the ruler of Liddesdale and let him take care to be our friend.'

THE ARMSTRONGS

Johnnie Armstrong returning to Gilnochie Tower, 1530. Painted by Henry Hetherington Emerson in 1880. *By kind permission of The National Trust.*

They set out on the following day, making a fine show, each mounted on a sturdy Border horse, wearing helmet, breastplate and sword and carrying a lance. The people lined the roads in villages which they passed and cheered their Johnnie, the finest chief of all. His uncle Will rode alongside Johnnie but his sombre face contrasted with the happy one of his headstrong young nephew. It was wrong to go. Their strength was here, where their kinsfolk lived. Their blood ties crossed the border. Even when raiding Cumberland, they had spies, refuges and help. They had guerilla tactics — in and out before armed resistance could be organised — mobility on their horses, and knowledge of the country and how to cross the treacherous Solway Moss, where pursuit was impossible. They had done well as a clan and had land, cattle and wealth. Because of their fierce reputation, they had attracted outlaws and broken men who had enlisted with them and been glad to take the surname Armstrong, which struck terror far and wide.

Now they were taking a terrible risk - marching north with only fifty men. away from their area and allies, to parley with a king who was an unknown quantity. They did not need to go. James had only a tenuous hold on his army and not enough money to keep it together for more than a few weeks. Then he would go home again and leave the Armstrongs alone. He had not dared come to them but had played on Johnnie's vanity, daring him to put the clan into his power. He must have known that Johnnie would accept the challenge —

Johnnie who, since his earliest days, had been daring, fearless and vain, the hero of a hundred raids, his name sung in ballads and now probably wealthier than his monarch. No, Johnnie would never refuse a challenge.

Will thought of his home, his fortified bastle-house not five miles up the River Esk from Hollows, his wife and the three surviving children. They were all grown up now, he assured himself, so even if the worst were to happen, he had left heirs.

They rode into the royal camp in style. There were many men there but it was not an impressive army, just conscripted farm labourers brought by their lairds and poorly clad and armed. Even the nobles were outshone by Johnnie, whose armour and jewelled belt sparkled in the morning sun.

They dismounted as ordered and handed their horses to soldiers before approaching the king. A great mistake, thought Will. The reiver fights on horseback: once dismounted he is an ordinary soldier.

James stood among his lords while Johnnie approached with Will and two other members of the family. The king's face darkened when he saw them.

The messenger galloped all night and at dawn brought the dreadful news to Old Thomas Armstrong, laird of Mangerton, chief of the clan. 'They are all hanged!' he cried.

At first, the party had been friendly but the king had made many references to Johnnie's fine armour, jewels and wealth. 'Too good for an over-mighty subject,' he said and, at a signal, his men had overpowered the Armstrongs, Will and several others being badly wounded in the fray. They were all hanged from the trees nearby then James awarded the Armstrong lands to Lord Maxwell.

1815

Richard Armstrong was seventy-two but still active. He sat on the front of the dray with the reins of the two horses in his hands while Robert, his eighteen-year-old son, walked up the hill, leading the near-side horse by its bridle. The load was heavy and there was still a long way to go to Longtown. They had set out from Arthuret at six that morning.

Richard could scarcely write his name but he had a prodigious memory and liked to while away these journeys thinking of the stories his mother had told him of glories past. For the family had not always been poor. He did not know how much to believe as some of the stories went back many, many years to the time of Johnnie Armstrong of Gilnockie Tower at Hollows. He knew the tower. It was a ruin, now standing on a bend of the River Esk on the other side of the Scots Dike. She had told him that he was related to Johnnie, who was a chief and had been hanged by King James. Hard to believe, he thought, thinking of how they lived today.

But there was no doubt about his father John. He had owned land and a large house at Bewcastle, had been quite prosperous, in fact. But he had lost everything, including his life, for a stupid cause, thought Richard — that of so-called Bonny Prince Charlie. Richard had been only two years old when that dashing prince had landed in Scotland, rallied the clans to his cause, defeated the English at Prestonpans and marched into England at Carlisle. John the romantic, the impulsive, with stories of his famous namesake ringing in his ears, had enlisted with the prince despite his wife and family's protests. The Highland army had marched proudly from Carlisle to Penrith and even as far south as Derby. They expected the English Jacobins to join them and a few did so, but most waited to see what King George would do. Then disaster struck. The clans wanted to go home. They had already ventured too far into England; all the prince's arguments and promises could not hold them. They left in droves and the prince could only follow them back to Scotland. King George sent his son, the duke of Cumberland, in a pursuit which ended on a moor near Inverness called Culloden.

Although only three years old, he clearly remembered the day that the soldiers came for his father. The rebellion over, 'Butcher' Cumberland was going to make an example. John had been denounced by the good folk of Canonbie, those who had cheered the prince as he passed but failed to find the courage to join him. John was tried at the Carlisle special assizes, found guilty as a traitor and hanged together with many others. His mother had always told Richard that he could have fled to the American colonies to avoid retribution but was listless. He had set his heart on this romantic cause and had been let down. He considered himself a loyal Scot, filled his mind with tales of past daring and felt devastated by the lack of tenacity in the prince's army. Moreover, he argued that if he was taken and hanged, there would be an end to it whereas if the family fled, they would lose the farm and everything that they possessed. He was hanged all right but he had failed to understand the laws regarding traitors. Everything was forfeit to the Crown.

Richard, his mother and baby sister were evicted with only the clothes they wore and everyone was forbidden to give them food or shelter. But blood is thicker than water and one poor relative had taken them in. He was a bachelor who lived at Bewcastle and earned his living by carrying goods short distances with his old horse and cart. Richard liked horses and soon made himself useful, working long hours until at last the business was left to him. Now he and Robert had three carts and drays and good horses to pull them.

The horses plodded slowly onwards as Richard day dreamed. How foolish of his father to throw away everything on a dream! Though they had done well enough not to want, they had had to struggle. Dreams of reiver days and glories had almost ruined the family. Yet those times were long, long gone. The union of the crowns in 1603, when James VI of Scotland became James I of England, had put an end to it. Now there was nowhere to hide. James had sent his army and those of the Armstrongs, Elliots or Grahams who survived were scattered to Ireland and England or became mercenary soldiers in the continental wars. James had succeeded in doing by force what his grandfather had failed to do by treachery.

6TH DECEMBER, 1862

'Sign here and witness here, please' said the solicitor. John William did so and then, turning, kissed his wife Eliza. 'It's ours now,' he said, 'for the next thirty years. The George Hotel in Penrith is ours by right of the lease and thereafter; perhaps we will be able to buy it outright'.

The great day had come at last — the third good thing to have happened in the last fifteen months, thought John. The first was, of course, his marriage to Eliza in Newcastle on the 9th September, 1861: the second the birth of Robert last July. Life was a bed of roses just now but it hadn't always been that way.

His father, Robert, had died in 1839, one year before his grandfather, Richard, who survived into his ninety-seventh year. Long years but sad ones, as Robert had taken to drink and little by little lost the carrying business that Richard had painfully built up, while Richard was too old and feeble to repeat his earlier success. His widowed mother, Ann, had run a small boarding house and John became a domestic servant in a large house in Haltwhistle which stands on Hadrian's Wall.

It was while working there that John met Eliza Ward. Her father, Bernard, had brought his family to stay at the house and, much to her parents' dismay, Eliza fell in love with John. They reacted as most parents would whose daughter loves a man of lesser status and removed her promptly to Newcastle, forbidding them to meet. Then fate took a hand. Bernard Ward was the agent of landowners in Ireland and during the troubles there, he was shot and killed by the Fenians while collecting rents. Eliza's mother was left a wealthy widow but, being of a somewhat weaker nature than her strong-willed daughter, eventually gave in and allowed them to wed, even putting up the necessary funds for them to start married life as the proprietors of the George Hotel.

It is no wonder that John was pleased with his lot. The long-established George Hotel was the largest and best placed in Penrith, an important market town. Standing on a corner in the middle of town, it had twenty-four bedrooms, a large assembly room, a courtyard and stabling; and from it the coaches ran a service to Ullswater in the Lake District. Indeed, it was where Bonny Prince Charlie had stayed on his journey to England — an irony not lost on John, whose namesake had spent both his life and fortune in the venture.

The hotel prospered by dint of hard work and Eliza's strength of character and six more children were born. But the curse of the father was visited upon the son and John, who had always been outgoing and good company, began to spend many hours drinking with his customers. The end came in 1882 when cirrhosis took its toll.

Robert Ward Armstrong (called Bob) was twenty by that time and took command of the family, seeing to his brothers' and sisters' education. But Bob was not cut out to be a hotelier. His interest was horses and he had ridden a pony since he was three years old. He was well known as a jockey, riding all over Britain wherever he could get a mount and bought a racehorse with his

CUMBERLAND LAKE DISTRICT.

TO HOTEL KEEPERS, BREWERS, WINE MERCHANTS, & CAPITALISTS GENERALLY.

PLANS, PARTICULARS, AND CONDITIONS OF SALE

Of that very Valuable Old-established, Well-accustomed, Freehold, Family and Commercial

HOTEL & POSTING ESTABLISHMENT,

KNOWN AS

"THE GEORGE HOTEL"

Advantageously situate in

DEVONSHIRE STREET, PENRITH,

With the spacious and popular ASSEMBLY ROOM adjoining thereto, and the very ample Range of

STABLING & COACH HOUSES,

And other accommodation of a like nature at the rear thereof, as now occupied by Mr. R. W. Armstrong, whose lease will expire in February, 1893; together with the conveniently arranged

IRONMONGER'S SHOP

And numerous Store Rooms in the Basement thereof also situate in DEVONSHIRE STREET, adjoining "The George," as now in the occupation of Messrs. Thos. Altham and Sons, as yearly tenants, which

WILL BE SOLD BY AUCTION

(Subject to conditions herewith),

By Messrs. M. DEROME & SON,

OF KENDAL,

IN THE ASSEMBLY ROOM,

Upon the Premises,

On TUESDAY, DECEMBER 6th, 1892,

AT TWO O'CLOCK IN THE AFTERNOON.

Messrs. GEO. WATSON & SON, Architects, of No. 3 St. Andrew's Place, Penrith, will shew the Premises.

All enquiries respecting the Property must be addressed to A. N. BOWMAN, Esq., No. 3 Castle Street, Carlisle; or Messrs. CURREY, HOLLAND, & CURREY, 14 Great George Street, Westminster, London, S.W.

Bill of Sale for the George Hotel, Penrith, 1892. Bought by Fred Armstrong (Bob's Brother).

Bob on his horse, 1915.

brother Fred. So he began his career as a trainer while Fred ran the George, which he eventually bought when the lease expired in 1892 and kept until his death in 1945.

Bob soon gave up riding as a jockey and concentrated on training, first in stables at Penrith and later a few miles away when he bought a stable yard at Eamont Bridge. Here, he attracted the attention of the local landowner, the earl of Lonsdale, for whom he trained horses for many years. One of the services Bob provided for Lord Lonsdale was to find the seventy-eight matched chestnut horses of sixteen hands in height, which were needed to pull the carriages when Kaiser Wilhelm visited Lowther Castle in 1894. Lonsdale was also a patron of boxing, presenting the well-known Lonsdale belt.

Christmas 1896 and Bob was extremely nervous. The Lamplough family were gathered in the large salon of the Manor House hotel at Leamington Spa, which they owned. They were all tall so Bob was dwarfed among them; they were wealthy farmers and two were doctors. There had been an archbishop of York in the family. They looked down on Bob in more ways than one but he could put up with that. The prize was well worth the pain. The prize was Eleanor, Nellie to all. Good-looking, intelligent and with a mind of her own,

Lamplough family at Manor House Hotel, Leamington Spa, 1907. Bob Armstrong, *second from right back row*; Nellie *fourth person from right second row*; Gerald *far left second row*; Do middle of the children.

Nellie had defied her family and married Robert just three weeks before. The northern race horse trainer, even if the owner of a hotel (but not one in the same class as the Manor House!), was clearly not good enough for Robert Lamplough and his family. But Nellie had decided her future and that was that.

They moved into the Eamont Bridge house and stables and it was there that Doris was born in 1897, followed by Gerald in 1899 and Fred in 1904 (always known as Sam to differentiate him from his uncle).

Bob was a good trainer and Nellie ran the stable yard with its team of thirty men and boys and sixty horses very capably. The household was also large because it accommodated not just the family, but also the constant stream of visitors who owned horses with them and would come for up to a week at a time to watch their horses work on the gallops in Lowther Park.

Nellie was intrepid. She was one of the first women in Cumberland to learn to drive and drove Bob to the races from 1906 onwards in a Gladiator car. It soon became apparent to all that Nellie wore the trousers in the Armstrong household.

Nellie had a dream and that was to build a house to her own design. The result was Clifton Hill, a few miles from Eamont Bridge, and she joyfully moved

Clifton Hill House, Eamont Bridge, 1914, showing Sam, Gerald and Bob.

Clifton Hill Hotel, 1980.

the family in in 1912. But her pleasure was short-lived. The 1914 war saw the ploughing up of grassland to plant corn because food imports had been interrupted. Lord Lonsdale allowed Lowther Park to be ploughed up and consequently Bob had nowhere to gallop his horses. A move was imperative as racing had been largely stopped in England for the duration of the war.

Broken-hearted, Nellie had to watch her beloved house being sold after having lived there for only two years. The family moved to stables called Ruanbeg on the Curragh in Ireland with their staff, horses, bags and baggage. At that time, The Curragh was a military camp and Gerald, who was then seventeen, persuaded his father to allow him to leave Rossall School and join the Fifth Lancers regiment. He was commissioned as a second lieutenant but the war was to end

Gerald in uniform, 1917.

Middleham Village about 1800.

Middleham 1908 — as Bob would have seen it when he first went to Tupgill in 1904.

Capt. J. Fielden, Bob and Lord Lonsdale at Newmarket Bloodstock Sales,
14th July, 1936.

war was to end before he saw active service. This was just as well as they trained with the bamboo lances of the last century and tanks, barbed wire and machine guns had already made the cavalry obsolete.

In November 1904, Bob had travelled by train on that lovely scenic route from Carlisle to Garsdale station at the top of Wensleydale in Yorkshire. There he hired a pony and trap to take him to Middleham, an historic town dominated by its ruined castle which had been a centre of horse racing for centuries and where great trainers like Dobson Peacock, Harry Hall and John Osbourne dominated northern racing. He lunched at the famous White Swan pub and rode up Coverdale to look at Tupgill Park, which was for sale.

Tupgill Park was the very same farm that had been owned by the Maid of Coverdale's family over 800 years previously, though Bob was not to know it. Now it consisted of a good house, fifty stables, fifty acres of land and the necessary cottages, barns and stable boys' accommodation to make it an ideal training location; especially as it had direct access to the Middleham Moor gallops. It was a bargain and he bought it as an investment. As he had no immediate need for it, he leased it to a Captain Scott, who trained there until 1920.

The First World War over, Bob looked to return from Ireland to England. Clifton Hill had been sold so the family went to Tupgill Park. Nellie, as so often, took charge but insisted that the house be totally remodelled and enlarged before she moved in. It had started life as a farmhouse in the seventeenth century, and been extended later but was still relatively small in 1920. Nellie had bow windows added both downstairs and upstairs on the south side, and a dining room and conservatory built.

THE RACING ARMSTRONGS

Bob was now sixty but the family fame spread in the racing world. Gerald the gentleman, sportsman and keen 'amateur' helped his father to train. But his great love was riding and he won over 100 races on the flat as an amateur jockey. Sam was for a while a professional jockey, a very 'professional' trainer and business-man and made a fortune. Sam, the younger son, persuaded his father to buy Ashgill, an adjoining stable to Tupgill, in 1924 and there he began his career as a trainer at the age of twenty, the youngest ever to hold a licence from the Jockey Club. Today, it is the Arabs who hold the purse strings in racing; in the last century it was the British aristocracy; but in the 1920s, it was the Indian princes. The Maharajah of Baroda sent Sam three horses. These were successful and Baroda's string of horses increased to the extent that Sam had to rent extra stables all around Ashgill to accommodate them. Finally, Baroda asked Sam to buy him a large stable in Newmarket in 1946 and to move into it as his resident private trainer. Sam bought Warren Place and, selling Ashgill, moved his sixty horses, family, staff and all in a chartered train from Leyburn station to Newmarket, the heart of British racing.

Meanwhile Gerald assisted Bob and rode winners, played rugby, squash and flew his two-seater monoplane, called Thankerton after a horse he had trained. Flying was then a simple affair — one learned to fly, got a plane and was away. There was no radio and no air traffic controls, and one navigated with a map, flying low enough to be able to follow roads or railway lines. If you ran out of fuel, you landed in any field and hitched a lift to the nearest petrol station, carrying a five-gallon jerry can. Of course, not everyone cared for this hazardous way of travel. Gerald once flew Charlie Brown, his stable jockey, from Tupgill over the Pennines to race at Carlisle. They got lost in a snowstorm and, having finally landed at the racecourse, he said jokingly: 'If you don't win this race, Charlie, you can find your own way home.' Charlie replied: 'Win or lose, there's no way you'll get me in that plane again.'

It was the 31st August, 1934 as the horses lined up at the starting gate at the Bank Holiday meeting at Ripon. Gerald was drawn as number one, which did not please him as he could get trapped on the rail if he was not quickly away. He wanted desperately to win this race because this would make this his best season yet with twenty wins. There was an even greater reason: he was wearing the royal colours of purple, red sleeves and gold frogging for Whitehead was the king's horse. 'Under starter's orders' — 'don't turn now, boy', he pleaded to the excited horse, which was dancing on the spot. If the tapes went up and he were sideways on, it would cost him the race.

Gerald and Bob, 1938.

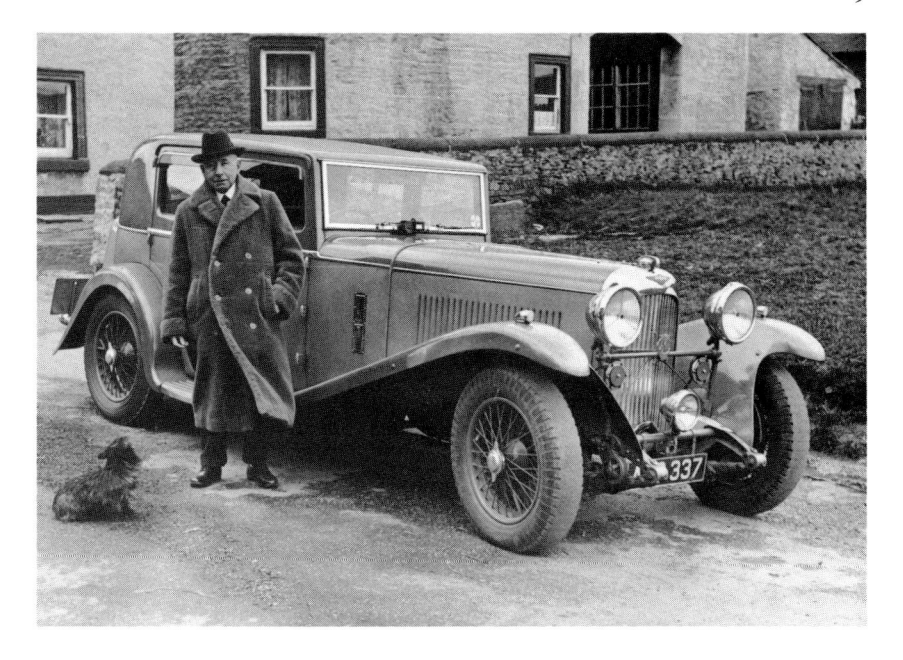

Bob by his car, 1938.

'They're off.' Thank God, he had done that right, a mile to go and well positioned before the turn. That was when the jostling would start, away from the eyes of the officials. He knew all the riders. They were all amateurs, some titled, and his immediate neighbour was an 'honourable'. But that, thought Gerald, was a misnomer. There was nothing at all honourable about Jack Stoutt, who had a foul reputation as a cheat. But because of his position, nobody was prepared to complain.

Right on cue, he glanced sideways and was in time to see the blow coming. By now, Gerald and Jack were well ahead of the field. The race was between them. The whip was aimed at his face and, flinging himself flat on to Whitehead's neck, he heard it whistle over his head. At the same time, he used his own whip on the horse's flank. He gained a stride as Jack had unbalanced his own mount. That was enough for the big colt which, seeing itself in the lead, pulled strongly ahead and won by five lengths. His majesty's racing manager graciously presented Gerald with a gold-mounted riding crop.

Ripon Race Company had been founded in 1899 although race meetings had been held in the town since the seventeenth century. There was a public subscription for shares and Bob had bought some, later becoming a director and finally chairman. There were four principal families involved at the start, the Hutchinsons, Wells, Wilmot-Smiths and Armstrongs. All four are still

Gerald riding H.M. horse 'Whitehead' at Ripon, 1934.

represented on the board in their third or fourth generations. On Bob's death in 1956, a race was sponsored and this Armstrong Cup is still held annually on the first Monday in August.

Jockeys have many falls in their careers and many bones are broken. Gerald was no exception. In August 1937, he flew his plane to Lewes racecourse, where he was to ride a horse call Fad. After three furlongs, the saddle slipped and, though he tried desperately to hang on, Fad swerved and hit another horse and Gerald came off. His foot caught in the stirrup and he was dragged some way. When it finally came free, he was galloped over by the rest of the field. He was rushed to Brighton hospital and a top brain surgeon summoned to attend him. It was touch and go whether he would live or not, but he survived and, with a metal plate inserted in his head, eventually left the hospital. On regaining consciousness after the operation, his first thought was for his plane. 'Will I be able to fly again?' he asked. 'I suppose', said the surgeon, 'that compared to riding, you would be safer in the air'.

That accident ended Gerald's riding career — a notable one with 100 wins to his credit, one of only two men living in England at the time who had done so as an amateur. As there are relatively few amateur races and as amateurs are not allowed to ride in professional races, this was no mean achievement. It was also very expensive as these races were for serving officers and members of the race club. Gerald had to subscribe to every club to be eligible to ride.

September 1939 was notable for the British and French declaration of war on Germany, and for Gerald's wedding. Margaret, always known as Tiggy, was the fifth child of Joseph Wilson, hat manufacturer of Denton, Manchester, whose home was at Greyfriars, a very attractive house in Chapel-en-le-Frith in Derbyshire. Today, few women wear hats and even fewer men wear bowlers or trilbies (the latter almost confined to the racing fraternity). But look at any photo of a crowd of people in the early twentieth century, and you will see that everyone did. So Jo. Wilson and Co. was a large and prosperous business in its third generation.

Tiggy had gone to school at Queen Ethelburga's in Harrogate, then on to the Royal Academy of Music in London, where she gained her LRAM for the piano. She had a short spell as a trainee nurse before dedicating her time to her real passions of horses and dogs. This began on the hunting field, went on to point-to-point races and inevitably led to racing. She had met Gerald through one of his best friends, Becket Henderson, who had married her sister Diana two years previously. Becket and Diana lived at the Manor House, Kettlewell, fourteen miles from Tupgill and Gerald was a frequent visitor there. Becket, whose family was in the wool trade in Keighley, owned hunters and kept horses

'Tiggy' Wilson (*left*) with her sisters Diana and Kathleen outside Greyfriars, Chapel-en-le-Frith, 1939.

in training with another of their pals, Colonel Wilfred Lyde, who had the Thorngill Stables adjoining Tupgill.

With the war, Wilfred Lyde rejoined his regiment and Bob bought Thorngill for Gerald to train because, unlike the First World War, racing did continue in the second. However, they were not immune from the effects of the war. Gerald was not fit for active service because of his age and the disabilities caused by his accident, and became a captain in the home guard. Moreover, Tupgill was commandeered by the army for the use of an armoured regiment. The army moved in and built Nissen huts, canteens, latrine blocks, ammunition stores and parade grounds on the area where the Forbidden Corner is today.

Bob and Nellie would have been evicted as Tupgill House was required for officers' quarters but Nellie was ailing. She had Parkinson's disease and was cared for by her daughter, Doris, who ran the household and by this time had given up all thought of marriage. (She was part of the generation of girls for whom there were insufficient husbands because more than 1,000,000 British men were killed in the First World War.) Doris (Do), who had been painfully shy as a child and stood in awe of her formidable mother as a girl, now blossomed

Do, 1960.

into a very capable administrator, very much the centre of the Armstrong world. Sunday lunch was held at Tupgill with Gerald and Tiggy, and Sam and his wife Maureen, who were still at Ashgill at this time. Perhaps the friction between Gerald and Tiggy was caused by the closeness of the relationship between Do and Gerald, with she the stronger and he the more pliant. Perhaps it arose because she had been brought up in a financially secure world which he was not able to maintain after his accident. Or perhaps Gerald had not been her first choice of husband but had caught her on the rebound. Whatever the reason, it was not a marriage made in heaven.

On the 9th September, 1945, Gerald was in the bar of the University Arms Hotel at Cambridge, having been racing at Newmarket that day with a further race meeting on the next. It was towards midnight and the bartender was eager to go to bed but Gerald sat and sat on his own, continually looking at his watch. At last the call came. 'A call from the Doris Court nursing home for you', said the hall porter. Gerald ran for the phone. He put it down and beamed at the barman and porter. 'Let's open a bottle of champagne,' he said. 'I've got a son.'

Colin Robert, he was christened: Colin for Tiggy's brother, who had been killed in the war while bombing Germany, Robert for old Bob. Now Gerald

Kate, Colin (on the donkey) and Jane (*leading*) with Nanny Bobby Reynolds, Thorngill, 1946.

Jane, Kate and Colin on donkeys at Whitby, 1949.

had three children, for Jane had been born in 1941 and Catherine (Kate) in 1944.

Sadly, Nellie lived to hold the baby only once before dying, though Bob lived until his ninety-fourth year, dying in his sleep in 1956.

The war over at last, both Gerald and Sam continued their careers. Gerald was now known as Captain Armstrong at Thorngill and Sam, after giving up the tenancy of Warren Place, bought St Gatien, another Newmarket stable, and trained on his own account, having found the Maharajah of Baroda a rather fickle owner.

Sam was the successful brother and over a fifty-year career trained over 2,000 winners in such important races as the St Leger, the Two Thousand Guineas, the Irish Derby, the Stewards Cup, the Ascot Gold Cup and the Cesarewitch, although he never won the Derby.

Trainers do not just train horses. They train future jockeys through the apprenticeship of stable boys who sign on from perhaps the age of fifteen to work for board, keep and pocket money, with the hope of one day becoming famous jockeys. Harry Carr, who became the queen's jockey, began his career with Bob his father, Bobby Carr, was the stable head man. Willie Carson began

Kate, Colin and Jane in 1998.

with Gerald and passed on to Sam and the rest is history. Josh Gifford, who went on to become champion National Hunt jockey, also started with Sam.

Willie Carson's first winner was at Catterick races on a horse trained by Gerald called Pinkers Pond, which was named after a small pool on Middleham Moor. This pond only came into being after trees on an escarpment above it were cut down during the Second World War. As a little girl, Jane had two favourite blankets, Bluey and Pinkie, so, as she and Tiggy went to the nearby town of Leyburn each day to shop, they would stop at the pond and open the door, and Pinkie would get out (metaphorically) and wait at the pond until they returned to pick it up. After a while, Gerald would order his boys to 'take the horses down the road as far as Pinkers Pond, circle around up to the moor and canter back'. So Pinkers Pond was put on the map where it is today, thanks to Jane.

Though Sam had a lot more success, Gerald too had his share of winners. Thankerton won the Jersey Stakes at Ascot in 1936 and was third in the Derby of that year and Sailing Light won the Lincoln Handicap in 1953. Of course, even the best trainer cannot win races without good horses and then, as now, the money and the best horses were in the South. Sam saw this plainly but Gerald was content to stay in the North. But he did once train for the Maharajah of Gwalior, an Indian prince, and told stories of transporting horses by ship to Bombay and from there to Gwalior by train and of seeing the splendour of the palace, the elephants, the private army and the jewels.

Gerald retired as a trainer following a serious car accident. This almost cost him his life and showed how bad luck dogged him at this time. A trainer receives commissions (orders) to buy horses and the great time for buying is in the autumn at the Doncaster or Newmarket yearling sales. All racehorses, regardless of when they are foaled which can be any time between January and June, have an official birthday on the 1st January when they change from foals to yearlings. In 1961, Father had commissions to buy five yearlings, which was excellent news for his small stable of twenty. He set off for the Newmarket December sales with a friend and owner, Teddy Watson, who was driving. They stopped for lunch at the well-known Ram Jam Hotel, which stands on the A1 between Stamford and Grantham. After a good meal, Teddy was foolish enough to back his car out of the car park in front of a speeding car. He was killed and father was very badly injured, staying in hospital for months so the yearlings were never bought for Thorngill. In 1962, he sold Thorngill to the trainer Joe Hartigan, moving only half a mile uphill to Ferngill, a small dower house on the Tupgill Park estate. There, he lived with Tiggy until she died in 1975 and he moved into Tupgill with his sister Doris, living there until he too died in 1979.

Sam had also retired as a trainer following a heart attack but he had a son, Robert, who took on the business at St Gatien and was a successful trainer for many years before retiring to live in Jersey, where his wife's family live. Sam's daughter, Susan, is another woman fascinated by horses and racing. After leaving school, she assisted Sam most ably in the running of St Gatien and in entering horses for future races (the trainer's worst chore). When she married in 1960, it was to a jockey following the example of Nellie Lamplough, to whom she has a striking resemblance, sixty-four years previously. The similarities do not end there because Susan, like her grandmother, is a mover and a doer, all energy and action. However, there was no opposition to this match. Both families were in racing and had known each other for many years. Susan became Mrs Lester Piggott.

Their two daughters continue the racing tradition. Maureen married William Haggas, who trains at Newmarket, and Tracey is a sports correspondent for the Dublin television station RTE.

1945 ONWARDS — COLIN

THE MOMENT OF MY birth has already been established. It may sound a bit heartless that my father was away racing at the time. But a nervous and restless father-to-be is pretty useless outside the maternity room so he was better employed at work.

From the nursing home in Manchester where Tiggy went to be near her mother, I was brought back to our home at Thorngill. Standing a mile from Tupgill, Thorngill is perhaps the nicest of the collection of 'gill' houses, having been enlarged in Victorian times with larger and better proportioned rooms built on to the south side. Like Tupgill, it had land, stables and barns but was short of living accommodation for staff. At this time, Gerald's uncle Fred died and when the George Hotel was sold, he received an inheritance which enabled him to build an accommodation block of two cottages and a stable lads' hostel. Unfortunately, being built of brick and with steel windows and a red pantiled roof, it has always been an eyesore among Coverdale's attractive stone-built buildings.

From the age of four, I shared a teacher with half a dozen other children of similar age who came to Thorngill each day. Then, when I was eight years old, I was sent to Huyton Hill preparatory school near Ambleside in the Lake District. Jane and Kate were not far away at Blackwell on Lake Windermere.

Being a tall leggy boy, I was quite good at running and won several events each sports day. But neither work nor team games came easily to me. The one colour I achieved in my five years there was for estate work. The Butler brothers, who owned the school, were dedicated to re-landscaping the large grounds, transforming rhododendron thickets into playing fields, and all the boys were press-ganged into this work with pick, shovel and wheelbarrow. It was, perhaps, where I acquired the taste for landscaping that I applied many years later at Tupgill.

Cold water was then considered an essential aid for developing the minds and bodies of young boys and the Butlers strongly believed in it. During winter terms this meant a cold bath on getting up, just a quick in, under and out. In the summer term, we were called by dormitories, and with pyjamas off and towel around waist, ran down the garden to the end of the jetty, dropped the towel and dived in. Then we swam back and out as fast as we could. It may have been summer but Lake Windermere never warms up. After a while, this became quite a spectator sport for local residents!

Like other children at boarding school, I remember longing for the holidays, counting the days to go. Then having returned home, there was depression at finding nothing had changed. Gerald and Tiggy would be bickering, or rather she would be getting at him as he would take it and say little, and this would be worse in the evenings when she had had a drink.

Because Thorngill is in the countryside two miles from the village of Middleham and four from the market town of Leyburn, we did not have many friends of our own age to play with. Jane, who was four years older than myself, would not often deign to play with Kate and I, so we sometimes played together. As Father was a trainer, we all had ponies but Jane and Kate were much keener than I. I was more often on my own, playing with an electric train, air-rifle or my stamp collection and at one point became a fanatical photographer, developing and printing the photos and selling them to the family or anyone else who would buy them. I also liked fishing and would go after trout in the River Cover. I was always keen on reading books and filled many hours in that way.

There was another girl of our age: Wendy, the daughter of Jimmy Lee, the travelling head man who lived in the cottage next to the big house. She was always with us when we were smaller but tended to play more with my sisters later. Jimmy Lee would transport the horses to races and represent father when he was at another meeting. Charlie Brown, the former jockey, drove the horsebox and Fred Asker was the head lad at home. Curiously, we children had to address them by their surnames as Asker and Lee, while they referred to the family as Mr Gerald, Mrs Gerald, Master Colin and Miss Jane or Kate. It was a curious snobbery of those days. We had a winners' bell and whenever the parents called from the races announcing a winner, we kids scrambled to ring the bell. It is always a joyful sound in a racing stable.

Trainers travel to races a great deal and we had a series of large cars including a Standard Vanguard, a 'Maigre' type Citroen and our favourite, a mark 10 Jaguar and, more often than not, we had a chauffeur. Although Mother liked to drive, Father rarely did so as his accidents had impaired his eyesight.

Having failed the Common Entrance exam at first attempt, I spent a miserable summer holiday being 'crammed' in Latin by a local vicar before finally getting into Rossall School at Fleetwood, near Blackpool, in 1958. I was not a great success there either, not being very good at either work or sport, and known in Rossall parlance as a 'spare'. But by that time, I had made up my mind what I wanted to do. I wanted to be a farmer. So I spent a great deal of my spare time in the last year or so there reading the farming press in the school library. I had worked out how I could make a living on the combined 100 acres of Tupgill and Thorngill. This included intensive pig and poultry rearing and I shudder at the thought today as both are particularly unsightly and smelly.

To further my plans, I checked up on agricultural colleges and applied to all four English establishments for information. I discovered that I could be admitted with just O-levels (today's GCSE), without needing A-levels. This was just as well, as Father was preparing to retire and making it quite clear that there was no money to keep me on at school.

At that time, summer holidays normally involved just one long stay at Thorngill. When we were younger, we had gone to Scarborough, Blackpool or Torbay with Mother. But those days were over. In my case, a good solution was found when, for several consecutive years, I was packed off to Rockbourne, Hampshire, to stay with Mother's bachelor brother, Stuart Wilson, for six weeks at a time. Uncle Stuart owned the Manor Farm at Rockbourne — 800 acres of rolling downs. It seemed to suit both of us. He quite enjoyed having a nephew about at certain times of day, especially in the evening, as long as I kept out of his way during the daytime.

For my part, I made friends with his gamekeeper who was called Philip Hood (and had a brother called Robin Hood). Philip would build me hides of straw bales and I would take sandwiches and sit out all day shooting pigeons with the twenty-eight bore double-barrelled shotgun which had belonged to Father in his youth. I have happy memories of warm afternoons and the smells and sounds of summer. I became quite good at this pastime and, after shooting each bird, I would stake it out as a decoy in a natural position and thereby attract more pigeons. Some of these birds were eaten at Rockbourne but I would travel back to Thorngill on the train with a dozen or so to proudly show to my parents. They were not very keen on eating them and would pretend to be enthusiastic but most of the birds were thrown away.

Uncle Stuart had many interests apart from farming. He collected old glass and antique furniture, sailed a barge called the *Goose Of Wessex* which he kept at Southampton, and was quite proficient in French and Spanish. One of his great loves was cooking and he would prepare wonderful dinners while his guests sat chatting to him in the kitchen, he wearing a butcher's apron over his suit. When everything was ready, he would move everyone into the dining room and get 'housemaid' Thomas to serve it. She was not a housemaid at all but a lovely old widowed lady who had a grace-and-favour flat in the house and who would invite me to tea with her each afternoon. It was always china tea, which still reminds me of her today.

Stuart had a large number of friends and the dinner guests who I met ranged from William Hill of betting shop fame, who had a stud adjoining Manor Farm, to Augustus John, the bohemian painter and friend of gypsies. He intrigued me as he looked 100 years old and had wild beard and hair (in fact, he was eighty-one and was to die three years later) and he was driven in an old London taxi. It was whispered that he was not married to Dorelia, the mother of several of his children, which, of course, was quite true as was also the fact that he had dozens of children by other women. He was said not to know quite how many there were but thought there were more than fifty, the most famous son being Admiral of the Fleet Sir Caspar John GCB.

It was while I was staying at Rockbourne that the telegram arrived one August day (people used telegrams more in those days). It said 'All bar French, well done, Mum' and referred to my passing eight O-levels, which were more than enough to get me into agricultural college. However, I had not been at all certain just how well I had done at the time so had asked Father for one more term at Rossall, just in case. I did not need this as it turned out but, as a school career could not be terminated without a term's notice, I went back into the lower sixth form for one term and passed my French O-level at the second attempt.

During that term, the Cuban missile crisis flared up and the world was threatened with war. I remember thinking that it might decide my career for me as I was seventeen and eligible for the draft. But Kruschev blinked and I applied to Harper Adams Agricultural College. I had, in fact, chosen to go to the Royal Agricultural College and been accepted but, for one of the few times in his life, Father put his foot down and said: 'No! that's for playboys.' So Harper it was. One of the admission requirements was that if one was not a farmer's son, and I did not qualify on this count, one had to have eighteen months' experience as a farm pupil. I had gained a little hands-on experience because the fifty acres at Thorngill were run as a small farm by a series of farm men who seemed to come and go fairly frequently until Doug Weatherill arrived while I was still at Rossall.

We hit it off straight away and I was always to be found helping him. We milked twelve cows in those days and Doug asked if I would do the milking for him one Sunday afternoon. Even though I had helped him often enough, I had not really been concentrating on the job, as I soon found out when I had to do it alone. We had a small Gascoigne milking machine on wheels, which you pushed up the byre and connected to two cows at a time. I started with this and rushed to the front of the cows to give them the required food ration. This startled them and, without waiting for the food, they cleared off into the field, taking the machine with them. I had forgotten to chain them up first! Well, they did not get milked that afternoon and it was late the next morning before we had recovered the machine and cleaned it.

It used to brighten up my day at Rossall when I received Doug's letters telling of the calves born or sows farrowed. Yes, I really wanted to be a farmer.

My Rossall career finished at Christmas 1962 but shortly before then, I had a couple of days off for sister Jane's wedding to Peter Conway. Jane had left school after O-levels and, after a job with an estate agent, had helped Father for some time as general assistant and secretary (after going to secretarial school). She developed a prodigious memory for horses' pedigrees and past form and was the only one of the three of us to take an interest in racing. She gave that up when she married Peter and soon afterwards emigrated to South Africa, where they still live today. My parents really pushed out the boat for the wedding and a large marquee was hired and erected in the field in front of Thorngill, with heaters installed as it was November. In fact, it snowed. A huge number of people were invited including numerous aunts, uncles and cousins on the Wilson side (some of whom I have never seen since). It was an excellent 'do' and marked not only Jane's departure from home, but also the Armstrong decampment from Thorngill.

Father had decided to retire from training (and stop losing money as Mother had acidly put it!) and had sold Thorngill. He had a quiet chat with me previously, the tenor of which was that, if I wanted to take the business on, he would continue for a while longer and help me. But no — I had no interest in horses or racing and, having seen him struggle with poor horses and bad luck for years, there was no way that I wanted to be a trainer. However, my dreams of farming the land had taken a knock because thirty-five of the precious 100 acres went with Thorngill. Well, there would just have to be more intensive pig and poultry rearing!

Meanwhile sister Kate had left school and started on a succession of jobs with horses and animals which included a spell with Chipperfield's circus, helping in a hunting stable, and with a Mr and Mrs Holmes, who trained the animals which appeared in films and television. Aunt Diana (Becket Henderson's wife) had tried to encourage Kate to get an office job and sent her to secretarial school in Leeds but she was, and is, an outdoor person and preferred her work with animals. There was evidence of this years previously, when she had a pony called Freddy and trained him to do all sorts of tricks, such as rearing up and walking on his hind legs.

So it was home alone for Gerald and Tiggy in Ferngill, which stands on the hill above Thorngill, a pretty house of four rooms up and four down with two staircases. The idea was that a couple of bedrooms were for family, the others for servants. Curiously, it was built gable-on to the south so only two rooms caught the sun. All the other houses in the area face south. (This defect I partially corrected when enlarging the house in 1977).

Father and Mother now swapped roles. Mother had always been the gardener at Thorngill, and a large garden it is too. She prided herself on growing most of the vegetables that we ate and, in those post-war years of food rationing, she made jams, salted beans and preserved all sort of things. Now it was Father's turn, and he gardened and grew tomatoes in a small greenhouse while Mother took not the slightest interest. Father's big day of the week was his 'Douglas day', when Doug Weatherill, who had now taken tenancy of the land at Ashgill and lived there with his wife Margaret and four children, came to help him with the heavier digging and gave him company as much as anything. Father's eyesight was deteriorating and he could no longer drive, so Doug drove him about as Mother never seemed to find it convenient.

There had been a change, too, in my relations with them both over the years. In the early days, it was Mother, the caring, efficient, capable one who brought up the children, wrote letters to us at school, organised holidays and was a severe disciplinarian. But she was often outspoken and on several occasions let father down badly. The custom of owners staying overnight with the trainer was less prevalent at this time than in Bob's day due to better transport. But they did often come to inspect their horses, especially at weekends and sometimes without warning. Often we children had to give up the family roast beef on Sunday and eat something else in the kitchen while our parents

Margaret and Doug Weatherill with Florrie Hammond at Kate's wedding, 1967.

entertained owners in the dining room. One of them, a Mr Greenwood, had five horses with us. He was reputed to be a war profiteer and was a vulgar, loud man. Mother disliked him intensely but put a brave face on it until the day he appeared with a girlfriend in mink and jewels and proceeded to tell everyone just how much each item had cost him, to the girlfriend's acute embarrassment. Mother took her aside and said 'Why don't you drop this creep? He will never marry you.' The idiot girl (who deserved her fate) repeated this to Greenwood on their way home. The next day motor horse-boxes arrived to remove the five horses, a quarter of Gerald's stable.

At that time, Father was preoccupied with his business, gave preference to business friends and contacts over family and was somewhat distant to us. I remember avoiding him when playing outside at Thorngill as, each time he came across me, he would think of a 'little job' that I could usefully do. These normally involved a certain amount of graft like sawing logs, filling pot holes in the drive with gravel or painting the garage doors. He was a great one for keeping up the property. Apart from these tasks, I had my regular chores to do. Mother kept chickens and during the school holidays it was my job to feed them, collect the eggs and occasionally kill one for lunch.

In later years, I switched my allegiance to him as, once retired, he took much more interest in me, In fact, he was desperate for my company which, to my shame, I begrudged him although we did become quite close. My relationship with Mother deteriorated as she retreated to her own world where her dogs (Yorkshire terriers by then) reigned supreme.

MEVAGISSEY

I THINK I PICKED a farm as far away from home as I could get, which was near Mevagissey in Cornwall. I had seen the advert in the farming press for a farm pupil, who would be a source of cheap labour for the farmer, requiring only board, lodging and pocket money and who would be expected to put in the same hours as a paid man. The learning would be by osmosis as there would be no formal academic training. Home Farm was owned by Freddy James, an irascible seventy-year-old bachelor, and his sister, who lived in an ancient farmhouse with only a cold tap in the kitchen and outside 'long drop'. They bathed in a tin bath with a couple of inches of water in it heated by the kettle in front of the kitchen fire. I do not remember how privacy was ensured at such times but I do remember having very few baths in the six months (February to July) that I was there.

Freddy James was old-fashioned in his farming methods too, and I suppose I was lucky in seeing farming of a sort that was already consigned to the museum elsewhere. He grew oats and these were cut with a binder. Although it was at least now pulled by a tractor, it had been adapted as it was made for horses. The corn was stooked in the farmyard until the threshing machine arrived. A great day it was too, as neighbours came in to help to feed this voracious machine which was huge, wooden and had a cat's cradle of whirring belts. It was tremendously hard work, interrupted by many breaks for consuming pints of tea to remove the dust from the throat, and afterwards there was the great harvest-home supper.

Freddy kept South Devon cows which were milked by hand, and it is not bad to wake up slowly on a cold winter's morning, tucked under a warm cow with the sweet smell of milk. By breakfast time, you have come to terms with the day.

I have found that happiness always eludes you when you are looking for it but crops up at the most unexpected moments. I experienced one such occasion at Mevagissey.

It was a March night and we had started lambing, which required the farm men to take turns wandering around the field, helping ewes to lamb, encouraging new-born lambs to suckle their mothers or rescuing orphans to be raised in the farmhouse. The night was freezing cold but starlit and I was awoken at three o'clock for my stint. I went with a bad will and grumpily stomped around the field trying to keep warm and wondering why I had chosen farming at all. After an hour or two of this, I came across a ewe having difficulty lambing. Only one leg of her lamb was protruding and she was showing signs of stress. Panic! I had prayed this would not happen while I was on duty. I had been told and seen what to do but now I had to do it by myself.

The operation involved removing coat and jacket, rolling up shirt sleeves, lying on the frosty ground and getting my arm into the sheep's vulva, then pushing, turning and fighting with the lamb and ewe until the two parted company. That was the theory — but I hesitated. The wind was icy and I was already cold despite having several layers of clothes on. But something clearly had to be done so, like jumping into a cold bath (shades of Huyton Hill school), I did it quickly. What I did not appreciate was the strength needed to push against the contractions. The ewe and I struggled for what seemed like hours, and every now and then I removed my arm to get the circulation going again. Although I had hardly forgotten the cold, it was at least partially ignored now. One more go — I had to get the lamb out. Finally it came, whether due to my help or not I do not know. But I had done it. I rubbed the wet and smelly lamb with straw and watched it suckle like a proud father as its tail wagged vigorously. Then the first rays of the sun appeared on the horizon and I was overcome by inexpressible happiness.

David Burnett was the farm foreman and became a very good friend of mine. He took me around with him on Sundays, generally to churches because, despite limited formal education, he was a lay preacher and bell-ringer. We would occasionally go to Truro Cathedral and I would watch as a team of half a dozen went through the process of change-ringing. Not that David let me have a go — those bells can weigh many tons and they are perched upside-down on a beam. The first pull dislodges the bell and if one is not careful, it can take the ringer up to the roof of the belfry.

David was a very down-to-earth and convincing preacher and I think my time with him brought me closer to believing than I had been before or have been since. He later went on to an ecclesiastical college and was ordained and sent to Manchester. Sadly, we lost contact when I went abroad.

I bought a second-hand BSA 250cc motorbike in St Austell and rode this supremely unreliable machine around the Cornish lanes, nearly killing myself when (admittedly after several pints of Guinness) I hit one of the earth and stone banks that pass for fences in Cornwall at speed. I was unconscious with concussion for twenty-four hours and this incident — together with a childhood accident when Kate dropped a large stone on my head — may well account for some of my eccentricities today.

FLINTON

July 1963 brought an invitation to cousin John Henderson's twenty-first birthday and I decided that it would be a good time to leave Home Farm and look elsewhere for farm experience. I packed everything (there was not much) on to the bike, which had now been repaired, and rode off to the North. It would have been a lovely ride but by the time had I got to Bristol, I had had enough of breakdowns and put both bike and self on the overnight train to Leeds. There, I rode straight to Stainton Cotes, Becket's lovely house standing in his 3,000-acre estate near Gargrave in Yorkshire. Becket Henderson had not been born poor but he was a very shrewd businessman and increased his wealth enormously in the wool trade until, finally selling at the right moment, he bought land and became the local squire and master of foxhounds. John was his only son and Becket and Diana gave him a huge twenty-first party, my recollections of which are of my trying to impress the girls by doing some very fancy footwork in the Charleston; the trainer Jeremy Hindley telling me what a fool I was to have given up the chance to be a trainer when he was desperate to do just that; and old Becket, who had spent a fortune on the party, rather furtively collecting up bottles of champagne and hiding them in his study. 'Treasure trove' he told me.

In fact, it was Uncle Becket who arranged the next stage of my farm pupil career by arranging for me to work for John Caley, who farmed a large farm at Flinton, near Sproatly outside Hull. This was a very different operation from Mevagissey. Crawler tractors were used to plough the heavy clay soils and wheat, potatoes and peas grown in a very organised way. Here, I was lodged with a Mrs Bemrose, who fed me terrifically. Not that I put on much fat — I have always been a beanpole. You consume so much energy through manual work and I suppose that I was still growing at eighteen. The motorbike was still with me and took me to Hull on Saturday nights to pursue the girls at a dance club which I joined, not often successfully, if I remember rightly. John Caley kindly invited me to join him and his son Henry, who was a bit older than me, from time to time. But Henry had money and a car and I had neither, so I could not keep up the pace.

This led me to mix with the village lads and we had many a pub binge, which on one occasion led to a fight with a group of Irish navvies. I had been in a gang of five when the fight started but somehow I was left on my own under a pile of labourers and, when pulled out by the village policeman, had a broken nose, black eye and three cracked ribs. However, I had apparently put one of my opponents in hospital so my stock rose in the gang. They had, they explained, just left me to fetch the policeman, call an ambulance, buy a last drink, go to the loo or whatever!. We stayed friends although I was careful to avoid more fights with that crowd of pussycats at my back.

John Caley squared the policeman and no charges were brought but he gave me a hell of a lecture about a chap of my background getting into this sort of scrape, and drinking too much too! It is difficult to play the gentleman with no money.

HARPER ADAMS

OCTOBER 1964 AND I was a fully-fledged student. I had been for an interview with the North Riding of Yorkshire county council education committee and duly obtained a 100 per cent grant on account of father's penury. Then I went by train to Shrewsbury and bus to Newport in Shropshire and arrived at Harper Adams Agricultural College. The motorbike was left at Flinton with my mate Roy, who promised to sell it and send me the cash but never did.

Life at Harper Adams began in a fairly robust way as all freshmen had to go though an initiation ceremony. This consisted of being pelted with wheat chaff and coloured water after which, once cleaned up, they went down to the pub for a monumental booze-up. It broke the ice and first friendships were made. I knew only one person: 'Beng' Franklin, who had been at Rossall with me and whose father, Colonel Franklin, had a poultry farm near Oswestry, where I was once or twice invited to stay. An early new friend was Winston Suarez from Santa Cruz in Bolivia, a small, dapper Latin American with a Clark Gable moustache. He had been a pupil on the college farm, knew his way around and had a great sense of humour.

I once took Winston home to meet my parents and Aunt Do. The conversation turned to a book written by Cecil Beaton called *My Bolivian Aunt*. It referred to an aunt of Beaton's, who had married a Bolivian called Pedro Suarez who was the country's ambassador in London. He took her back to Bolivia and she told of the hardships of the journey, which involved travelling by mule for days on end. Winston told us that Pedro Suarez was the brother of his grandfather, who had married a Miss Sisson from Eamont Bridge, where my grandfather use to train horses. Do improved the story by saying that her father had courted a sister of the lady in question so, but for fate, Winston and I might have been related.

Early in my time at Harper Adams, I had acquired a car for £30 in an auction. It was a green Vauxhall Wyvern and, as I had passed my driving test (on the third attempt) at Hull, I was now mobile. Well, mobile on and off. All sorts of things happened to that car. One day, while driving down a steep hill near Helmsley in Yorkshire, a back wheel came off and overtook me while I followed on three wheels. I was unable to stop because the brakes would not work. Both wheel and car eventually ploughed into a hedge and came to a halt. As luck would have it, I was near the farm of a friend, who was a very keen mechanic and he came to the rescue. However, his solution to the problem was to weld the wheel disc to the half shaft — a good solid job. But half shafts, as I found out later, are made of tempered steel and do not take to being welded. A month later, while returning to Harper Adams, the half shaft snapped in the high street of Bishop's Stortford and I caused a monumental traffic jam. Eventually an old half shaft was procured from a scrap-yard for £5 and off I went again.

Winston, who did not have a car, would often come with me on hunting expeditions to the local teacher training colleges or nurses' homes. We took it in turns for the use of the back seat.

Rag week came early in the Michaelmas term and we set out with a vengeance to raise money for charity and have a wild time too. One of the stunts involved building cages of wood on several of the college farm trailers, which were then driven into the marketplace of Newport with students dressed as pirates. We 'kidnapped' the shop girls and, having locked them in the cages, auctioned them back to their employers or relatives. It amazes me now to think that we got away with it — just seizing girls, putting them over our shoulders and running for the cages. Very few girls refused to cooperate. It was a great day and all the girls were invited to our dance that night.

The kidnapping of a goat caused more trouble. It was no ordinary goat, but the mascot of the Shropshire Yeomanry (or some such regiment). This wretched creature was hidden in someone's room and the military and civilian police roamed the place and interviewed people all the next day. Only when we were promised that there would be no reprisals was it was finally returned. All ended well except for the poor fellow whose room the goat had been in, and who had to live with smell for ages.

Rugby was another passion. Although I had been pretty poor at it at school, my farm work had made me a lot stronger and I rediscovered the game. Although I was not good enough for the first team, I was a leading light in the second, playing either three-quarter back or flanker. Winston was fly half and, having taught us 'derecha' and 'izquierda' for right and left, helped us to steal a march on the opposition. We travelled far and wide to play against rugby clubs, colleges, the armed forces and even a remand home. After a hard game and tea at the latter, we felt very sorry for the inmates because, when we left in our bus for a local pub, they were lined up in the rain on the courtyard for gym.

The 'apres-ski' or after-match was, of course, a big part of the attraction of rugby and I soon developed into a notable bar-room singer who knew all the words of the 'Jockstrap Ensemble' type of songs. Once when we had a free day, we played the first team and, to their chagrin, we beat them. We had developed into a good team of ordinary players while they were a group of outstanding individualists. There is a lesson there.

Of course, work did interrupt play, and gradually we laid aside the worst of our silliness and got stuck in. We took a college diploma at Harper Adams and a National Diploma at Leeds University. Happily, I passed both, gaining a distinction in management in the NDA, and was therefore offered a place on the agricultural management diploma course at Essex Institute of Agriculture a year later.

Meanwhile, before term ended, we were all beginning to think of a career. Although I had filled my head with dreams of the family farm venture at Tupgill, I joined the others when Father put a stop to it. He said that it was all very well to milk cows and muck out pigs when I was twenty-one, but I would be doing exactly the same thing when I was fifty-one and would not have a penny to my name. I should 'Go and get a job'. This must be the best advice I have been given in my life!

During my Harper Adam days, I had grown a beard, for the simple reason that I could. I thought it quite fetching but this was not a universal opinion, as I found out when I attended and failed a string of job interviews. One of these was with ICI and I know that the beard was the problem, because they took me on two years later — or perhaps I had improved in other ways in the meantime?

As the interviews had not proved to be a success, I had to look around for something else. This turned out to be an advertisement in a student magazine for IVA — International Voluntary Service, the British branch of Service Civil Internacional of Switzerland. I applied and was accepted, attending a short induction course at a college in London and then a two-week international camp in the French Pyrenees near Lourdes. Students from all over Europe, and one or two from the States, were brought together to mix, improve international relations and more specifically to dig a pipeline from one poverty-stricken village to another about three miles away. So we were out in the sun digging all day, stripped to the waist. In the evening, we would be given a lecture and then feast off local bread, meats and wine and sing around the campfire. With my limited knowledge of (or fluency in) French, let alone Rumanian, I tended to stick with the British group. One American had no language but English and managed to communicate with and make friends with everyone by force of his personality, which was very impressive. On the last day, monsieur le Maire, his councillors and the local press turned up to see how the work was progressing. However, being French, they ignored all the hard-working lads and gathered round two German girls with spectacular figures, who worked in the tiniest of bikinis.

So back to England and my twenty-first birthday. My parents would not countenance a party at Ferngill but Aunt Do took pity on me and let me have the use of an empty cottage at Tupgill, and I set to to clean it and make it presentable. Then I made a fair impression of a grotto with garden netting (borrowed from the raspberries) and green lighting. My girlfriend at that time was Catherine Adamson, the doctor's daughter, who had just graduated from the Royal College of Music in London, had a lovely voice and could accompany herself on the guitar. We invited everyone that we knew locally, although there were not many as we had both been away from the area for some time. However, the party went with a swing and my birthday was duly celebrated. Cathy sang a lot that evening and I treasure the memory. My parents did not attend the party as it was just for the young people, but they gave me a gold wrist watch and a pewter beer tankard with a naked lady as handle. In Mother's words, this was so I could combine my favourite pastimes. I still use both today.

Cathy, with her blonde hair and striking good looks, was my second serious girlfriend and we went out together for over a year. This ended when I went abroad and she eventually married a Sudanese doctor and moved to Khartoum. The first was Pauline Chesswood, who was at a teacher training college at Wolverhampton. I was smitten but she was rather less so as she had never quite given up the previous boyfriend and one call from him set her all in a whirl. We went out for six months and when she ended the relationship, I became so terribly drunk that the landlord of the pub had to bed me down in the bar. Ah! young love (and belated thanks to the former landlord of The Pheasant at Harmby).

SWAZILAND

Then it was hey-ho for Swaziland, for that was where IVS was sending me. Twenty-one and my first journey by plane: a BOAC VC 10. It was a night flight and I clearly remember the magic of looking down and seeing the sand dunes of the Sahara desert in the moonlight. We landed at Nairobi airport to refuel in the morning, then went on again to Johannesburg.

I will just return to Nellie Lamplough, who had married Bob, for a moment. She had a sister who married a man called Harry Clark, producing three children, Christine, Jimmy and Eleanor. I was now bound to Jimmy's house. He had emigrated to South Africa many years before and, as well as becoming the country's champion golfer, had founded several companies such as JL Clark Engineering (PTY) Ltd, JL Clark Cotton (PTY) Ltd, JL Clark Textiles (PTY) Ltd, all sharing a head office at Lamplo House in Johannesburg. In fact, Uncle Jimmy had done very well indeed. He lived in style in a white house at Morningside, an up-market suburb of Johannesburg, with eighteen acres of garden where he had a golf course, a pool and a small farm with Jersey cows, all topped by lovely blue flowering Jacaranda trees. The house was a large bungalow with gables in the Dutch colonial style.

Although I had hardly been close to Jimmy before, he was kindness itself. He picked me up at the airport, took me to his home and, after a few days' rest, put me on the night train from Johannesburg to Piet Retief, which is the nearest station to Swaziland in South Africa. I remember looking out of the train window in the night as we crossed the African veldt and being excited about what the next day would bring.

I was met at Piet Retief station by a tall Afrikaaner, Derek Van Zuydam, who drove me to Mbabane, the capital of Swaziland. I was briefly introduced to some people in the agricultural department including the development officer, Alan Dicks, before we continued the journey down from the mountains of the Swazi high veldt to Malkerns on the middle veldt.

Swaziland remained a small British protectorate after South Africa became a republic and is today an independent country. Situated between South Africa and Mozambique, it can be divided into three distinct areas by altitude: the high veldt is mountainous with pine forests; the middle veldt has undulating farmland where pineapple, citrus fruits and cattle are farmed; and the low veldt is much hotter and sugar cane is grown there. Swaziland is a monarchy and the old king, Sobutu Dlamini, was about seventy years old and I believe that he became the world's longest-reigning monarch. He took a new wife of about fifteen years old each year and had dozens of offspring, so one continually met

SWAZILAND

THE IMMIGRATION PROCLAMATION, 1964
(NO. 32 OF 1964)

TEMPORARY RESIDENCE PERMIT
(Under Section twenty-one)

No. T.1150/66

Particulars of passport:—
Nationality ...... British ...... No. LO.127672
Date of Issue d..... Liverpool ...... Date of Expiry 27.5.71
This permit is granted to ...... Mr. Colin Robert ARMSTRONG
* and the following children under 16 years of age

Swaziland residence permit, Colin, 1967.

princes and princesses. Not that they were very rich or impressive — most lived in the traditional rondavel or round, thatched mud hut. But, like all Swazis, they were happy, friendly people and very welcoming.

The Malkerns valley boasts a university and an agricultural research station, one at each side of the road facing each other. I was attached to the research station as an assistant agricultural officer but lived in a bungalow at the university with four other IVS volunteers who taught there. Their names are fading with time but they include Richard Green, Paul Kafno and Veronica (or Ronnie). Paul, whose surname was Czech, remains in my memory for saying that I had 'quite a noble face' when I finally shaved off my beard. Pride is based on such small things.

My job there was to run, with the help of a Swazi agricultural officer, the Eluyengweni Settlement, a newly-formed co-operative of some 200 farmers who had been resettled nearby and given a small concrete house, two dairy cows and five acres of land. They had been moved from a badly over-grazed area to prevent erosion of the land but were not at all pleased to have been uprooted in this way. It was a difficult start but I did make some progress in the year that I was there.

I had to organise the daily milk collection and make sure that the churns were taken to the refrigerated tank at the research station. Once a week in the wet season, and every second week in the dry season, all — and I mean all — cattle in Swaziland were dipped in insecticide to control the ticks which would otherwise cause red water fever and death. This meant starting before dawn and counting every animal in my area through the dip. We had a large book and all births and deaths were recorded — such was the efficiency of the old British colonial agricultural department, which was still retained. I tested its efficiency once, quite accidentally. During a routine inspection of a dead cow,

I searched for symptoms and diagnosed anthrax using my Harper Adams animal husbandry book. This set the cat among the pigeons as there had not been an outbreak of the disease in Swaziland for many years. Had this been the case, all the animals in the vicinity would have had to be slaughtered. Veterinary officers raced to the scene and a general alarm was raised. Of course, it was not anthrax and my moment of glory quickly passed with mutterings about college students today not being worth their keep and so on.

One venture I started while in Swaziland was the growing of peas for freezing and sale in South Africa. We signed a contract with a large Johannesburg firm, received the seed and fertiliser and began work. Each family was to plant an acre or two on their plots where they had access to irrigation water. All went well until harvest time when we discovered that we did not have enough hands to pick the peas which were all ripening together. To solve this problem, I organised farm trailers, old buses and my own pick-up so that we could collect children after school and bring them in for the harvest. They worked well and happily, the tradition of communal work being strong in Africa. So we began to fill our quota of sacks of peas, which were collected daily by a truck from Johannesburg.

However Africa, or at least Swaziland, has other traditions which can impede progress. A death in the community would stop all work for two days and there were 200 families there. Of course, this happened and more than once during the harvest. I attended several councils of elders, sitting in a circle on the ground, passing the gourd of kaffir beer (fermented millet) from hand to hand and being as eloquent as I could although the interpreter was clearly not sympathetic to my cause. But I could not persuade them to continue the harvest. As a result, empty trucks returned to Johannesburg and there were claims for compensation. However, I believe that the venture was a success on the whole and it continued in subsequent years.

Apart from work, we were able to see a lot of the country and ate numerous barbecues of steak and boerewors — that delicious, thick sausage of the Afrikaaner — beer and South African brandy. Four of us once went to Lourenco Marques (present-day Maputo) in Mozambique, hitching a lift with a Portuguese driver. It is only a few hours' journey. Lourenco Marques was still colonial Portuguese and boasted excellent street restaurants under jacaranda and flame trees where the seafood was accompanied by piri-piri, a fiery chilli sauce. We went to the bullfight and saw terrific horsemanship as the matador placed his banderillas in the bulls' shoulders, using both hands and controlling his beautiful horse with his knees. The horse danced around the bull, always keeping clear of its horns but close enough for the rider to work. In the end, bullocks are let into the ring and the bull runs out with them. I suppose that they are later killed for meat as I understand that they cannot be allowed to fight again because they know the tricks.

Following the bullfight and animated by the spectacle and the beer we had drunk, we headed for the dockside bars which were the haunt of sailors and ladies of the night. Finally, having spent all our money, we took one room for two people at a cheap hotel, then let the other two in through the window. I do not recall how we got back to Malkerns the next day.

A new university lecturer had driven from Lusaka in Zambia with his family and needed someone to return the car for him. What an opportunity! Richard, Paul and I volunteered. We drove from Swaziland to Johannesburg, that long, straight, east-west road, where the afternoon the sun is permanently in your eyes. From there, we went north to Beit Bridge on the Rhodesian border (now Zimbabwe) and crossed the 'great, green, greasy Limpopo river'. Actually, it was not very impressive — unlike the mighty baobab trees with their light green, enormously swollen trunks and stubby branches. They have adapted well to the semi-arid conditions and store water in their trunks. From Beit Bridge, we took the road to the Wankie game reserve, which we drove through, staying a night at the guest house in the centre. We saw most things, including elephants, giraffes, rhinos, hippos, and warthogs but lions were absent.

After Wankie, we visited the ruins called 'Zimbabwe'. Built by some unknown civilisation, possibly Arabic, they consist of a huge enclosure walled with stone to a height of twenty feet or so and containing any amount of fallen masonry. I do not think anyone knows exactly what its purpose was: whether it was a fort, a temple or both. It is particularly impressive in an area of Africa where all building is of wood or mud bricks.

From there, we made our way to Salisbury (present-day Harare) and admired the width of the main streets. We were told that they were wide enough to turn twelve oxen pulling a cart. We had been give the name of someone's friends there and stayed with them for a day or so.

I was never left wing like my friends but, being with IVS, we were extremely sensitive to apartheid in South Africa, which they considered the very devil's haunt. We were all pleased, therefore, to find Rhodesia much more relaxed on this score. I think that this was because the separation of races was a quasi-religious affair in South Africa, whereas in British-colonised Rhodesia, it was had mainly economic causes. Buses and restaurants were not segregated but there were fewer black people in the more expensive ones. This was before Ian Smith's Unilateral Declaration of Independence and the civil war which hardened racial attitudes.

We had arranged to hand over the car by Victoria Falls at the Zambian border, so took the opportunity to see this most magnificent sight, and be soaked by the permanent cloud of spray which comes from it.

Now without a car, we took a bus to Bulawayo and then hitched a ride on a night train to Gaberones, the capital of Botswana, another British protectorate. This was a romantic journey. It was a goods train and we rode in the cab of the steam engine with the driver, drank beers and watched the African night. Botswana is a large desert country and quite cold at night. We were glad of the heat from the boiler. It was totally illegal for the driver to take riders on his train and I forget how we persuaded him — perhaps by providing company on a long routine run. We had to disembark before arriving at Gaberones station so were dropped in the desert some miles away and walked to the road where we caught a bus into the 'city'.

It was a most extraordinary place as it had been only a native village before becoming a capital city some time earlier. The small dirt road suddenly blossomed into a tarmac dual carriageway and rondavels changed to high-rise flats with the obligatory parliament buildings, banks, hotels and so on. A mile farther on, it returned to a dirt road between shacks. There was not much to do here so we headed east back to Swaziland, hitching rides of usually only a few miles at a time from farm to town or vice versa. One afternoon, we had a lift with an Afrikaaner farmer, who invited us to stay at his house. We bathed and smartened up as best we could and joined the family in the kitchen for supper. We were starving and the food smelled wonderful but, before we could start, there were prayers which seemed to us to go on for ever. These were very devout folk of the South African Bible belt. But they were generous and kind and sent us off the next day with sandwiches and their best wishes.

In July 1967, I received the offer of a year's course at Writtle (the Essex Institute of Agriculture). Even though I was asked to stay a second year in Swaziland, I decided to leave in September and fly back to England.

Before leaving, though, I had one last job to finish. I had been asked to organise a trade fair near the settlement. I had no experience of this sort of thing but set to with great energy to make it a success. I contacted all the farm input suppliers and tractor representatives and they all agreed to take part. We marked out an area of ground with streets and exhibition areas, found flags and bunting and advertised in the local press. The great day arrived and it was most impressive, I thought, even though we did not attract the sort of crowds we expected. One aspect of my organisation landed me in trouble, however. I proudly hoisted the Union Jack over the fairground. I was soon told to take it down and quickly. Swaziland had recently become an independent country and flying the British flag was seen as a deliberate provocation by a local politician.

In many ways, I was sorry to be leaving Swaziland. I had enjoyed the job and Africa with its big skies (the moon and stars look much larger there than in any other part of the world I know). The people were all very friendly and, as bad luck would have it, just after deciding to leave I had met a very lovely girl, Dina Heslop. Dina was from Rhodesia and I am not sure why she was in Swaziland. We knew each other for only a month before I left. I was very smitten but the course of true love was somewhat complicated as her boyfriend, a British army officer, turned up in Swaziland .He was not at all pleased to meet me and did his best to monopolise her time. However, we did contrive to meet.

We wrote to each other once or twice afterwards and the last time I heard from her, she was in Sydney. She introduced me to her younger sister, Elizabeth, who was studying in Oxford and I took her to Newmarket races once when I was at Writtle. But there it ended. The attraction was Dina.

After a few days' holiday with uncle Jimmy in Johannesburg, I decided on a trip to Cape Town. He offered to buy me a ticket on the famous Blue Train but I foolishly said that I would hitchhike. His driver set me on my way, dropping me off outside Johannesburg in the Mercedes, where I hung about for ages waiting for the first lift. Eventually a car came and slowly, through a series of lifts, I came to Kimberley but once again foolishly did not pause to see the diamond mines. I ploughed on but finding lifts was becoming more difficult in this desert part of the Free State and eventually I gave up and took a train the rest of the way.

When I arrived at Cape Town, I called Jimmy's manager who had kindly offered to put me up for a couple of days. He and his wife were very good to me and even lent me a car so that I could go to see the wine-growing area. I was most impressed by a tour of the Stellenbosch vineyards and particularly the sampling of their products. I attended a lecture on the merits of different wines. There was a rack with six glasses in front of each chair. These ranged from sherry and white wine, to red wine and brandy. The lecturer described each and we tasted them in turn. Two American ladies in my group were teetotal and offered me theirs too. So, with three glasses of each drink, I was one happy chappie.

During the course of my stay in Johannesburg, I had borrowed a car from Jimmy too and driven to the movies in Hillbrow in the centre of the city. Coming out late at night, I completely lost my way back to Morningside. Time after time, I stopped in one suburb or another to ask the way but there was no one in the streets and each time I knocked at a door, a voice would shout: 'Go away', 'I'll call the police' or 'I've got a gun.' No one would even give me simple directions — a city that lived in fear. Or perhaps I was walking where wise men feared to tread. In the end, it was dawn before I returned home and Jimmy and family were frantically calling the police to look for me. Cape Town, by comparison, seemed much more relaxed.

Our close group of friends disbanded and the others left Swaziland at the same time. Richard went in for publishing in London, Paul to the BBC and I do not know where Ronnie went. Richard, Paul and I met up once in London and Paul took me to the BBC canteen at Bush House where they served haggis of all things, it being Burns Night. Then we lost contact, partly, I suppose, because I spent the better part of the next thirty years abroad but also perhaps because our friendship was based on having been thrust together in Africa, rather like passengers on a ship. Once we were back in the UK, we were less compatible. Sadly, I heard later that Derek Van Zuydam had committed suicide over some financial problems. I wrote to his wife — they had been very good to me while I was there.

WRITTLE

ONE MORE TRIP TO Northallerton secured another 100 per cent grant for Writtle and I drove there in an old Austin Cambridge, which I had again bought at the car auctions. Writtle is near Chelmsford in flat, farming country and, like Harper Adams, has its own adjoining experimental farm. I went there as a postgraduate (or rather post-NDA) to take a one-year college diploma in management. I joined the rugby club, made friends and it seemed like Harper Adams all over again.

The Austin Cambridge did not last long as, after one prang, a lot of the bodywork seemed to disintegrate and it appeared to be held together only by rust. At that point Aunt Do came to the rescue. Until then, she had been a rather strict maiden aunt although she had given us shares from time to time when hers had new allocations or 'pups', as she put it. Without the least prompting, she gave me £500 for a new car and I bought the most fun car I have ever had, a second-hand Mini Morris Cooper. It was a Mini with a souped-up engine which went like a go-kart. As I am over six foot tall, it took some getting into and out of and I sat with my knees up to my shoulders but it was a great car to drive.

During the Easter break from Writtle, I joined a party of twenty for a skiing trip at Solden in Austria. This involved taking a night train across Europe, which was full of ski parties and even had a disco carriage, and lots of fun deciding who slept where in the six bunk cabins. As a result, I was in love by the time we arrived (although I now forget her name). Then there was frustration as she preferred one of the ski instructors who, in turn, was chasing someone else! The skiing was fun although I never progressed further than the nursery slopes, the snow plough and cries of 'bend ze knees'.

Towards the end of the year at Writtle, the interview season started and (now beardless) I received three job offers. The first was from a large firm of land agents, Strutt and Parker, which offered me a starting salary of £600 a year. The chinless gentleman who interviewed me said: 'Of course, on this salary your father will have to continue supporting you for a year or two.' This was out of the question. The second was from the now defunct Milk Marketing Board, which offered me £800 a year. But when I asked about promotion prospects, I was told: 'As you have only diplomas and not a degree, you can reach only grade B3 or some such level.' That bureaucratic monster deserved its fate.

Finally, I went to ICI, which promised £1,200 a year and considered my three years of higher education as equal to a degree — nectar! But I did not

Colin, studio portrait, 1968.

have just one quick interview. Following the first at Writtle, I was summoned to the ICI agricultural division headquarters at Billingham on Teesside. There were four candidates and we were told to arrive at four o'clock in the afternoon at the company guest house. Then there were drinks with a group of eight managers followed by dinner (to see if we could use a knife and fork) and formal interviews by several department managers on the following day. It was the drinks party that decided my career. Only two of the managers' names now come to mind. Mr Parfect, the personnel manager, was very smooth but had the sort of handshake that made you wipe your fingers afterwards. The other entered the room, announced in a booming voice 'Jenkins, exports' and crushed my hand. When he asked if I would like to work abroad, I had no hesitation at all in saying yes.

One further, and rather comical, interview followed. It was made clear that I had been given a job but that they would like me to visit the Plant Protection Ltd (later to be ICI Agrochemicals) head office at Fernhurst near Haslemere in Surrey. This is a very attractive site based on an estate with a large German-looking house (Schloss) and Second World War-type accommodation for offices, all on a large farm. The directors' offices were in the house and I was led up the stairs to meet Dr Watts-Padwick, who had once been the 'Imperial mycologist' in India many years before. He was now approaching retirement. On being introduced, he looked up from his desk and said 'Play rugby?' Then 'welcome aboard'. And that was that.

USA

THIS INTERVIEW took place in May 1968 and it was decided that I would start with ICI in October. Meanwhile, I had plans to see the United States.

All sorts of special travel deals were available through the student union. One offered a charter flight to New York returning three months later for £90. It sounded just the thing. I talked to someone who had tried it the previous year and who had worked in California on a pear farm at Walnut Grove near Sacramento. He gave me the address and I contacted the farmer, Dennis W Leary, who offered me work when I arrived. We flew by Aer Lingus from Manchester via Shannon to New York, where we were stacked for two hours, circling JFK airport and drinking the plane dry. When we finally reached New York, it was hot and noisy and we were all booked in to a cheap hotel downtown, where we were astonished at the number of television channels available, there being only two or three in the UK at that time.

We split up on the following day. I went to the Greyhound station as I had already bought a ninety-nine dollar ticket in the UK, which allowed me to go anywhere for ninety days. This was good value as I calculated that I had travelled over 10,000 miles by Greyhound before I left the States. The first leg of the journey was to Sacramento via Chicago, Omaha, Cheyenne and Salt Lake City. I did it in one go (taking about 72 hours) and did not stop off at these towns. The buses went on night and day, stopping every three hours or so for a break at a roadside restaurant. This was fine in daytime but at three o'clock in the morning the cry of 'Wakey, wakey folks — this is Lone Cactus' before being bundled out of the bus to drink an unwanted cup of coffee was less welcome. Of course, there were times when these breaks were all too short. Once, I was just making friends with a very pretty waitress who had opened the conversation with 'Gee I just love your accent' when the idiot bus driver was calling 'OK folks, all back on the bus please.'

You see lots of maize while driving from east to west across the States — millions of acres of it for about sixty of the seventy-two hours. Things improve as you cross the Rockies and the Pacific coast is a dream. Dennis Leary met me at Sacramento and I was driven to Walnut Grove.

I shared a cabin with a couple of American students and we were the only non–hispanic members of the labour force, as the other hundred or so were migrant Mexican 'wetbacks'. It was the harvest season for pears and the Mexicans had ladders and bags and went from tree to tree. I drove a tractor with a large wooden bin on the front loader and took the fruit to the packing house, where it was washed and packed into boxes ready for despatch to the supermarkets. The work was hard and the days long but it was a cheerful time and I acquired a taste for Mexican food. After three weeks of this, I collected my wages and took the bus to San Francisco for a day or so, then went down the coast to Santa Monica, Santa Barbara and Los Angeles.

Uncle Sam Armstrong was a great one for supplying the names and addresses of business contacts overseas who would be 'delighted' to meet you. Father had told him that I was off to the States so I was given a list. I had tried this out in New York but, strangely enough, the business tycoon who had once had a horse with Sam was somewhat less fascinated in meeting his penniless nephew, who was backpacking around the country. However, of the dozen names, six of whom I contacted before giving up, one turned up trumps. This was in Los Angeles and the lady in question 'knew everyone in Hollywood'. She did indeed and took me to a studio where an episode of the television series *Bewitched* starring Elizabeth Montgomery was being filmed. We watched the filming and then she showed me around the studio and drove me around Hollywood, pointing out where each of the stars lived — a lovely day.

Los Angeles did not impress me. I stayed downtown and the noise of police sirens did not cease, day or night. I had developed an ulcer on my leg from an infection and this was getting more painful, especially when walking, so finally I looked for a doctor. I asked where I could find one at my cheap, five-dollar-a-night hotel and, with a fine sense of humour, the porter sent me to the most expensive medical centre in town, all marble and glass and pretty, immaculate nurses. The doctor bound up the wound, gave me a prescription and then took about two of the three weeks' wages from my pear harvesting as a fee. He asked me to return to see him in a week's time but, calculating that I could either eat or have a second appointment, I chose the former. The leg finally healed itself.

From Los Angeles, it is only a short bus ride (by US standards) to Las Vegas. By this time, I had worked out a routine which involved travelling by night on the Greyhound to avoid paying hotel bills but Las Vegas has the perfect answer to this problem. As long as one occasionally places a bet in the casino, the owners are perfectly happy to feed and water (or whisky) you, as well as give you free shows.

I was no stranger to casinos having, while at Writtle, become a member of Charlie Chester's Casino in Soho. For four glorious Saturdays, I played black and red on the roulette table with the simplest of systems. It is an even chance of black or red coming up except, of course, for that rotten zero where the house wins (or, even worse, the double zero as well in some casinos). I would bet, say, a pound on red. If that failed, I would double up and so on until red finally came up and I was ahead. For four Saturdays, everything went splendidly and I had won some £300 (remember that my Mini Cooper had cost £500) and I gave thought to becoming a professional gambler. I had obviously a talent for it but the fifth Saturday in Charlie Chester's removed that option. Black came up eight times running, then zero.

Luckily, I had my train ticket back to college but absolutely nothing else and had to contact Father as I had blown most of my term's grant money. I had to put up with a fairly lengthy lecture on my stupidity, but he saw me right.

Back to Caesar's Palace in Las Vegas. I had bought a decent, light brown cotton jacket in Los Angeles and, having somehow pressed my trousers, I left the rucksack at the Greyhound depot and stepped into the exciting world of Las Vegas, every inch the smart tourist and gambler. I played the tables carefully all night and emerged at dawn, having had an enjoyable time with the same amount of money in my pocket as when I had gone in.

From Las Vegas, Greyhound carried me to the Grand Canyon, Albuquerque in New Mexico and El Paso, Texas. Tourism, I have since found out, is a game for two or more players. You can take photographs of each other, exclaim at the size and beauty of whatever you are looking at, and generally ooh! and aah!

It is a bit limiting on your own. I got out of the bus at the Grand Canyon viewing point, looked over the edge, stared at it for ten minutes, then went to look for a beer.

Having had brief contact with Mexicans (limited, as I spoke no Spanish) and Mexican food at Walnut Grove, I now thought I might see the country. As the Greyhound ticket was only valid for the US, this presented a problem. But having crossed the Rio Grande at El Paso into Ciudad Juarez, I managed to hitch a lift with two Mexicans, who worked in the States and were returning to see their family in Mexico City. We would share the cost of the petrol and they were happy to take me. The journey was 1,000 kilometres long and the Mexicans usually spoke to each other in Spanish so I looked at the countryside, which is remarkably barren between the odd, irrigated valleys, and listened to the car radio. I kept hearing the newscasters getting very excited and mentioning Czechoslovakia and Prague so I asked my hosts what was happening. They told me that the Russians had moved in to Czechoslovakia to put down a bid for independence. It was the 20th August, 1968.

I stayed in a remarkably cheap hotel near the centre of Mexico City and wandered around, admiring the cathedral, which was slowly sinking into the ground, the elegant La Reforma avenue and the Garibaldi Square, where there are dozens of mariachi bands, which will play for the tourists there or be hired by Mexicans for parties or serenades elsewhere. After a couple of days, I took a bus to Acapulco, where I met up with a group of British and American hippies who had been there for ages on the beach. Two days of their company was quite enough but one of the group, who was travelling back to Texas in a battered van, agreed to take me on the same petrol-sharing basis. Petrol was remarkably cheap in Mexico, which was lucky as my funds were running low.

Once back in the great USA, I again used my bus pass to go to Miami. Here I had to work as I was only eating once a day after paying three days in advance at the cheapest hotel I could find. I asked if they knew of any work to be had and was sent to a multi-storey car park nearby, which specialised in storing cars while their owners were away. The owner was a tough old bird of about sixty years old. Yes, she needed someone to park the cars and I started at once. As the cars arrived, they had to be taken up in a lift and manoeuvred about according to their date of collection so that those which would be first to leave were not trapped behind those staying longer. It was easy enough and I got on well with the old bird who would call out 'Mr Armstroooong' whenever she needed me. I worked there for about three weeks (denting only one or two cars through my enthusiastic parking) and recovered my financial situation, as wages for manual employment in the States are good, the living cheap and everyone friendly. Everyone, that is, except for the lift operator at the hotel where I stayed. It was an old-fashioned lift with a brass concertina gate and a handle (as on a ship's bridge to communicate with the engine room). The lift operator was a Cuban who was built like 'Odd Job' of James Bond fame and had obviously suffered some severe shock in the country's revolutionary wars. One day, as he was not there, I climbed into the lift and operated it myself up to the third floor. When I arrived, an absolutely furious Odd Job came belting up the stairs and berated me for taking the lift when he was not there. 'The next time you do it,' he said, 'I'll kill you with these hands! I've done it before. In Cuba I've killed many men.' Well, what can one say but 'sorry'.

From Miami, I moved as far north as I could go in the USA to Buffalo, before crossing briefly into Canada to see Niagara Falls. It was wonderful, but again I suffered from the lone tourist syndrome. From there, I went back to New York and, as it was mid-September, I had three weeks to fill before Air Lingus was due to return me to the UK. I checked in at the YMCA in downtown Manhattan, saw the sights of New York and then, even though my funds would have lasted, I went down to the employment exchange and looked for a job. It occurred to me that I could actually return to the UK with more cash than I had brought to the States, have all of this fascinating trip for nothing and be ahead of the game.

I was the only white person at the exchange and was selected to wash dishes in a restaurant in Queens with three black people. It was more than a restaurant as it had a small chocolate factory attached to it. On the first day, the owner said: 'Eat all the chocolates you want.' I did — and did not touch another in the three weeks that I was there! In fact, I did not wash dishes. I was the bus-boy who picked up the dirty dishes from the tables and took them to the kitchen where my black companions operated the dishwashers. They lasted three days on average, then with 'mother' this and 'mother' that as to hard work and exploitation, they left. At the end of the three weeks, I was considered a veteran. In fact, although I say it myself, the manager congratulated me on my good work and offered to make the job permanent. I declined, saying that I had an appointment with ICI in the UK. Interestingly, the wage that I was offered was the same as the ICI starting salary.

ICI

Monday the 13th October was my first day at work at Fernhurst. I had driven down from Yorkshire in my Mini Cooper the day before and checked in to The Swan at Haslemere, which had been booked for me by ICI.

Now I presented myself at reception, dressed in a new three-piece suit. I was shown to Gerry Jenkin's office by his long-time secretary, Barbara Wall. Gerry in turn introduced me to Scott Wischart, the team leader of the Far East group, his assistant Nick Geach, Ric Stobbe (a Dutchman), Mike Hartley and Leslie Thomas, our assistant. Apart from a few secondees already abroad, this was the team that controlled sales over the whole of the Far East. Other areas of the world (divided into six groups excluding Britain) were of equal size. Gerry Jenkins was world sales manager with two assistants, one of whom was Keith Moores, the other Ronnie Hampel, who finished his career with ICI recently as chairman and Sir Ronald.

During my first few weeks with ICI, I was expected to learn about the products. Plant Protection Ltd had been formed by ICI and Coopers McDougall before the last war to sell the pesticides used in those days such as DDT, BHC and derris. During the war years, it invented the hormonal herbicides MCPA and 2,4-D and in the 1960s the total herbicides Gramoxone and Reglone. I also had to get to know who was who and generally fit in. I was not given much work to do, which at first came as a pleasant surprise. I had not known what to expect but thought that it would entail long hours of graft. After a while, however, I became bored and I was looking for more to do. One day, I suggested that we needed better maps of our territory. Scott, who was busy, said 'You organise it'. So I did. I rang a map publisher in London and said 'Armstrong, ICI here, we need the best maps you have.' These duly arrived by special delivery together with a huge bill and I had a bollocking. Scott had intended me to ring Plant Protection office supplies department at Fernhurst.

In those days, Plant Protection Ltd was very departmentalised and part of the acclimatisation process involved knowing what you could and could not do. Often there were complaints that I had failed to follow the correct procedures. I had talked, for instance, to the factory people at Yalding in Kent, directly instead of going through production liaison department or whatever. I was a bit too keen for all tastes.

Meanwhile, I had found digs with a Major and Mrs Page at their delightful old house, The Chimes at Lurgershall, about three miles from Fernhurst. The house stands besides a stream just down from the church, hence the name. It is very ancient, crooked, half-timbered and quite delightful. To add to its attractions, there were two teenaged Page daughters, Liz and Alex. Mrs Page rented me a small flat at the back of the house with bedroom and sitting room and I shared their kitchen. Major Page was a lecturer at a university in the Midlands and generally away from home. Inevitably, Liz and I became good friends and went out together until fate, determined to protect my bachelorhood, saw me abroad again.

During my indoctrination at Plant Protection Ltd, I attended two family events, one happy one sad. The first and happy one was Cousin Robert Armstrong's wedding in November 1968. He married Elizabeth Marsh, the daughter of trainer Marcus Marsh, in a huge ceremony at Ely Cathedral. All of the racing world was there. As this involved wearing a morning suit, I hired one (as I have done on the only other three occasions since that I have needed one) and set off in the Mini Cooper to meet my parents on the way. We had arranged to meet at a pub just off the A1 towards Huntingdon. That day was a good one for us — Father looking smart in his own morning suit (not a hired one as he had found plenty of use for it over the years) and Mother looking very well in a new suit and hat. They were on best behaviour and getting along well. I changed quickly into my togs in the pub gents and off we went to Ely and a great wedding in the cathedral and reception afterwards, where my parents knew loads of people. We later separated and they drove home north and I south. Unfortunately, Robert and Elizabeth's marriage did not last many years, but they did give us a great day.

The other family event was the death of Uncle Bert Armstrong. He was Father's cousin as his father had been Bob's brother and brought up with him at the George Hotel in Penrith. Bert had worked in insurance in London and I first met him when he was delegated to help me across London from Kings Cross to Waterloo station, when I went to stay at Rockbourne each summer. He would always appear wearing a bowler hat and seeing me, a small boy with two cases, would ask: 'Which is the heavier?' I would point it out and he would say: 'You can carry that' and pick up the other.

He talked little about his past, even in his later years. He had fought at Gallipoli in the First World War and had risen to the rank of major, although curiously I found this out only towards the end of his life. It struck me as strange when father was so keen on his rank as a captain in the home guard and military titles were so often used in civilian life, that he kept his hidden. Perhaps it was the trauma of that brutal campaign that affected him. Tragedy followed him when his young wife died while having dental surgery in the 'twenties. He then went to Argentina to work in the oil industry with Fred Madlener, the husband of Do's great friend Di, whom she had met while studying French in 1914. He did not enjoy that so he returned to England and spent the rest of his working life in an insurance office. When he was well in to middle age, he met his second wife, Ann, and, when they retired, bought Lane Cottage at the bottom of Tupgill Park from Do and spent their time gardening.

Now Bert was dead, and I headed home for the funeral. Bert, self-effacing to the end, was cremated so he did not occupy a piece of Coverham churchyard where my grandparents and father lie (but not Mother, who asked for her ashes to be scattered on Flag Moor in Derbyshire, where she had spent so many happy days hunting). Ann, who lived to the age of ninety-one, died in September 2000, independent to the last in her cottage.

Gerry Jenkins called me into his office one day in December and said that Brian Higgins, who was currently seconded to ICI Malaysia, was returning home and asked if I would like to go to Kuala Lumpur for a year. I would love to. In those days, you were given a clothing allowance by the company when you went on secondment and pointed at Tropiccadilly, the tropical outfitters, in Picadilly. Wandering around, I was fascinated to see that you could still get pith helmets of the sort that 'won The Empire'. However, I resisted the temptation and got myself a biscuit-coloured tropical suit that I still have today (and can still get in to thirty years later.)

The day of the UK expatriate secondee is almost over. Today, international companies use locally employed executives overseas, and send them to head office for training, rather than the other way around. They have the advantage of knowing the language and local conditions but perhaps something of the energy, pioneer spirit and clubbiness of the old system has been lost. Dare I say it, but perhaps there are not the same number of volunteers in Britain today who are prepared to give up their parents, home, social life and girlfriend to go overseas (because these postings were strictly bachelor). In my case, there was less difficulty. Britain was passing through one of the worst stages of its history with labour unrest, discontentment, high taxes, and nationalised industries and was falling behind the rest of the world according to every economic measurement. My relationship with my parents was only polite, those with Venus still optional.

MALAYSIA

Ric Stobbe left for Indonesia and Mike Hartley for the Philippines at the same time. I flew to Kuala Lumpur in January 1969 and was met by Brian Higgins at the airport. Driving into town with him, I said that I had heard of the millions of acres of rubber plantations in Malaysia. Where were they? He laughed: 'We've been travelling through them since we left the airport.' Only then did I realise that what I had taken for woodland was rubber. The trees are tall and grow in straight lines and each one has a panel cut into the bark and a little cup attached to it to collect the latex. Every day the workers take off the slimmest slice of bark from the panel to continue the flow of latex.

Kuala Lumpur was impressive. In the centre of the city is the Padang, a sort of central park, with the famous Selangor Club (The Dog) on one corner. The railway station is on the opposite side, housed in a very attractive mock eastern building of the British colonial period. There were a few high-rise buildings but nothing to compare with what exists today.

I was put up at the Lake Club for a few days before finding a flat. This was curious as Norman Smith, the sales manager of ICI Malaysia, made it very plain that 'You will join The Dog. You will not join the Lake Club, which is for your elders and betters.' Polo-playing Norman had been in Malaysia all of his working life and knew practically all the planters, many of whom were still British, and particularly Scottish, at that time. Rubber was still the biggest plantation crop but oil palm was increasing quickly and pepper was also important.

After a week, I had found a furnished apartment at a development called U:K: Heights at the end of Jalan Ampang (the Ampang road), where ICI had its offices. A Chinese 'amah' was contracted to cook and clean and I moved in. Work began, as at Fernhurst, on learning the products. Apart from Gramoxone, the big seller, there were old and specialist products such as Fomac for root diseases and Fylomac for panel fungus in rubber. Then I was despatched (having acquired a car) to conduct some market research among the British planters.

I approached this job rather nervously as, fresh from England and freshly in to agrochemicals, I was conscious of how little I knew. However, I need not have worried because each and every planter was an expert, knew all the answers and had nothing to learn (though they had widely differing opinions!). All I had to do was keep my mouth shut and listen. The ICI name normally gave me access to the plantations and I began with 'Greetings from Norman Smith' although this did not always go down well. Some seemed to have less than pleasant recollections of their last meeting and I had to back-pedal several times or face ejection from the property.

After a while, I got the hang of the jargon and, having heard from Mr Campbell that he had a serious problem with fomes fungus on the roots, I had only to carry this to Mr McDonald, as a bee pollinates flowers, and we could have a fine discussion. No doubt I was given credit for being a sound technical man. Actually, Fomac, which we sold for this problem, had a disadvantage. You had to clean the roots of the rubber tree (which could be twenty-five feet tall) of all soil and apply the product to the diseased roots. How this was done without either cutting through the roots or bringing down the whole tree I never found out.

In the course of my year in Malaysia, I got to see most of the country, firstly with this market research project and then by selling Gramoxone. I was also sent over to what was then Eastern Malaysia, Sarawak, where the Borneo Company was the ICI agent. I flew to Kuching via Singapore and was met by a Chinese salesman who was (very correctly) somewhat dismissive as to the use of sending a wet-behind-the-ears expatriate who did not speak the language to sell Gramoxone. However, he had his orders and after a hold-up of forty-eight hours, when I had the worst stomach upset in my life, we embarked on a dugout canoe with an outboard engine and headed inland up-river.

After many hours' journey through the jungle in intense heat, and with my head aching, we arrived at the Dyak village. The idea was to show the villagers the wonders of spraying weeds with Gramoxone so that they could grow their rice more easily. It seemed a fairly futile exercise as they did not look as if they had any money, anyway. The Dyak Indians are very primitive and live in communal longhouses. Traditionally, their women are bare-breasted but some years previously the League of Decency, or missionaries, had struck and now the women wore large, white Madonna-like conical brassieres. No blouses, just a traditional skirt and these wretched brassieres — the church has a lot to answer for!

Well, after sploshing about in paddy fields with a knapsack sprayer for some time, feeling unwell, the chief invited us into the longhouse for lunch. With great ceremony, I was seated next to him with one of his giggling daughters next to me — a lovely girl (well sort of), perhaps fifteen, plump and with black teeth from chewing betel nuts. A live chicken was brought and offered to me; looking to the Chinese salesman for guidance, I was told to nod. I did so and the chicken was garotted in front of me, which did little for my wellbeing.

Following the meal and numerous speeches, the time came for us to depart. We climbed into the canoe and so did the girl, who had taken quite a shine to me. I was told that she was a present from the chief. In panic, I said that I did not want her but the salesman told me it would be rude to refuse and that she should go with us to Kuching and be sent back after a few days with some money. He seemed very keen on the idea and so it worked out. He enjoyed the lady's favours and I had to give the money and return her to sender.

I returned to Sarawak several times and once went to Brunei, that fabulously wealthy sultanate, though, as I remember, the wealth did not appear to have been spent on the town. I admired the huge white marble mosque, which stood out very prominently among poor bamboo houses.

I was also once sent to Medan, the chief city in the north of Sumatra in Indonesia. This led to trouble, but not of my making, as the ICI Malaysia franchise did not cover Indonesia, where a large British trading company, Harrison Crossfield, had the rights to sell ICI's agrochemicals. It complained to Fernhurst and that finished the business for us.

Before then, in Kuala Lumpur it was thought that there was business to be had by selling across the Malacca Straits, and I was despatched with a Mr Reg Bull, who knew Sumatra and had contacts there. We flew from Penang to Medan and got started.

Since the Dutch had been expelled from Indonesia after the last war, there had been practically no investment in Sumatra. We visited oil palm plantations where the trees were huge and, having passed their productive age, were beginning to fall down. The plantations were over-grown and roads dreadful. This contrasted with Malaysia, where everything was spick and span and planters competed over the appearance as well as the productivity of their estates. Medan was very run-down, the houses had not been painted for years, the electricity worked only spasmodically, and the telephone wires all had knots in then from frequent repairs of old wire.

Reg was a man prone to sudden fits of terrible anger and during the week or so that we were together, I witnessed this many times. At first this was very frightening, but I soon found that I had a hitherto unsuspected skill of calming anger, which has stood me in good stead over the years. Together, Reg and I did good business with the Chinese traders still operating there and, as we flew back by sea plane to Penang, I heard the news that Neil Armstrong had set foot on the moon. It was the 21st July, 1969.

Malaysia offered a huge variety of things to do in your spare time. I had joined 'The Dog' and on Saturday afternoons the club put out two rugby teams, two hockey teams and one soccer team. In fact, most of the Padang was given over to the club's use. I played rugby for the second team and was once nearly drowned in a game. In Malaysia it rains all year round, normally at 5pm. On this day, the sky opened up during the game and so heavy was it that the water could not sink into the ground. I was tackled and the entire scrum landed on me, forcing my nose into the water. I struggled to raise my head but the team was tired and thought that they would take a breather before getting up. So there they lay on top of me and kept my head down. Thankfully they rose to resume the game just before my lungs gave out. The only fellow player I remember from those days was an insurance man from the Hartford Insurance Company of Connecticut in the States, called Jean Dumas. I did not know him well then but our paths crossed again some years later in Guayaquil, Ecuador, when he introduced me to my future wife.

'The Dog' has several bars but we all headed for the long bar (which was stag) after a game and a bath and there began the evening's festivities. To get into the restaurants, you required a jacket and tie, but the club had a selection of these and would kit you out rather than turn you away. On the subject of dress, it was normal to see men in safari suits of bush jacket and matching shorts with knee-length socks. We used them outstation and even for the office. I adopted a form of night attire there which I still use today, the sarong. This is a piece of cloth sewn in a circle which you step into before pulling it tight around the waist, doubling it over and turning it down at the waistband. It is more comfortable than pyjamas and in tropical climes a jacket is not necessary.

Norman Smith, whom I grew to know and like, was a stalwart at the Kuala Lumpur Polo Club and one day suggested that I help to exercise the ponies. I am not sure how this came about, as I had not ridden since giving up my pony at the age of eight and had no interest in horses. Possibly it arose from a dinner conversation regarding my father and comments like 'You must ride very well.' Perhaps, full of good humour and wine, I had agreed to go to the Polo Club but I went with mixed feelings.

Obviously I could ride but did I want to take it up again to the detriment of other leisure activities? Well, I did enjoy it and went on doing it for several weeks: exercising the horses that is, not playing polo. I tried having a swing with the sticks but quickly found that I did not have the necessary strength in my wrists for it. The date of the amateur races in Singapore was approaching and they were a jockey short so I was asked to ride in a race. Thinking of Father's happiness when he heard of this, I accepted. Then I had to go to a Chinese boot maker and have some lightweight racing boots made. One week before the race, I was weighed in boots and silks and holding my two-pound saddle. Disaster — I weighed ten pounds more than the horse's handicapped weight. There was no way that the owner was putting up an overweight jockey, especially one with no previous experience. I was about to be discarded at the first fence. But I had set my heart on the race by this time (and no doubt already told Father) so I promised to lose the necessary ten pounds within a week. And I did too, by practically not eating at all. I now know the horrors of losing weight, something that I have only had to do on this occasion. I was miserable all week.

I drove from Kuala Lumpur to Singapore, the day before the race and presented myself at the Orchard road racecourse on race day. I watched the first four races from the stand as mine was the fifth race, a five-furlong sprint. I was beginning to have second thoughts about the wisdom of doing this. Most of the other jockeys were Chinese and looked very competent, and the horses, mainly polo ponies, were not very large while I am over six foot tall. When we entered the ring before the race, having changed into britches and silks in the weighing room, I knew I was going to look ridiculous. The other jockeys were five foot nothing and I stood out like a sore thumb. Worse was to follow, as the pony I was to ride was perhaps 14½ hands and the stirrups were so short that my knees literally touched over the saddle. When I rode on to the course and paraded in front of the stand, I received a great deal of laughter and a cheer from the crowd. But by this time, I did not notice them as I was concentrating on getting down to the starting gate and staying on board. My mount might have been small but it had mettle and, as an old campaigner, knew the excitement of the racecourse.

It nearly unseated me with a few unexpected bucks and then we set off for the gate, while I almost stood in those short stirrups to prevent a headlong gallop, which would have worn it out before the race had even started. On arriving at the gate, which was the old-fashioned sort consisting of one tape across the field, I walked in a circle with the others until the starter called us into line. Twice I came into line beautifully and twice an idiot jockey was facing the wrong way, and aborted the start with calls of 'Not yet, Sir' to the starter. On the third time, it was my horse that was facing sideways but the starter had waited long enough. 'Under starter's orders, they're off.' I lost my chance to get away quickly and, although both horse and I made great efforts to catch up, we never had a chance of winning. We did, however, come fourth, which was not bad for an inexperienced jockey and the horse that no one else wanted to ride. I do not remember its name.

After the races, we had a night out in Singapore, that dynamic, clean, city with a huge harbour full of ships. Stamford Raffles got it right when he set up a colony here. Today, it is one of the powerhouses of the world but even thirty years ago it was a booming city. In those days, a night out in Singapore would finish in the early hours of the morning in Bugi Street, where food stalls served satay, that delicious chicken on a stick dipped in peanut sauce, all night long. The street had another claim to fame which was the crowd of transvestites who would hang about there until a sailor, who was so plastered that he could not tell chicken from rabbit, picked them up to the great amusement of their mates and passers-by. The story is often told of the drunken Scottish sailor who went off with one. The following day, he was questioned by his shipmates as to what happened when he had found out that he had not picked up a girl. He said: 'What do you think? I had paid my money by that time.' It was not at all easy to tell the difference, even when sober, as they were very attractive 'girls' and I must admit to being deceived myself (at a distance mind, at a distance!)

Malaysia is an ethnic mix of approximately sixty per cent Malays, thirty-five per cent Chinese, four per cent Indian (Sikhs or Tamils) and one per cent European (chiefly British). The reason for this is that when the British colonised it and planted rubber, they needed labour for the plantations. The Malays did not take to this sort of work and labour was brought in from China and India. The Chinese gradually took over most of the economy with the Malays working for them. On independence from Britain, the majority Malay government tried to correct this by giving land to Malay peasants (the Bumiputra programme) and made ethnic quotas compulsory.

But relationships between the two main groups would occasionally break down. This happened while I was there. Riots had broken out in the poorer areas of Kuala Lumpur, which led to the killing of over 2,000 people. Malays attacked Chinese where they were in the majority and vice versa. There were stories of fights with parangs (the machète-like weapon), of people hacked to death and of girls and women being mutilated with their breasts hacked off. The government called a state of emergency and total curfew for several days. The British High Commission called on all expatriates to help the relief services, as we were neutral. I was given a large red cross for the car (the only way a vehicle could move about at all) and detailed to help move food supplies to devastated areas. There were road blocks everywhere, manned by soldiers who looked very fierce until you waved to them and then they would put down their guns and wave back. As the days passed and tension eased, the curfew was gradually relaxed although it was maintained at night until I left Malaysia. As all my British pals had the necessary Red Cross plaques, we could still go out at night and party in each other's houses.

I had several short romances while in Malaysia, two of which were with Malaysian girls. They were from professional middle-class backgrounds and had a certain amount of liberty, although going out with foreigners was frowned upon by their families. There was also always the risk of being caught by the Muslim religious fanatics. There were stories of courting couples being dragged from their cars and beaten as the Muslim law prohibits close proximity between men and women outside the family or marriage. Still, we preferred Malay girls as girlfriends to the Chinese, who were thought of as cold and calculating while Malays were warm, sweet and loving. They are probably both grandmothers by now and I hope that they are very happy, with large families. Indeed, I hope that they are still the best friends that they once were, despite a certain strain on that friendship when I changed from one to the other. Ah well, that was thirty years ago.

There is one more memory of Kuala Lumpur which I have quoted ad nauseam to my employees. A lecture was given to a group of salesmen in ICI Malaysia by a Mr Da Silva, an old man who had retired from business and was now lecturing on good business practices. He drew a graph to illustrate his point with one parameter enthusiasm, the other experience. 'When you start work, you have 100 per cent enthusiasm and zero experience and when you retire, you have 100 per cent experience and zero enthusiasm.' It is true and I can feel myself crawling slowly up that scale.

December 1969 and I had my marching orders: 'Be in Fernhurst on the 3rd January for debriefing and prepare to go to Mexico by end of March.' Well, I was not at all keen on leaving Malaysia and went to see Norman Smith to see if he could help me to stay. He said that he could not as Gerry Jenkins had asked for me to go to Mexico and there was no gainsaying Gerry. I made one further attempt by lobbying a director of the company but got nowhere and so made plans to leave.

I could choose my own way home, provided it did not cost more than the direct Kuala Lumpur to London route. I asked a travel agent who came up with a bright idea. Why not fly Aeroflot to London with three free days in Moscow? Thinking back, I must have been daydreaming or in love to have accepted this wonderful offer because it was December. The flight came from Australia with a stop in Singapore, so I went there to pick it up. There were very few passengers on board: only some of the Bolshoi Ballet returning from a tour of Australia and one or two idiots like myself who had forgotten what cold is like. The stewardesses lived up to Aeroflot's reputation. They were built like wrestlers, slopped food in front of us and vanished to the back of the plane to chat, appearing one or two more times on that long flight to renew the plate of black bread and sardines.

We arrived at Moscow's airport at nine o'clock at night and the temperature was 23° Celsius — below zero! There was no tunnel from the plane to the building so we walked and almost froze solid in that 100 yards. I had only tropical clothes with me, not even an overcoat. Once inside the building, however, it was warm and I soon thawed out. The arrival area was huge and the luggage was delivered at one end but the buses and taxis could just be seen at the other end, about half a mile away. As I was going home after a year away, I had four bags. I looked for a porter (no trollies then) and saw two or three lounging together. However, despite pointing out my predicament in sign language, none of them was prepared to help. Let the capitalist roader do his own thing, there is no service in the People's Soviet Republic. There was nothing for it but to make two trips, each with several stops to rest and uncurl my hands, until finally all four bags were at the bus end of the lobby. I had been instructed to make contact with the Aeroflot desk on arrival and I would be provided with the necessary vouchers for the hotel and meals. After some delay, the officials did so, and did so well, explaining that I was to go by their bus, waiting nearby, to the Aeroflot Hotel at the airport. Tomorrow I could see the sights by taking a bus to the Hotel Metropole near Red Square. They gave me a card with Hotel Aeroflot written in Russian on one side and Metropole on the other, and off I went to the former hotel. It was a drab, modern place but at least it was warm.

The following day, after a surprisingly good breakfast of lovely greasy food to keep out the cold, I put on almost all my clothes until I looked like the Michelin man and waited for the bus. When it came, I showed the driver my card and he could not have been more helpful, detailing a passenger to tell me where to get off. Despite there being snow on the ground during the daytime, it was not unbearably cold because the sun was shining. I wandered about the centre, the Kremlin and Red Square and then had lunch at the old-fashioned and very ornate dining room of the Metropole Hotel. My vouchers seemed to work well.

I had been entrusted with an expensive camera which Bill Kapoor, an ICI man, had asked me to take as a present for someone in England. I was to use it on my trip so that it should not look new and attract duty. Well, I had hardly ever used a camera since giving up photography at ten years old but thought that it would be a good idea to take photographs of Moscow. However, after lunch at the Metropole, I left it on the chair and I did not remember it until some hours later. In a panic, I rushed back to the restaurant and the head waiter was waiting for me with the camera in his hand. Although very different now, Russians then had a reputation for honesty, and friendliness too. On my frequent trips between the hotels by bus or Metro, everyone would help me when I asked and some were keen to practise their English as well. One evening, I went to see the opera *Rigoletto* at the Bolshoi Theatre, which is huge. There were two intervals and everyone got up and filed into the aisles, into the lobby, up the escalators and on to the top floor, where there was food and drink on sale. There was no pushing whatsoever and if anyone should brush against you, he immediately apologised. I enjoyed the opera, the first I had seen, but the only aria I knew, *La Donna e Mobile*, sounded strange and guttural in Russian. The journey back to the hotel was memorable. The temperature had returned to 23 below and I had to walk quite a distance from the Kremlin Theatre to the Metro station. It was so cold that it took your breath away and the only way to progress was to pop into the many liquor shops selling vodka, where the hot air curtains at the door revived you, and then you could make the next 100 yards. So finally I arrived at the Metro, blessedly warm, then the hotel. I had more or less enjoyed my stay but was keen to be home and left for Heathrow the following day with relief. Then I went from London to Northallerton by train and Mother picked me up from there.

Whenever I returned to Ferngill from abroad, I was struck by how much my parents had aged. It came as a shock each time. They had not just aged but grown smaller, and although one quickly said how well they looked, one did not mean it. I cannot remember who was there for Christmas that year. I rather think that Jane had left for South Africa, so Kate and I, my parents and Aunt Ann who would have had Christmas lunch at Tupgill with Do. I think that Micky Wilson would have been there; after his mother died, he came every year until Do too departed. 'Micky's mother was a man,' as father used to put it. Well yes, she was Dorothy Mann before marrying Harrop Wilson, the owner of a large textile mill in Leeds. A generation previously, a Mr Mann had married Nellie Lamplough's sister so that was how we were related.

Micky lived at Harrogate until he died in August 2000 aged seventy-five. He never married, dedicating his life to field sports, particularly shooting and fishing. During his last few years, he would come and shoot with us although he was used to a much better class of shoot than ours was. He had some funny stories to tell of the people he had met while shooting. Once he was invited to shoot at Six Mile Bottom near Newmarket and was placed next to a chap whom he described as an 'extraordinary little man'. He told him, during the intervals between drives, how he worked in London and, as travel was so very expensive, he took a lift with some good lady to the station each day, which was cheaper than leaving his car in the station car park. At the end of the day, Micky's host provided him with the names of their fellow guests and he discovered that the man was the chief executive of one of Britain's biggest companies.

In his will, he left his matched pair of shotguns to our son Nick, who was delighted to receive them. Ceci and I inherited the roulette table which had belonged to Do, who had left it to him in her will, so now it returned home to Tupgill. But I am jumping ahead thirty years.

We had had the same Christmas routine for as long as I can remember. We would walk from Thorngill (later Ferngill) to Tupgill at 12 o'clock, drink a glass of champagne, have lunch at one o'clock, drink coffee and watch the queen's speech at three and leave at about four o'clock. At this time, Do had an old companion, Mrs Weymes (I think she was called Margaret but she was Mrs Weymes to everyone.) She was the widow of Jack Weymes, who had been Bob's head man. When Bob gave up training at Tupgill, Jack became the trainer and on his death his son Ernie took over. Ernie also trained at Ashgill for many years before in turn handing over to his son last John year. Mrs Weymes kept house for Do and the two old ladies would chat in the evening. She lived in West House, which was connected to Tupgill though a series of rooms which were the apprentices' dining room, stableman's dining room, kitchen, stores and so on of yesteryear. Now they were filled with dust and jumble but served as a covered way for Mrs Weymes to enter Tupgill. Mrs Weymes always came into her own on Christmas day. A great fuss was made of her. Mother and Ann brought dishes of stuffing or mince pies and a general inspection of the turkey and smacking of lips would ensue until the great moment when she announced 'Lunch is served' in her Scottish accent.

My parents still had a daily help at this time — a tall, thin woman called Florrie Hammond. She had been with us for many years, since we were small children. Florrie's son Peter was one of my playmates and I used to go and stay with her at her mother's house in Carlton, about two miles away. Florrie's husband had been killed in the war and, as well as looking after us, she had her own boy and widowed mother to care for. Poor Florrie — hers was a hard life and perhaps because of this, she did not have much patience with us as children although we got on much better when we grew up. Florrie and Mother, however, were great friends. She found it much easier to confide in Florrie than in Father. Florrie gave up her job when Mother died, but sadly did not live many years longer.

After spending my end-of-secondment leave at Ferngill, I returned to Fernhurst and rejoined Plant Protection Ltd, if it was still called that by then. It became ICI Plant Protection Division, then ICI Agrochemicals, then five years ago Zeneca Agrochemicals and now Syngenta. But my time with the Far East section was over and I transferred to the Americas. Gerry Jenkins was still in charge of world sales and John Robinson headed Latin America with Mike Chambers as technical manager and David Lloyd-Williams looking after part of the area.

I had to write a report on my work in Malaysia and that was the end of my contact with the country, although I hope to visit it again some day. I needed to learn Spanish for my new job and was sent to Berlitz Language School near Marble Arch for three weeks. I have never had a great facility for learning languages. I had battled away with French and passed my O-level in it but, despite further attempts later in life, I have never been able to speak it at more than a very basic level. Spanish seemed annoyingly similar to French, which caused me to regurgitate long-forgotten French words instead of Spanish ones. The course I took at Berlitz was intensive: three weeks, five days a week, nine hours a day, and one-on-one teaching. They started with the present, past and future tenses of verbs and, before I was halfway into these, we were on to subjunctives, completely baffling me. I did not use those subjunctives for years to come and got along quite happily, so perhaps they were a bit over the top.

Soon after getting back to Fernhurst, Roger Ball, who had just come back from a secondment (in Japan, I think) offered me a bedroom in the house that he was renting with one or two others in the delightfully named hamlet of Titty Hill, a couple of miles from Fernhurst. I stayed in England for three months between leaving Malaysia and my next posting in Mexico and remember the delightful parties we had in that house. On several occasions, full of bonhomie at closing time at the Red Lion in Fernhurst, we would invite everyone still in the pub back to Titty Hill, having bought those four- or eight-pint giant cans of beer between us.

John Robinson decided that I needed to gen up on sugar cane and coffee before arriving in Mexico so I was sent via Trinidad for two weeks and Costa Rica for three weeks. Both were very enjoyable. Phil Manning was the secondee in Port of Spain and he and his wife Carol showed me around and took me to the beach at weekends. One evening, we went to the Trinidad Hilton, where I saw limbo dancing for the first time. It was put on for tourists and the trick was to get a girl wearing a short skirt to volunteer to do it. Several did and it is very revealing!

Phil and I duly went from one sugar estate to another and I took note of how the crop was grown and how Gramoxone could be used for weed control. The work aspect does not stand out in my memory very clearly now, although the social side certainly does. There seemed to be a lot of parties, almost every night, and we went to the races once. It was there that a very beautiful girl, Faith Power, showed what I thought to be great character. She was wearing a strapless dress and no bra and the lads were milling around her when one went a bit too far and unzipped the back of the dress from top to bottom, expecting her to squeal. Not a bit of it — clutching the dress to her at the front, she turned around, slapped him hard across the face and said: 'Now do it up.' He did so very shamefacedly and it was he who was the butt of the jokes from then on.

There was just one rather frightening experience. After a party in which I had taken a shine to a lovely mulatto girl, she suggested that I walk her home as it was not too far. I did so and, arriving at her flat, was asked in for the proverbial coffee. Not long afterwards (which was very fortunate), there was a hammering at the door and the girl cried: 'It's my boyfriend — he's terribly jealous!' Now she tells me!

The flat was on the first floor but there was nothing for it. I went out of the window just as the boyfriend, who was black and looked seven feet tall, broke the lock on the door and charged in with a knife in his hand. He saw me in the garden and came down the stairs while I took to my heels. The chase went on for several blocks and the streets were empty as it was three o'clock in the morning. I can run and fear gave wings to my feet but I was not losing him. In panic, I rounded a corner, saw a garden hedge and dived over it. He raced past and, in due course, came walking back, looking around for me but I played possum long enough. Finally, shaken and somewhat dirty and scratched, I made it back to my hotel.

I arrived in San Jose and was met by David Blows, an Australian and again the ICI secondee. David was a bachelor then and a very popular one he was, too. He seemed to know dozens of girls, so once more I was in party mode, although it is now hard to recollect any individual parties because they seemed to be continuous. Not to say that David did not get any work done — on the contrary, he was terrifically successful in increasing ICI's sales in all of Central America. We went to see coffee farms, which are very well run there, and drove down to Puerto Limon on the Atlantic coast to see banana farms. David was welcomed everywhere we went. He had the sort of personality which makes friends easily. Years later, when Standard Fruit Company was opening up in Ecuador, every one of their executives who had been in Central America knew or knew of David. He made it much easier for me to get in with them.

Puerto Limon has another claim to fame apart from its banana plantations. The people there are of Negro descent and speak English (of a sort) in a Spanish-speaking country. Apparently a slave ship had been wrecked there and they stayed together in that one area.

Ecuador has a similar area, Esmeraldas, on the northern coast, again with the story of shipwreck. Were there so many wrecks or were slaves once imported and now no one wants to admit it?

Costa Rica is a very attractive country with coffee and dairy farming in the range of hills which run from north to south in the centre of the country and banana and oil palm plantations and cattle ranching on the coasts. Today, it is a great tourist country with eco-tourism to the fore. I have got to know it well from many visits there, especially since I bought a share of a company there in 1992. But that story comes later.

David left ICI some years afterwards and, having met and married Vanessa in England, went to farm in Australia. Today he owns and farms a large cotton spread near Wee Waa, New South Wales, with his three sons and we stay in contact through our mutual friend, Bob McIntosh, who is the Zeneca distributor in Panama. David and his family came to stay at Ferngill a couple of years ago and we talked over old times. But, as both our wives were present, the Costa Rican adventures had to be censored.

MEXICO

I ARRIVED IN MEXICO in April 1970. An ICI de Mexico already existed but until then it had not handled the agrochemicals business, which was done through the Mexican office of the US company, Chevron Ortho Inc. My job, as second-in-command to John Waghorn, was to set up an agrochemical department within ICI de Mexico and close down the agency agreement with Chevron Ortho. Of course, all this had to be done without losing sales and in fact with the ambitious target of increasing them. This was my eventual remit but in the beginning it was of a more technical nature: establishing Gramoxone in the coffee and banana areas of Veracruz, Tabasco and Chiapas. As I remember, John Waghorn did not arrive until after I had been there for six months, so during that time sales must have continued through Chevron Ortho Inc.

I was given a company car (an Opal) and sent down to Jalapa in Veracruz where I had to set up trial plots in coffee plantations to demonstrate Gramoxone's ability to keep the coffee free of weeds. I was told to report back to Mexico City on not more than one weekend, plus a couple of working days per month. Otherwise I was to stay in the bush. This was rather daunting as my Spanish was still rudimentary and very few people spoke English in these southern provinces. I had to force myself to make interviews with farmers and no doubt they suffered almost as much as I did just by having to listen to me. Using the telephone was even worse as, without seeing the other person, you cannot use your hands to help to explain. I used to end up bathed in sweat after a phone conversation. As the area I covered was large and I had some twenty demonstration plots at a time which needed checking and reapplications, I changed base and hotel about every three days. To this day, I am an excellent packer, leaving everything on hangers which I transfer from case to wardrobe to case.

My Spanish gradually improved but I would end each day in my hotel room reading an English novel so as not to have to speak to anyone. However, there came the day when I met a girl called Margarita in Jalapa and suddenly I wanted to be able to speak Spanish well. Our affair was short-lived but I had crossed the divide in terms of Spanish by the time it ended. Although to this day I make any number of grammatical errors, I have never since considered speaking Spanish a barrier to work or play.

However, my over-confidence had repercussions. I was invited to a cocktail party in Mexico City, given by the president of ICI de Mexico and with most of the company executives and their wives present. They were both British and

Mexican and both languages were used. I thought that I would try out my newly learned Spanish on one or two Mexican ladies. Well, this was not a success. They very soon turned away from me in disgust and the president of the company hurried over to ask me to speak in English, or go home. I had unknowingly used what they described as pure 'Alvarado', the name of a small town in Veracruz famous for its crude language and obscenities!

The central plateau of Mexico is very arid, broken up only by irrigated valleys, but on the Gulf coast there is much higher rainfall and Veracruz and Tabasco states are verdant. Veracruz produces coffee in the hills and has citrus, maize and pastures, while Tabasco has bananas and pastures. Veracruz City is a port and has a lovely centre, with a large plaza surrounded by restaurants where one can sit and drink a beer, listen to the music of 'conjuntos Veracruzanos', and watch the girls go by.

The mariachis are famous all over the world as the typical Mexican folk group but they originate from the northern state of Jalisco. Each state has its own culture, music and food. In Veracruz the 'conjunto' or group dresses in white tropical clothes and plays guitars, double bass and a small harp, rather than the trumpets and violins of the mariachis. Villa Hermosa, the capital of Tabasco State, translates as beautiful city but this is not the case at all. It has grown from nothing into a petroleum town and has few redeeming features. Jalapa is in the hills, surrounded by coffee plantations, and is attractive but is not, to my mind, as good as Veracruz City.

These, then, were the three poles of my early Mexican days. Round and round them I went, conducting Gramoxone trials and visiting the agrochemical dealers to push sales. Occasionally, I travelled to Chiapas State — which has many thousands of small farmers, many of them indigenous and growing coffee and maize — and stayed at the town of Tapachula, working for a week or two at a time. While there, I visited the Honorary British Consul, whose name I forget, for advice on the area. It was my first contact with this office, a local British businessman who agrees, for a small stipend, to look after the interests of the British community in the area. It was my first contact but not the last; I have been one myself for the last nineteen years.

The Yucatan peninsula is very dry and did not merit a great deal of my time although they did grow hemp for fibre. The chief attraction of going there was to visit the Mayan ruins, which I did once at Xuxmal. The lone tourist syndrome struck once more and I did not really appreciate them, until many years later when I went back with my wife and saw them again, together with the even better site of Chitsenitza.

When my boss, John Waghorn, had arrived in Mexico, he came with me on a tour of my area — I considered myself an old hand by now! One night, we stayed in San Andres Tuxla, a small town in Veracruz State. We had had a hard day and in the evening I offered to take him to the 'zona rosa'. Most Mexican towns have one of these: an area outside the town limits where prostitution is tolerated but which also has good food, beers and music — in fact a night club area. He said: 'Well OK, but let's be discreet and not go in the ICI car with the company logo on the door.' 'Don't worry', said I 'we will be in good company.' And off we went. When we arrived, he saw why. The car park was full of company cars: Dupont, Dow, Bayer, Monsanto and others. All our competition was there; they greeted us with cheerful insults and we enjoyed a good evening.

I will admit, rather shamefully, that some time previously, in a similar place, the evening had become so riotous that the police were called. Not accepting excuses from anyone, they had locked us up for what was left of the night. Now a Mexican jail is no fun place and we were greatly relieved to see a lawyer arrive at nine o'clock the following morning to get us out. Work hard, play hard was the order of the day. In fact, the two could often be combined as one's customers were often to be found in the 'zona' and, even if no business was conducted there, it gave one the 'entrada' to the client's office or farm the next day.

I have mentioned that I enjoyed Mexican food before but that was the 'Tex-Mex' of California. Here the food was seriously hot with the chilli peppers included in the recipe and not as an optional sauce. I suffered for the first three months but then got to like it, and today no meal is complete without it.

Folk culture is very strong in Mexico and different in each state. I saw one example of this in Veracruz: the 'Flying Indians'. This is a tradition going back to pre-colonial times but is now performed for tourists. A very tall pole is erected with a platform on top, which four Indian flyers mount by rope ladder. The pole is wound about with ropes and each man ties a rope around his ankles. At a signal, all four leap off the pole and 'fly' in circles around it as the ropes unwind, getting further and further outwards and downwards until they land. It is very impressive to see. At the same place, they grow vanilla vines and the two go together in my mind as the vanilla is made into sweet-smelling dolls and figures and sold to the tourists.

The Ballet Folklorico de Mexico, which plays continually at the Palacio de Bellas Artes in Mexico City, is one of the gems of the country, providing a sample of the dances from all over Mexico. This normally starts with the terrific deer dance, an athletic dancer with a deer's head pursued by two hunters. Then there are the polkas of the revolutionary period and fishermen's and farmers' dances in brilliant costumes. It all makes a very memorable show. I am a fan and have seen it nine times so far.

Once John Waghorn had arrived in Mexico, and I was appointed his assistant manager, I spent more time in Mexico City and needed somewhere to stay. Having found a flat in Las Lomas de Chapultepec, a very pleasant residential area, I advertised so that I could share it with someone. Not only was it expensive but I was still travelling a great deal, so I did not want it to myself or to have to open and close it every few days. Roy Slingsby became my flat mate. Roy, somewhat older than myself, had had a career as an engineer in British industry and was now with a large partnership of consulting engineers, which was tendering for the contract to design and build a new steel complex in Mexico. It eventually won the huge contract and Roy became a partner in his firm.

Roy and I became very good friends and he gave me much good advice about all sorts of things, including the financial front. One of the benefits of the secondment system was that one was paid two salaries. The UK salary was paid into a bank account in Jersey by ICI and was tax-free as you were a non-resident for the period that you were out of the UK. There was also a local salary paid by ICI Malaysia or Mexico. In addition, as I was travelling and staying in hotels in Mexico, I was living on expenses for a lot of the time. So I not only saved the UK salary but part of the local salary too. It was a great time to accumulate capital, which I just left in the bank earning interest. Roy knew a lot about British companies and was a keen player of the stock market. We could get hold of a *Financial Times* which was just a day or so old and we pored over this and put together a portfolio of shares for me. It was 1971 and there was a good bull market at the time. I had savings of about £4,000 and I doubled the amount in that year. It was this capital which was to change my life quite dramatically a year later.

While living in Mexico City, I met Cristina Guerrero, and she became my girlfriend until I left the country. She was a tall, elegant girl who lived with her parents in a large Spanish-style house near my flat. I would go to pick her up in the evening and be let into the house by the maid and shown to an elegant drawing room, which was clearly not used by the family. Here, I would wait for her to come downstairs. The same thing happens in other parts of Latin America. The family (or those who have large houses) live upstairs and the downstairs hall, drawing room and even dining room remain pristine and museum-like and are used only for entertaining. Another custom, but one peculiar to Mexico, is the serenata.

I was never romantic enough to do this for Cristina but saw it performed for a girl who lived above my flat. Her boyfriend, probably after a fight with her, became completely drunk. Then, feeling amorous at about two o'clock in the morning, he drove his pick-up truck to the Garibaldi Square where there are mariachis for hire, piled a group into the truck and drove to the girlfriend's flat. I was awoken by a terrible din as they played right outside my ground-floor bedroom window. Going out on to the patio, I saw the band with the lovesick swain singing his lungs out, the daughter and her mother on the balcony in floods of tears, and her father beaming, obviously recalling his youth. I was somewhat less fascinated and thought a bucket of cold water was more the order of the moment!

Before leaving Mexico, I was sent to visit most of the states and once drove the thousand kilometres from Mexico City to Ciudad Juarez, in the state of Chihuahua on the Texan border, non-stop apart from petrol and food. Together with a Mexican salesman, Jorge Ramirez, I took in the exciting night life of Ciudad Juarez. I also crossed the Rio Grande into El Paso, but this was totally dead at night, just paper blowing around in the canyons between high-rise offices. Once or twice, I went to Acapulco with friends and this time, with rather more cash in my pocket, I enjoyed it tremendously. There is a spectacle of a diver diving off a rock some 150 feet into the sea below. This takes place at night and is floodlit, and one can watch it in comfort from the balcony bar of a hotel nearby.

There is a small town on the road from Mexico City to Acapulco called Cuernavaca and, in my early days in the country, I tried to sell Gramoxone to an agrochemical retailer there. My Spanish was hopeless at that time and I battled as I tried to find the relevant words while he sat watching me impassively but offering absolutely no help whatsoever. After half an hour of my presentation, when I thought I might as well get up and go as I could not make the slightest headway with this potential customer, he said to me in English: 'Good try but you are going to have to improve a lot yet if you are ever going to sell anything in Mexico.' I gaped at him and he laughed and said that he was American. I could have punched him for making me struggle in Spanish. But he had made clear just what had to be done. He made it up to me by taking me to a delightful restaurant called Las Mañanitas, which is in a beautiful garden behind the walls of a Cuernavaca street. In fact, the town has lots of beautiful houses but you would not guess it as you pass through the dusty streets. The delights are all behind those doors.

I must have made some headway both in Spanish and sales skill because I was the top-selling salesman in our team before I left Mexico in November 1971. I had not wanted to leave as I very much enjoyed being in Mexico but Fernhurst gave marching orders. I was told to go to the Venezuelan embassy in Mexico and get a work permit for Venezuela. I tried to do this, but it was no-go. It was, and is, very difficult to get into the country for anything other than tourism. As this failed, I was to report back to the UK. I did so reluctantly, not fancying the idea of returning to head office.

On the way home, I decided to have a look at Bermuda (why not — it's on the way?) and flew there with Quantas. By coincidence, I had met and made friends with the Quantas pilot at a party the day before. So, just before we were due to land in Bermuda, I was called into the cabin and sat in the extra seat for the landing. What a view of Bermuda — the transparent green of the sea showing the much greater extent of the island underwater and the coral reefs, as well as the tiny island itself laid out like a map.

I spent only a day and night on the island but I hired a moped and travelled around to see as much as I could including the perfume factory, the Blue Grotto, the fort and the old naval dockyard. That night, I wandered around the bars on the waterfront and eventually got talking to a middle-aged Ulsterman — a sailor, who was very drunk and belligerent. Now I have always enjoyed imitating accents so I turned on my best Ulster brogue and away we went. He looked at me slyly and said: 'You're a policeman, aren't you?' I denied it but he kept asking all evening until eventually, to make him happy, I suggested that I was indeed. Shortly afterwards, he excused himself to go to the bathroom and did not return. I wonder what he had to hide — or was the joke on me? I had to pay for both our drinks. No doubt he is telling the story of a young Englishman with a phoney Ulster accent being left with the bar bills.

Many years later, I returned to Bermuda with my wife, Cecilia, and children, Nick and Diana. We hired a scooter for two and two mopeds and beetled around the island, seeing all the same sights. But how much nicer it was to be able to share it with those you love — no more the lone tourist.

As I had been on secondment for eighteen months, I was due six weeks' leave. Having arrived at Heathrow, I called my boss, John Robinson, from the airport, just to let him know I would be in Yorkshire. He said: 'Make it two weeks' leave and then get back to the office. I have a job for you in Ecuador.'

Meanwhile, before going to Yorkshire, I had an appointment in London. At that time, ITV had a programme hosted by Eamonn Andrews called *This Is Your Life*, in which a celebrity would be confronted with people from his or her past who would tell a story concerning him (or her) and then take a seat on the stage. At the end of the show, Eamonn would present a red book to the celebrity with all the details the company had managed to research, supposedly without his or her knowledge.

Today it was Willie Carson's turn and, as Father had first taught him to ride and put him on his first winner, he was part of Willie's story. I met Father at the Cumberland Hotel, where he was staying courtesy of ITV, and we went to the studio together. I was to sit in the audience while Father was hidden backstage until the moment came for his surprise appearance. It all went very well and Eamonn, reading Willie's story, told of his childhood in Glasgow and asked him how he got into racing. Before he could reply, Father's voice came from off-stage, telling of how he had met Willie and their first talk together. Willie looked suitably surprised and Father walked on to the stage to audience applause and shook hands with Willie. They exchanged a joke. then Father sat down and the show moved on.

After it was all over, Willie invited us all to Mirabel's Nightclub where we partied for the rest of the night. I remember it as a very expensive sort of place full of the young and rich beautiful people, with titles well to the fore.

The next day, when we finally got up, Father and I made our way by train from Kings Cross to Northallerton, where Doug picked us up and drove us back to Ferngill.

ECUADOR

When I arrived at Fernhurst on the 20th December, John explained the job to me. ICI had an agent in Ecuador, a pharmaceutical company called Life SA. It had built an agrochemical division over the years but had now been partly acquired by a competitor, Dow Chemical Inc, and there was a conflict of interest over certain products. John Austin, who was seconded to Colombia and covered Ecuador, had been asked to find a replacement agent. He looked at the existing agrochemical set-up and did not see potential in any of the candidates. Then he met Tom McDougall, who held ICI agencies for plastics, explosives and other chemicals and offered him the agrochemical agency. Mac, as he was known, said: 'Yes, but give me a man who knows the business for two years to set it up.'

We all met at Fernhurst: Gerry Jenkins, John Robinson, Mac McDougall and I, and the deal was done. I still have the notes on the meeting. Afterwards we had a celebration dinner at the Spread Eagle hotel in Midhurst, that splendid 400-year-old inn where I have stayed on many occasions since. Over dinner, we tried to think of a name for the new company. Mac already had a company called Cipac and another Quimipac so we decided on Agripac Compañia Ltda. Out of that brief meeting, an institution was formed which today ranks among the top businesses of Ecuador. The 'Compañia Limitada', or private company, was later changed to 'Sociedad Anonima', which is a public company with shares that can be traded.

I was to fly out on the 17th January, 1972 in the guise of a technical visitor to Life SA and see what the market was like. Then the company would be given notice of the termination of the contract in March and Agripac, which was to be set up in the meantime, would take over the business in June.

Then it was home to Yorkshire to spend Christmas with my parents and Do at Tupgill. On the 3rd January, I drove Father down to Fernhurst as he badly wanted to see where I worked. We stayed the night with Peter Hampel, Ronnie's younger brother who had none of his brother's drive but of whom it was said 'Peter is as charming as Ronnie is ambitious.' We had a conversation that night to the effect that, although we grow older, we do not feel any different to ourselves. Father was then seventy-three, Peter possibly forty and myself twenty-six. It is something I have remembered over the years.

I had promised to take Father, for the only time in our lives, for a brief holiday together in Portugal. Here he had an old friend, Allan Parry, a retired army colonel who lived at Estoril. We went by train from Haslemere to Waterloo and, while waiting for a taxi to Heathrow, I met my contemporary, Ric Stobbe, in the queue. He had left ICI after returning from Indonesia and had moved to another agrochemical company. We had only a brief chat as, when you are in no hurry, the taxis come infuriatingly quickly. I have not heard of him again since then. We flew to Lisbon, drove to Cascais and Estoril, and had a quiet but pleasant holiday. I am glad we were able to do it.

I flew to Bogota via Miami on Saturday, the 15th January. Here, I met up with John Austin and stayed with Sally and him at their apartment before John and I flew to Quito the next day. I remember taking John a bottle of duty-free whisky as a present. He thanked me and put it away in his bar but I could not help noticing all the other bottles of whisky — there were gallons and half gallons! Mine looked very small beside them. He explained that whisky was very expensive there and he regularly stocked up at the duty-free for parties.

Quito, the capital of Ecuador, is a lovely town surrounded by mountains. Some of them are covered in snow, as they are up to 20,000 feet high. Quito stands at 10,000 feet. This can be a problem, as the least exertion leaves you out of breath and the lack of oxygen can give violent headaches. Those who live there become acclimatised but visitors suffer and older people may need an oxygen mask at times.

Both John and I stayed with Mac and his very attractive wife Anne in the flat that they had there at this time. Mac was already forming the company Agripac Ltda. with his lawyer, ready for take-off. We all thought that I had better get straight on with finding out about the agriculture of Ecuador so, with John, I went to Life's head office, where we met the agrochemical sales manager, Oswaldo Maggio, a diminutive man with a gravelly voice. The next day, he was to go to Santo Domingo de Los Colorados, a town in the sub-tropical area about two hours from Quito. 'Los Colorados' is a tribe of Indians who paint their bodies with red and black stripes and their hair red. They can still be seen today, and will pose for photos.

We decided to go with him and see how the Gramoxone sales were going in the oil palm plantations there. We stayed the night at the Zaracay Hotel, which consists of cabins scattered around a large sub-tropical garden with a central restaurant and bar. It is covered with lichens, creepers and lots of vegetation and at that time had a number of monkeys in cages. It was also very damp and the rooms smelled musty. I was there again recently, twenty-eight years later. The monkeys have gone but the rest is just the same.

We returned to Quito and John flew back to Bogota while Mac and I took a local flight of forty minutes to Guayaquil. Then as now, as you fly into Guayaquil airport, it appears that you are about to land in a swamp because the rice fields are all flooded, especially in the wet season. You fly over a river, land suddenly and the town is all about you. It is one of the more convenient, or dangerous (depending on your point of view), airports in the world, being five minutes' from the centre for the city. Guayaquil is not everyone's ideal city. It stands on a large, muddy river about forty miles from the sea. The midday temperature ranges from the coolest of 25°C in September to 35°C from January to April, with humidity of almost ninety per cent. Over the years, I have seen it greatly transformed from a clapboard town to one of concrete buildings and high-rises. The population has increased from 800,000 to 2,500,000. Perhaps it has lost some of its character in the process, old sepia photographs of Guayaquil in the 1920s showing it as uniformly wooden and not more than three storeys high. But, for residents, the benefits of air-conditioning more than compensate for loss of character.

The flat which Mac had taken for me was in Las Peñas, the historic centre of town, which was then, as now, largely made up of wooden buildings along its one cobbled street. The flat, however, was in the basement floor of a concrete building. This building stretched from the street on the hillside to the river front so my flat was at river level (at high tide) and the water flowed past the windows, taking the flotsam and jetsam up- and down-river twice a day. It was, needless to say, terribly damp and clothes would turn green with mould within a week if not used. There was also no air-conditioning and I just used to lie in bed at night and sweat. Mac reserved one room for himself and Anne when they were in town; otherwise this was my home. It was equipped with the usual scruffy furniture of a furnished flat in Guayaquil and, as I had arrived in Ecuador with only two suitcases, I did not have many personal items with which to decorate it. A bit spartan it may have been, but it was a great place for a party.

Julian Sedgewick, a Briton of my own age, had the flat above and he too worked for Mac on the chemical side of the business. Through Julian and later my own contacts, I soon came to know lots of people. Stanley Wright, an Ecuadorian of British descent, worked in the Banco de Guayaquil. We became friends on my first visit to the bank to open an Agripac account. Then there was Holger Riebau, a German in a shipping agency; another German, Hans Schuback, and Eric Notarianni, surprisingly a Briton whose Italian forebears had moved to Edinburgh. We were all more or less of an age (actually Stan is a wee bit older) and bachelors. The parties were of the bring-a-bottle variety and there were always plenty of girls. At that stage, none of us was attached for long. Weekends would see us away in a group to the beaches, about an hour and half from Guayaquil.

But play, even the good fun that it was, definitely took second place to work. This was my first managerial position and I was not going to risk it being a flop. I had come to Ecuador as a technical secondee to Life, as the ending of the agency was still a secret, so I made contact with Life's office in Guayaquil, the manager of which was Andres Argudo, in order to play the part and get to know the country.

Andres is a born salesman and the most amusing of people, although one who is fond of practical jokes. As we travelled around together, he told me stories of visitors from ICI, some of whom knew very little Spanish (as Andres speaks very rudimentary English, I am not sure how they communicated).

While driving with one of them, Robin Addy, in the banana province of El Oro near the Peruvian border, he was stopped by a police patrol checking identification. 'What do I say to him?' asked Robin. 'Tell him "soy Ingles, hijo de puta",' said Andres. He did so and there was an immediate and very unfavourable reaction from the policeman, who levelled his pistol at Robin and ordered him out of the car. Andres sorted out the situation in fits of laughter and the policeman, with several angry backward looks, let them proceed. 'What on earth I did say?' asked Robin 'Oh just "I'm English, you son of a bitch!".'

While in El Oro, we met up with the Life salesman Antonio Zambrano, whom I recognised from an ICI advertising film called *Adelante Gramoxoneros* made the previous year. Three months later, Antonio became the second Agripac employee, after myself, and is still with the company today, very much the elder statesman.

Apart from the star product, Gramoxone, we worked with an insecticide for banana weevils called Primicid. The trial work on this involved making traps of pieces of banana stem and placing these at intervals in banana plantations, returning after a day or two to see how many insects there were in each trap, and thereby calculating the population per hectare. Now, there is an art to finding your way inside a banana plantation, one that I have never mastered. Bananas are planted in rows, but they move. That is to say, each generation sprouts from the base of the one before but on any side, so over a period of time they get out of line. A plantation can cover up to 500 hectares, so it is very easy to get lost somewhere in that green mass of leaves, especially when it is raining and you keep your collar up and head down. My early weevil trapping could take a lot more than the allotted time as, when I finally emerged on to a cart track, I had no idea which way to turn to get back to my Land-rover and ended by walking miles.

On Saturday, the 11th March, 1972 the moment came to fire Life as an agent (after many years of business) and hand over to the newly formed Agripac. John Robinson and John Austin arrived in Guayaquil with Mac and Anne, then we drove to a beach resort, Punta Carnero, to discuss our strategy. We returned to Guayaquil on Monday and flew to Quito, ready for the arranged meeting with the president of Life on Tuesday. Then there was a revolution on Monday night! Luckily, it was a bloodless one and the military took over, led by General Guillermo Rodriguez Lara and the five-times elected president, Jose Maria Velasco Ibarra, was deposed and sent into exile in Argentina, where he died some years later. A most extraordinary man, Velasco Ibarra was an exceptional orator who said: 'Give me a balcony from which to speak and I will be president.' Only once did he finish his elected term, being deposed either by military or civilian forces the other four times. He was basically a demagogue and rarely was his government an economic success.

However, this occurred at a very inappropriate time for us. John Robinson questioned whether it was the correct time to change the agency, with possibly negative consequences, while the country was in disorder. We all trooped to see the British ambassador, Peter Mennell, who, to my great relief, did not see the revolution as an impediment to our plans. Here was I, either on the brink of becoming the manager of the ICI Plant Protection Division agency in Ecuador, or continuing to count those wretched weevils for another year or so!

At the appointed hour, John Robinson, John Austin and myself, crossed Quito, which was full of soldiers, and negotiated military road blocks. We met Jaime Murillo Battle, the president of Life, and the notice was duly served. We gave him three months, until the 14th June, after which time Agripac would receive all stocks in good condition and take over the agency. Life did not appear surprised by the news and caused little difficulty. The management had already worked out that, when it was partially bought by Dow Chemicals Inc, there would be a conflict of interest with ICI.

The two Johns then departed and I was told to sort out the details. This involved me in several long and protracted sessions with Life's managers who, fearing for their jobs, were not nearly as friendly as Murillo had been. On several occasions, the talks about what I would, or would not, receive of its stock broke down with angry threats to offload those items which were easy to sell on the market at cost and spoil my business. I replied that Life would then have to get rid of the slower-moving stock against my competition. Eventually, all was settled, or at least it was until I had a look in their warehouse. Here, I found boxes containing tins of products which were more than ten years old. When lifted, they fell to pieces and the tins disintegrated, flooding the floor with foul-smelling chemicals. Then there was more hard bargaining I was not going to be in any way responsible for getting rid of this rubbish.

However, I was now, at least, in the open and could go ahead with looking for offices and staff for Agripac. Mac had two companies, Cipac and Quimipac, which were already established and the manager of Quimipac, Carlos Bucaram, was very helpful. Together, we found a warehouse which we could share at the corner of the streets Luis Urdaneta and Baquerizo Moreno in Guayaquil. It was the large ground floor of a two-storey building with doctors' surgeries above. It was a peculiar situation for an agrochemical warehouse, but in the six years we were there, we had very few complaints from the doctors about the smell of the chemicals. We built plywood offices inside the warehouse and, gloriously, had an air-conditioner installed. This office served both companies for less than a year, when Carlos had to look again for Quimipac's accommodation as Agripac needed all the available space. The company started with just two employees, myself and Antonio Zambrano. Then I hired a secretary, Patricia Aguirre, and, with Marcos Campusano as the other salesman, we made a start.

We were lucky in that 1972 saw the beginning of the petroleum era for Ecuador. There had been discoveries of petroleum on the coastal areas early in the century but these were declining. Then petroleum was discovered on the Amazonian side of the country in the 1960s. By 1972, this was being pumped through a pipeline hundreds of miles long over the Andes and to a terminal near the northern port of Esmeraldas. This radically improved the Ecuadorian economy and suddenly all sectors, including agriculture, blossomed. Shortly before, under the government of Velasco Ibarra, Ecuador, in common with most Latin American countries, had gone in for land reform in a big way. This, in effect, was the breaking-up of large estates and farms and the forming of co-operatives of their former workers.

Now that oil money was flowing, the military government, which was slightly left wing, financed these new co-operatives through the state-owned land bank, the Banco de Fomento. This meant putting a lot of money into hands which had no previous experience of handling it and, of course, led to all sorts of swindles. The co-operatives would elect their presidents and managers along with a host of lesser dignitaries. The ones who were elected were normally the smartest, but not necessarily the most honest, of the former workers.

We in Agripac would receive a visit from the señor presidente and señor gerente (manager) of the Rice Co-operative 31st May (or some such, they were generally dates). They would negotiate for a cash purchase of a goodly amount of Gramoxone or another of our products (we probably had twenty from former Life stock or new imports by this time). The deal would be done, and only then would it be indicated that a secret commission would have to be reserved for these two people and nothing said to the co-operative. When this was agreed, they would go off and appear again the next day with twelve other lads, all with straw hats but some without shoes. They would all be pushed into our tiny office, where the senor tesorero (the treasurer) would step forward with a large parcel wrapped in newspaper, which he opened to reveal wads of bank notes. The required amount was paid and off they went with the products in a hired pick-up truck. Some little while later, the señores presidente and gerente would pop back for their commissions. The system worked for only a couple of years. By this time, the legal representatives of most co-operatives had purchased not only agricultural inputs but cars, lorries, pumps, combine harvesters and whatever, needed or not, and then had disappeared to Colombia or Venezuela leaving the co-operatives bankrupt.

According to the law at the time, the co-operative movement could be created but never destroyed so there was no way for the Banco de Fomento to foreclose on the land and, as no more money could be lent, there was paralysis. The land grew weeds and the co-operative members returned to work for other farmers. Finally, years later, the law changed and some co-operatives survived by selling part of their land to private farmers, clearing their debts and farming the rest. But these were the exceptions to the rule. Most of the co-operative movement collapsed and has not reappeared to this day. Ecuador is a nation of individualists whose only allegiance is to the family. The self-denying kibbutz system did not catch on here.

But Agripac had had a good start and went from strength to strength. In 1973, the banana board, the Programa Nacional de Banano (PNB), called a

$1,000,000 tender for products to combat the banana weevil. Agripac quoted for Primicid but the competition was strong — it was, after all, worth thirty per cent of the total agrochemical yearly imports at that time. As it did not look as though we could win on price, we got in touch with John Robinson and he contacted a City company, Ralli Trading, which specialised in swap deals. Now it appeared that Ecuador wanted to sell bananas to Greece but that the Greeks had no foreign exchange to pay for them, but would pay in Hungarian clearings via Egypt, which would pay Ralli in whatever currency. Ralli would deliver the Primicid to Ecuador and everyone would be happy.

Sounds easy, doesn't it? There were just one or two snags. The PNB was adamant that, if a new market was going to be opened in Greece, it should go to the Federation of Banana Co-operatives (Urecobas) and not to large private exporters. Well, we had to accept this, but there were two Urecobas, one in the north near Quevedo, and one in the south near Machala. Both were noted for their unreliability and the very poor quality of their bananas. We had to work with both of them.

Then there was the problem of finding a reefer ship to transport the fruit. These were tightly held by the traditional worldwide banana companies and difficult to procure by an outsider. Ralli fixed this by contacting Geest Fruit Company in England, which chartered a Russian ship. The next problem was finance. The Urecobas had no credit rating whatsover and the box makers demanded cash in advance. Ralli had opened a letter of credit to an Ecuadorian bank (the Bank of Guayaquil and my new pal, Stanley) but it would not release funds until it saw a bill of lading, showing that the fruit was safely on board ship. Then the drivers of the trucks taking the fruit to the port demanded payment in advance. Eventually Mac had to sign as guarantor for all this and we were ready to start.

'Not so fast', said the director of the PNB (a naval lieutenant), 'We don't want $1,000,000 of Primicid. We would like fifty Land-rovers and the balance in Primicid.' Back to square one. Ralli said that there was no way of doing this as the deal depended on ICI making great discounts on the Primicid (which was proving difficult to sell.) However, British Leyland had no problem selling Land-rovers for cash and was not prepared to squeeze margins. Finally, the stalemate was resolved by Ralli, unilaterally deciding to substitute a cheaper specification Land-rover for the one PNB wanted, and thereby allowing the deal to go forward.

The logistics were horrific. I ran from one Urecoba to another, to the port to receive the ship, to the bank for cash, to the box factory and back to the Urecobas. Then, when we were finally loading the ship in Guayaquil, old John Van Geest (the chairman of Geest Fruit Company) turned up. He must have been seventy years old but impressed us all with the agility with which he ran up the loading ramp and down into the hold of ship to inspect the stacking of the boxes. Today, the ships are mainly containerised but loading was then by hand. The ships had side ports which were opened and wooden ramps were placed up to them. The stevedores would carry three boxes of forty-four pounds on one shoulder, and run up the ramp and down other ramps inside the ship to the lowest hold. The ships came into port for only twenty-four hours or so and loading went on by day and also under floodlights at night. Meanwhile, the trucks would arrive from the plantations before the ship, and form a queue outside the dock gates to be let in to the dockside two or three at a time. Under union rules, only one crew of stevedores could load a ship so the crews were hundreds-strong and worked in shifts, those off duty eating or sleeping on the dockside until the ship was loaded. John Heron was the Geest executive who was in charge of the operation of the three ships involved over a two-month period. John, who was a former Indian army officer, had the soldier's knack of making himself comfortable and Ceci, he and I had many a good dinner together.

So off went the first ship heading for Greece, the Urecobas got their cash and we relaxed. Then the proverbial hit the fan. The fruit was mainly ripe when it arrived in Piraeus. This is a capital offence in the banana business. The fruit must be green on arrival at the port of destination and is then taken to ripening houses, where ethylene gas is used to ripen all the fruit together, and off it goes to the supermarket shelf. Fruit which ripens on the voyage is thrown overboard, and this is what happened to a large part of the cargo. Greece is twenty days' sailing from Ecuador, near the time limit at which bananas will carry and stay green. To ensure that this was the case, they should have been below a certain size but the Urecoba lads, in a fit of enthusiasm, had included bigger fruit. The PNB was supposed to inspect the fruit at the dockside but had not done its job. As just one banana ripening in a box can ripen several surrounding boxes by generating natural ethylene gas, disaster struck. By this time, the second ship was already on the way to Greece and much the same thing happened. I am not sure how this situation was recovered; I think extra fruit was provided free or the insurance paid or both. Either way, the third ship was a success and it remained only for Ralli Trading to deliver the Primicid and Land-rovers.

These duly arrived but, when the PNB saw that the Land-rovers were of a much more basic specification, than that quoted, things got rough. This was a military government unused to the niceties of the law or to small print in contracts. It felt that it had been cheated and sent someone to arrest Mac (luckily he was the legal representative in the deal, not myself!). Mac hid in the British Embassy for a week, frantically telephoning Ralli Trading in London and John Robinson at Fernhurst. There was a lot at stake, not just for the fledgling Agripac but for the future of ICI business in Ecuador. Push came to shove, and it was agreed that the extra accessories needed to bring the Land-rovers up to the original specification would be flown out, together with people from the factory to assemble them. This was done and all ended happily. The then naval lieutenant who was the director of the PNB eventually became an admiral and, when I met him again twenty-five years later, we laughed about all the fuss. At the time, it was less than amusing and caused me no end of lost sleep.

There is a club called the Phoenix Club in Guayaquil. Founded in 1946 as a British club, it still exists today in a somewhat reduced form. At its founding, there were several British trading houses, a bank and several insurance companies, all of which sent out British bachelors. The Anglo-Ecuadorian oilfields also ran the petroleum installation in Ancon on the coast, and Ancon itself was laid out as a British town, with neat rows of clapboard houses, each with a garden. The small town boasted three clubs, each reserved for one level of management. There was an Anglican church and cemetery too. Today, the latter is the only part of the town occupied by the British, or indeed almost anyone, as the oil has run out and it is practically a ghost town.

When I first knew the Phoenix Club, it occupied the first floor of a large building on a corner of San Francisco Square right in the middle of town. It was already declining but had been important and was very well known. There were some 300 members, including many of the great and the good of Guayaquil who belonged to every club on principle. Although they rarely went, their subscriptions were paid annually in advance, which was a great help to club finances. The Phoenix was, and is, a place to meet friends, and play darts, pool or dominoes and it had a huge bar. There was a restaurant service but it hardly rose above snack level. The large rooms with high ceilings and ceiling ventilation fans lent themselves for parties.

I think Stanley Wright introduced me to the Phoenix, where the rest of my newfound pals were already members. We all worked until Saturday lunch time and the weekend would begin with a ceviche and beer at the Phoenix. Ceviche is raw fish or seafood marinated in lemon juice and served with hot chilli sauce and popcorn. It is found in several countries of Latin America but Ecuador claims to have invented it. At the Phoenix, weekend activities were planned: a party on Saturday night at someone's house, the beach on Sunday or even a rugby match. When we were all young and keen, we played rugby for Guayaquil versus Quito several times, but always in Guayaquil. Unfit as we were, we would have died playing at 10,000 feet. We grew quite confident in our abilities until a visiting naval destroyer, *HMS Liverpool,* came in and the crew challenged a combined Guayaquil-Quito team. It murdered us, and we gave up the game shortly afterwards and retired gracefully.

At this point in the story, our collective lives changed as the free and easy friendships we had with our girls gradually began to coalesce towards steady relationships. It is an insidious process. One chap — in our case Eric — starts it, then others fall into line and single chaps become talked of and invited as pairs. Eric and Isabel it was, Holger and Ximena, Stanley and Gussey, Hans and Rocio, Bruce and Sonia. Where was I in all this frantic pairing? Well, I did have a reasonably steady girlfriend whose name will not be mentioned here in the interest of domestic harmony. However, I again met Jean Dumas, who had turned up in Guayaquil, still with the Hartford Insurance Co. We talked of old days in Malaysia and he was invited to join our Sunday beach party. Just before we set off, Jean's car was broken in to and the bag containing the swimwear belonging to him and his girlfriend was stolen. I lent him another and my nameless partner lent his girlfriend a bikini. Once on the beach, I began comparing the figures of the two ladies and came to the conclusion that the bikini was shown off to much better advantage by Jean's partner than mine.

This was in December 1972, just before I left to go to Mexico and then, with Roy Slingsby, flew on to the UK for Christmas with the aged parents. Foolishly, as it turned out, I had completely underestimated the seasonal nature of agrochemical sales on the Ecuadorian coast as the rains begin. Within ten days of my leaving, we had sold out of stock and I was receiving frantic calls to return. So I cut the holiday short and rushed back. There was little I could do in the short term, as we had no stock and orders would take a month to reach us. It was terribly galling to have excess demand and no supply. However, there was one piece of business I could pursue and this I did with a will, very soon replacing Jean in the affections of Cecilia.

Cecilia Luna Lopez, who was then twenty, was working as secretary for a French count, Louis de Reiset (Don Louis). He had taken care of her when her parents divorced and had paid for her convent education in Cuenca, a quiet town in the mountains full of religious establishments. The Italian nuns who taught her wanted her to stay on and take vows, but that was not for Ceci. She returned to Guayaquil, took a secretarial course and then helped Don Louis in his farming enterprise, which ran to some 6,000 hectares and included banana and cocoa plantations and cattle.

Although Don Louis was French, his mother had been Ecuadorian. After the Second World War, he had come to Ecuador to take possession of his estates, which were then 10,000 hectares. As the family had lived abroad for many years, the land had been farmed on its behalf by administrators who had helped themselves freely to it. Old men on the farm tell of the day when Don Louis and a group of armed men appeared and arrested the administrators and took back the land. He was that type of man: strong, determined and as stubborn as a mule, who had resisted the land reform successfully and withstood several peasants' revolts to keep his inheritance together. However, from time to time he had had to sell pieces of it in order to invest in the rest. For a time, Ceci lived at his house at Hacienda Guarumal, where she was the teacher in the little primary school for the workers' children. But, like most girls, she preferred the city and moved to his house there. It was then that we met.

Shortly afterwards, I moved from the basement flat in Las Peñas to a sixth-floor flat in a building at the other end of the Malecon of Guayaquil from Las Peñas. Guayaquil fronts on to the River Guayas and traditionally all agricultural products were transported by water, hence the importance of the waterfront, or Malecon, in the history of the city. It was here that the coffee and cocoa was traded for fertilisers, tools and machinery. This area lost its importance with the coming of mechanised road transport but some of the old trading houses remain. In my early years, bananas were still brought down-river in barges and the banana ships would anchor in the river with the barges alongside. Then, with the building of the New Port on a salt water inlet south of the city, this trade also moved away and the Malecon became a residential area of high-rise blocks of flats.

My flat was brand new, air-conditioned and had a balcony with a splendid view across the river to the Isla Santay, which is an unspoilt island of grass and trees, that has so far escaped development. This flat was also partially furnished, although I was beginning to collect an item or two of my own and had had my old school trunk sent on from England. This contained whatever I had collected in previous travels, such as pictures, ornaments and several pangas and Malaysian knives. Now I see that I was unconsciously beginning to build a nest. One very conscious move was to have a bar made. I had always wanted a bar so I made a drawing of what I had in mind and asked a carpenter to make it for one corner of the room, in wood padded with imitation leather. Many were the evenings spent at its six stools.

Partying continued, of course, but we had settled down in pairs. The beach season is mainly between December and April, because at that time the cold Humboldt current, which flows up to the Pacific coast from the Antarctic (causing the deserts of Chile and Peru), is countered by the Niño current of warm water. This arrives on the equator from the west and pushes down as far as the north of Peru. It brings the hot, wet season to Ecuador and clear blue skies are followed on most evenings by heavy rain, rather like that of Malaysia but only for five months of the year. The rest are cooler and totally dry.

Our gang was getting organised and we lads rented a penthouse chummery in Salinas, the main beach resort, while our girls all stayed with the mother of one of them at a nearby house. We then had a base for weekends throughout the season and the parties moved from Guayaquil to Salinas. There was, of course, good bathing too with the sea temperatures getting up to 28°C, which is like tepid bath water. We would be asked out on friends' yachts (of the smaller working variety, rather than gin palaces) and went deep-sea fishing for black marlin and sailfish. This experience taught me that I was the world's worst sailor and I spent several miserable hours feeding the fish. Actually, I was fine when there was action. But hours of watching a grey horizon over a grey sea, unable to stand the heat of the sun on the deck or the smell of the diesel below (or even the smell of the fish in the hold), rather took away the joy of the occasion. One's so-called friends, who are as hale and hearty as old mariners, then offer you food or beer and rejoice as you rush once more to the gunwale!

But there was a moment to remember when one of the trailed lines, which the crew baits and watches for you, hooked a marlin. This is taken in strict rotation and this fish was mine. Into the revolving hot seat and fasten the seat belt, then the rod is thrust into your hands and you are on your own. My marlin pulled like a train and ran the line almost to the limit. The trick is to tire it out so that each time it stops running, you gradually wind it in. Then it feels the pressure and runs again. Occasionally it leaps out of the water for a glorious moment and all on board 'ooh' and 'aah' at its size and the lovely sight. Calculations are made as to its weight and how long it will take to wear it down. Mine was a big one and I must have wrestled with it for about forty minutes before it ran under the keel of the boat. Despite the captain's frantic efforts to turn, it broke the line on the keel and got away. It was probably 200 pounds in weight.

Others in our group did land marlin, which are ceremonially weighed when you return to shore and can weigh up to 500 pounds. You are lucky to catch a marlin every time you go out (and that is from dawn to dusk) but you can generally count on catching several dorado, which are snub-nosed fish weighing up to twenty pounds. As they are pulled out of the water, they have the most glorious translucent colours of blue, green and yellow. But the colour dies with the fish and they become grey. Dorado are good to eat but marlin are rather oily and are generally given to the crew of the boat to sell.

Despite the thrill of the strike and battle with a big fish, I could never come to terms with the sea. I had been violently ill on the ferry returning from the international camp in France and was even worse while crewing a yacht in a race from Port Swetternam to Penang in the Malacca Straits of Malaysia. This had gone well on the way north, but we returned at night and a gale blew up in the early hours of the morning, throwing me clean out of my bunk to land among a pile of tins of food on the cabin floor. The yacht was on its side with its mast parallel to the sea and waves were breaking over the whole boat. I was as sick as a dog and terrified, while my shipmates showed no fear at all. They secured me with a rope so I would not be washed overboard then merrily hauled down (or rather hauled in, as it was sideways on) the sail. The yacht righted itself, although it continued to make violent movements with the huge swell for hours afterwards. On reaching the shore, I was tempted to kiss the earth like the pope.

Shortly after Agripac started business in June 1972, Mac was asked by John Robinson to ensure the growth of the line by expanding the number of salesmen, each with a car. Life SA had had a larger sales force as it had several lines of products, notably from Dow Chemical and Rohm and Haas as well as ICI's line. Mac was rather put out by this. He said that his commitment had been to put in only three salesmen and one office and warehouse in Guayaquil; now ICI wanted six salesmen and a Quito office to be opened straight away. He had other plans to expand Quimipac and could not immediately find the capital to fulfil both at the same time. For my part, I was desperate to make a success of Agripac within my allotted two years and hoped that this would lead on to a brilliant career with ICI. So I offered to fund the expansion in part by lending Mac my entire capital of £8,000. He accepted and we drew up a loan agreement at twelve per cent interest. The expansion then went ahead.

In 1972 we sold US$200,000 and in 1973, despite my lack of provision for the main season, we sold the same amount in the first quarter of the year and US$1,000,000 for the complete year. We were riding on the crest of a wave, with instant success and profitability. Even the distraction of the Primicid banana deal (from which Agripac earned only a small commission), had not held us back. Mac then approached me with words to the effect that it was unfair to me to have invested my capital in a fixed rate loan when, if the business continued as it had started, I would be much better off as a shareholder. He did not know if I wanted to stay on in Ecuador or eventually to return to ICI but if I decided the latter, he would buy the shares back from me. I was thrilled. I was to be a twenty-five per cent shareholder in the company I had started, and which was doing tremendously well.

I enjoyed Ecuador and certainly did not want to return to Britain just then. I already saw myself staying in Ecuador in the long term. We agreed that this holding would be kept secret from ICI until I had made a final decision as to my future. I squared it with my conscience as, at that time, almost the only products that Agripac handled were ICI products so there would be no conflict of interest. The harder I worked and the better the sales, the happier ICI would be. The only other line we had was the CP-3 knapsack sprayer made by Cooper Pegler, of Burgess Hill, Sussex. It was made of plastic and was light and durable and we still sell it today, although it is now owned by Hardi of Denmark. Ecuador is a country which lends itself to the knapsack sprayer because of the very small scale of some of the farming, which precludes use of tractors or tractor-mounted sprayers. They are also the only practical way of applying herbicides and insecticides in banana plantations and rice paddies. We were to acquire many other product lines in the future as we tried to have an answer to every pest problem the farmer encountered.

Two more recruits to the company at that time were Mario Ramos, who eventually became a shareholder, and Manuel Suco, a diminutive man, not above five foot tall, but who is a brilliant accountant and is now the controller of the company. We also recruited secretaries, more sales personnel, including Pepe Zapata, who was based in Quito, and people to repack the products. This repacking was initially carried out in our single warehouse where the offices were. We needed small packs of products which small farmers could buy. In many cases, we imported in bulk packs of 200-litre drums or 25-kilogramme sacks and reduced these down to one-litre or even 100cc bottles or one-pound packs. This enabled us to make our own product labels in Spanish, which addressed the particular crops and pests of Ecuador.

It was a very primitive process, decanting liquids into small bottles using a funnel, weighing the bottle and then sealing it and sticking on a label. It was initially carried out sitting on the warehouse floor and the only protection was rubber gloves. The warehouse was hot and humid and we could not make people wear heavy overalls or masks. In those days, there was much less awareness of the hazards to human health of handling pesticides — a far cry from the situation today. Even so, I cannot recall having anything but very minor accidents and when this happened, we had recourse to the doctors' surgeries upstairs.

I can clearly remember one of the repacker's names today: Bolivar Vallejo. He was a cut above the rest as he had completed secondary education and soon became the foreman of the group, although only in his teens. A couple of years later, we were to install our first computer in the company and tested everyone we employed for computer ability — that is to say, potential to learn as none had had the least exposure before. I exempted myself from the test as I am a complete non-starter in such matters. NCR, which was to sell us the computer, was in charge of testing and, when we got the results, no one had scored more than two out of ten except Bolivar, who had nine. He then went on an NCR course of instruction and today is our head of systems, managing a vastly improved computer network covering our eighty shops.

Before 1973 was out, Eric Notarianni, who was the general manager of Coats Patons in Ecuador, was to be posted to Milan by his company. Clearly decision time had come for he and Isabel and they were duly married with great fanfare. This was significant to the rest of the gang and set us all thinking. We had all become steady couples by now. In June 1974, I took my next leave and on the way to England, I stopped off in the States, where Ceci was staying in Miami with her best friend, Graciela Real. We went to Orlando and Disney World together and my mind was half made up to pop the question. But I did not do so just then. We parted in Miami and I went on to England and to Ferngill to see the old folks. I then told them what I had in mind and tested the waters. Their reaction was natural for parents, I suppose. They had not met the girl, she was a foreigner, and would she want to live in England and so on. The very act of discussing marriage with anyone (I had not mentioned it to anyone in Ecuador, least of all to Ceci) cleared my perception and made me decide. I went to Ogden's the jeweller in Harrogate, bought a diamond engagement ring and set off back to Ecuador.

Well, it is said that one should never make an important decision within twenty-four hours of a transatlantic flight as your judgement can be impaired by jet lag. Ignoring this good advice, I went straight back and proposed to Ceci (actually the die was cast as I already had the ring!). She accepted and we then had to break the news to her parents. Don Luis was the most formidable obstacle to overcome because, although not related to Ceci, he was her guardian and employer. We went to see him and, after some severe questioning as to whether I could support her and seeing that we were both decided, he gave his consent and opened a bottle of champagne. The wedding was set for the 4th October and, having made that great decision, I went back to work.

In Ecuador one marries twice, once in a civil ceremony and once (optionally) in church. Ceci is a Catholic and I am nominally an Anglican so there was a little difficulty here. To be married in a Catholic church, the priest required me to take a course of instruction and promise to bring up any children as Catholics. I objected as I had neither the time nor the interest for religious lessons and the way that we brought up the children was our own business. There was an Anglican vicar in Guayaquil at that time, the Rev John Jones.

Although Ceci objected to being married in that church, we came to a happy solution that John would officiate in a ceremony in our flat. I had changed flats again that year and had a wonderful, large one on the twelfth floor of another building at the centre of the Malecon called Edificio Simon Bolivar. This was quite palatial, with large rooms and marble floors. Although it had air-conditioning throughout, there was also a constant breeze from across the river and a pleasant temperature was maintained just by leaving the balcony glass doors open. We were married there and spent several years in it until, sadly, the owner returned from living in the United States and we had to leave. We continued renting accommodation until we finally bought a flat in 1981. Until then, all the cash that was available went into Agripac or properties in the UK.

The fourth of October 1974 — in Ecuador, weddings are usually held in the evening and ours was set for seven o'clock for the civil ceremony and eight for the religious, both in the flat. I had a busy schedule at the office that day and a visitor from an American irrigation company, Rainbird Inc, which we were considering handling. He was somewhat surprised when he invited me to dinner that evening and I excused myself, saying that I was awfully sorry but I had a previous appointment — to get married!

Neither of my parents could travel to Ecuador but all our pals rallied round. Don Louis gave the bride away while I was supported by Mac and Stanley Wright, and Kingsley Fox, the Honorary British Consul, witnessed the event. At that time, the civil authority in Guayaquil was Johnny Govea, who must hold something of a record as he had officiated at some 40,000 weddings over a twenty-year period. He would normally marry people in his municipal office but would attend weddings at the couple's home for a fee. So along he came and read out the necessary phrases in the very loud voice that he had developed over the years to overcome chattering groups of well-wishers. Then we were legally pronounced man and wife and we and the witnesses signed the book. He then collected his fee and left before John Jones put on his vestments and we proceeded to the religious ceremony and blessing. This was followed by a great party before Ceci and I left in the early hours of the following morning and made for a Guayaquil hotel, the Atahualpa (named after the last of the Inca emperors). This was the best in town in those days, but was still very poor and later closed as other better hotels opened.

We stayed there for only one short night and the following morning headed for Cuenca, driving the small white Renault car that had been Don Louis's present to us. Cuenca is a very pretty town in the Andes and, standing at about 9,000 feet, has a more pleasant climate than Quito. Cuenca is also the home of the Canari Indians, those fierce fighters of old, who made the Incas pause in their conquest of what is now Ecuador. They were finally beaten and displaced to Cusco as a subject people. However, when Francisco Pizarro and his small army won their first battle against Atahualpa, the Inca emperor, the Canaris saw their future with the Spaniards and fought with them against the Incas, greatly helping them in the final outcome. But for all the charm of the town with its huge cathedral, narrow cobbled streets, neat red-tiled houses and Indian markets, Cuenca is 'un poquito' boring.

That might be an excellent reason to go there on honeymoon but then, as now, I was a restless soul and the building of my business could not be neglected. So, after two days' honeymoon, we began to visit Agripac customers in and around Cuenca. Then we drove from Cuenca to Riobamba on a tiny road, unpaved in parts, along the Cordilleras of the Andes, over passes and winding down into valleys, crossing a bridge over the river, then winding slowly up the other side. And the nature of our travel was slow as engines lose a great deal of power unless tuned for the altitude — and the Renault's was not. We also crossed a curious high desert where the sand was blowing over the road, partially obscuring it. So we reached Riobamba, where farming country began again and we stopped to visit Agripac's distributors, who were small shopkeepers in the high street who sold hardware, chicken food, fertilisers and agrochemicals. From there, we went on to Ambato, crossing the high pass by Chimborazo, the highest of Ecuador's mountains at over 23,000 feet. If it is clear, which is somewhat rare, there is a most glorious view of it. Today was clear and we saw it in all its glory — a perfect cone topped with snow.

Once again in Ambato, a very attractive colonial city, we did some business before driving on to Quito, where we were expected by Mac and Anne at their house. The following day, Mac and I settled down to discuss business while Anne took Ceci shopping. That day, we were due to meet Al Suter and, not having met him before, we expected a six-foot Californian who spoke no Spanish to appear. Al (which is short for Alois) is a small, dapper Swiss and multilingual. He was the representative of Petoseed, a vegetable seed company of Saticoy, California, whose line we were intending to represent in Ecuador. He flew into Quito and after a day there he drove down from Quito to Guayaquil with Ceci and I. So our honeymoon ended as a threesome! In fact, I had previously warned Ceci that there was little time for a honeymoon just then but that we would take a better one the following year, in the summer, on our way back to England.

Back in Guayaquil, we started our married life and acquired our first dog, a beagle given to us by Don Louis who, of course, had to be named Snoopy. My mother had always kept dogs and as a small boy I had had a rather long-legged Yorkshire terrier that slept on, or rather in, my bed while I was home on school holiday. This was Maxi and I grew terribly fond of him and was distraught when he disappeared one day. We searched for him day after day and I cried myself to sleep at night. He was never found. We supposed that he had been shot by a farmer for chasing sheep. Since that time, I had never had a dog (although I did keep white mice in a cage in my bedroom at Thorngill as a teenager!). I had grown from boy to adolescent to student to young executive (as I fondly imagined myself) and there had been no place in my life for pets. Now my latent love of dogs was awakened by Snoopy and I grew rather over-fond of him — so much so that after the birth of our first-born, Nick, our nanny was totally disgusted that I would spend more time with the dog than with my son. Snoopy lived only five years before being poisoned, probably by eating rat poison in the street, but he was the first of a series of beagles that have continued to this day.

Agripac continued to grow. We had added Petoseed and Chevron Chemical Co Inc to our list of suppliers, our staff was now up to twenty, and we had a turnover of nearly $2,000,000. As a partner in the business, I was starting to receive dividends and in fact recouped my initial investment in less than two years. At the time, I was still unsure which way my career would go — whether I would return to England and ICI or stay in Ecuador. Either way, I looked to put my newfound spare cash to good and safe use.

The year before, I had asked my father to look out for a cottage to buy in the village of Middleham, two miles from Tupgill. He found me Elmsville which I bought for £5,000 and then did up, furnished and rented. The following year brought another cottage in Grove Square, Leyburn, which, as I was by then courting Ceci, I named Cecilia House. Finally, I bought a larger house, Greystones, in Middleham, which had been the home of Edmund and Eileen Tennant, the parents of John and Rodney who are today well known for their fine arts business, Tennants of Yorkshire.

I was collecting a portfolio of properties but I had my eye on something much closer to my heart, Tupgill Park. Since old Bob had died in 1956, Aunt Do owned Tupgill Park and Ferngill, where my parents were living. Do was now in her late seventies and, although I had every expectation of inheriting something from her estate, she had five nieces and nephews so Tupgill would have had to be sold and the cash divided. I broached the issue rather nervously, not at all knowing how it would be received. Though Do was mellowing in these later years, and we would become extremely close at the end of her life, she was still very formidable. She did not agree at once but asked several people whom she trusted for their opinion. Her chief concern was for her security of tenure if this nephew of hers who appeared to be printing money at the moment should have a reverse of fortune. However, it was finally agreed that, with this provision, and for the sum of £42,000, payable over ten years with interest, I could buy it. I was over the moon. I have always had a strong sense of history and, living abroad, I badly wanted to own something that linked me to the family. The George Hotel at Penrith was long since sold to other hands but our link with Tupgill went back to 1904, exactly 1,000 years since Eric had first set foot on British soil.

And what did I get for my money? Tupgill House was still in reasonable condition although little had changed over the last fifty years. The fifty acres of land was, of course, in good condition but the rest was sad. Nothing had been done to the stables in many years and everything the army had left in 1945 was still there rotting quietly away: Nissen huts, latrine blocks, ammunition stores and other bits and pieces in brick and iron. The stables were rented out to two trainers, 'Jumbo' Wilkinson and 'Squeak' Fairhurst. They made do with the poor conditions as the rent was very low.

I had bought Tupgill to add to my three cottages but now my capital and bank overdraft were stretched, so there was no question of doing any repairs to Tupgill immediately. However, I did need someone to administer these UK assets and Father was really getting a bit past it so I advertised for an agent and, after interviewing several candidates, Elaine Foster got the job. Elaine was in her mid-twenties, blonde, buxom and secretary to the MP for Rossendale, Ronald Bray. However, Bray had lost his seat in the Commons and Elaine now worked only part-time for him and was looking for extra work. We hit it off at once and since 1975 I have kept files of our correspondence, at first by letter, which could take ten days to reach Ecuador from the UK, with the occasional urgent telegram, then in recent years by fax and now also e-mail.

What started as a business arrangement gradually began to involve her working with the family until she became almost part of it. She managed the affairs of Father and Do, including organising the 'Country Cousins' helpers and nurses of their later years and stood guardian to our three children during their boarding-school days. Apart from this, she was active as a Conservative agent and sat on numerous committees, school governing bodies and the local parish council. Elaine Foster became Elaine Lister shortly after starting with me in June 1975, when she married Charles Lister, who has a large sheep farm near Kettlewell, about fourteen miles from Tupgill. As well as all these activities, she found time to manage her household, bring up two boys and exercise hunters for neighbours. She was always known to the family as 'the efficient Elaine'.

Ceci and I finally got around to taking our honeymoon in June 1975, nine months after we had been married. I wanted to show her Mexico and we booked hotels through ICI de Mexico. The Presidente Hotel is in the very heart of Mexico City, where the famous 'charro' Cuco Sanchez would perform each evening, and the Boca Chica is in Acapulco. The first was a great success and we saw the Ballet Folklorico together and explored restaurants. Dear old Cuco Sanchez (who must have been seventy) caused hysterical tears in his audience, at least the female section, with his 'guitarra llora guitarra' and signed an LP for Ceci. We flew on to Acapulco and arrived in a rain storm. Only a few taxis were available so we shared one with several other people who were dropped off one by one at different hotels.

When only we were left, the taxi driver asked why on earth we wanted to go to Boca Chica when there were plenty of hotels with space out of season. But we said that it had been recommended to us (by Dick Burgoon, an American living in Ecuador who must have had more of a sense of humour than we had credited him with) and, anyway, the first night was paid in advance. We eventually arrived and saw to our dismay an old, rather dilapidated hotel, where the proprietor was sweeping water out of the foyer. Ceci was somewhat upset so I tried to make the best of it and ordered their best room. It turned out to

Colin and Elaine in front of the Tupgill gates just after they won planning permission in 1991.

be a suite with a close-up view of the (rather rough and wild) sea and a balcony. We left our luggage there and hurried out to see the sights.

There were Mini Mokes to rent — the Jeep variety of the Austin Mini. We took one and were immediately drenched as the sagging canvas roof had collected gallons of water which descended on us as we started. Ceci was by now giving me her opinion of what a fool I was to choose the worst hotel, in a water-logged Acapulco and then hire a mobile shower as a car. To add to the joy, I had toothache. Well, we saw the chap dive off the rock, had a reasonable meal and, with promises to change the hotel the next day, we returned in more torrential rain to the Boca Chica and so to bed. Now we saw that the room had two single beds set against the walls at right angles and a door led out on to the balcony, through which water was pouring into the room. The cases on the floor were already afloat. With bad tempers, we paddled about and went to our separate beds where I finally got to sleep after swallowing aspirins for my toothache and to the sound of Ceci's sobs.

The next morning, we tactfully told the rather glum proprietor that we had to return to Mexico City and could not stay for the three days that we had reserved. I think his hotel was empty after we left. Then we went down the beach to the Marriott, surprisingly getting an excellent room for less than the Boca Chica. The rest of the stay was spoilt only by the toothache.

Being who I am, I find it impossible to go anywhere without including some element of business and this second honeymoon was no exception. We flew from Acapulco to Los Angeles and were met there by our friend from the first honeymoon, Al Suter, who drove us to Saticoy where Petoseed has its offices.

By now, the toothache was getting bad and Al offered to take me to a dentist who diagnosed that a wisdom tooth had to be removed and said that he would do it at once. Well. I am a bit of a wimp for doctors and dentists so, with trepidation, suggested that he give me a complete anaesthetic. 'Of course not', he said, 'a local one will be quite enough and it will all be over in fifteen minutes.' 'Oh well, that did not sound too bad,' and off we went. Three hours and dozens of local anaesthetics later I sensed that something was wrong. The tooth had come out, but not the roots. He was cutting away at the gums and blood flowed profusely. The worst thing was that he seemed to be in more than a panic than I was and clearly at a loss as to what to do next.

By this time, I was arched in the chair like a taut bow and so tense that I was rigid. Then finally a 'miracle' — he extracted the root and we both collapsed in relief. He duly sewed me up and I staggered out of the surgery with Ceci, who had waited all this time in the waiting room. The next day, with spirits refreshed, we went to see Petoseed and afterwards to Al's house where he had a group of friends for dinner. When I told my tale, there was general astonishment and it appeared that only Al did not know that my dentist had only just set up in practice six months before. He had been a fighter pilot who had crashed in the Vietnam War and lost his nerve. After some time in a sanatorium, the air force had retrained him as a dentist and I must have been one of his first patients. Certainly I was the first difficult case he had attended. There was a tragic sequel to this story as he died suddenly of a heart attack the following year. I am convinced that his battle with my wisdom tooth was a contributory cause of this.

From Saticoy, we flew to San Francisco where we were to meet with Gordon Black, a vice-president of the Chevron Chemical Co Inc. We arrived in the evening and took a taxi to the Hyatt Hotel on Union Square, where Chevron has reserved a room on the thirty-fifth floor for us. It was a lovely room with a wonderful view over San Francisco. After dinner, we watched a recently released video in the room — *The Towering Inferno* — all about a skyscraper on fire. The building featured in the film was none other than the Hyatt on Union Square. Very reassuring indeed, as we saw how impossible it was for the fire brigade to deal with a fire above, say, floor ten!

Chevron had left an agenda for us at the hotel and I was due to be picked up by them at eight o'clock, while Ceci had her own schedule for nine. I visited its offices and research station facilities and then we went to Fisherman's Wharf for lunch, where we were to meet up again with Ceci. Well, no sign of Ceci. Then a stretch limousine drew up with darkened windows, the chauffeur opened the rear door and Ceci got out. 'What on earth are you doing in that?' was all I could think of to say, causing laughter all round except for the lady herself who was somewhat shy and timid in those days. In fact, she had had royal treatment with a driver and guide for a grand city tour.

San Francisco is a lovely city with its series of hills, elegant residences, high-rises, trams and waterfront. I had been there before on my US tour and we were to return years later with our teenage children, when we also visited the giant redwood forests nearby. These magnificent giants are prehistoric, or at least date from before modern history, as one can witness from the rings of a fallen tree on which is marked the year of the birth of Christ. In fact, the limousine was to reappear at this time as there were six people, including a friend of the family, and taxis can only take five.

Just before our stay in San Francisco was due to end, we received an urgent message through Agripac that my mother had fallen down the stairs of Ferngill and was seriously ill in hospital. We headed straight for England, flew to Heathrow and hired a car to drive to Yorkshire where we went straight to the Friarage Hospital in Northallerton. Mother was conscious but looked awful. She seemed tiny and had hairs on her face like a very old person although she was only sixty three. She had sent a very loving letter to Ceci on our wedding day, enclosing a sprig of heather but now the two were meeting for the first time in dreadful circumstances. We did not stay for too long as her mind was wandering but we were taken aside by the doctor and told that she would not last much longer — a month at most. Cirrhosis was claiming one more victim in the family. We left Northallerton and headed for home but before we had gone more than a few miles, I could not stand it any longer and pulled into the side of the road and wept. Although we had never been close and the gap had grown wider in recent years, the realisation that she was dying hit me hard. My memory went back to the early days when she was the one who had cared for us, the one who had packed school clothes, sewn on name tapes and written to us every week, and whom we longed to see at half term.

So Ceci came to Ferngill for the first time. With Mother in hospital, Father had moved into Tupgill with Do and we had Ferngill to ourselves. After unpacking and freshening up, we walked the quarter-mile down to Tupgill and I introduced my new wife to Father and Do. That went well and they became good friends, especially Do, who was to become very fond of Ceci. While we were there, the telephone rang and I answered to find that it was my Uncle Frank Wilson, Mother's youngest and closest brother. He said: 'Colin, give me the truth about your mother. Gerald and Doris will only say that she is doing well and will soon be home. How bad is it?' I told him that she was failing and that he had better visit her soon. We arranged to meet for lunch at the Golden Lion in Northallerton the following day and go to the hospital together.

He drove up from Hungerford with his wife, Eleanor, and presented Ceci and I with a pair of silver candlesticks, a belated wedding present, at lunch. Then we went to the hospital. I made several more visits during the month that we were in England but Mother lingered on and eventually we had to return to Ecuador. She died on the 14th September and her ashes were scattered on Flag Moor in Derbyshire by Frank. She had asked for this as her happiest days had been spent hunting there. I did not return to England for the funeral.

During the early years of Agripac, we had been extremely active in looking for new lines. In addition to ICI, we now represented Chevron, Cooper Pegler sprayers, Petoseed and even a line of irrigation equipment, and it was the latter that led indirectly to tractors and farm machinery. We had heard that British Leyland was looking for an agent for its tractor line and contacted it. While I was in England that summer, I had been to its factory in Leyland near Preston and met John Cubbin and Mike Keogh. They pointed out, rather as ICI had done to Mac, that a certain amount of technical expertise was necessary to run a tractor franchise and that I could have the line when I had the man to manage it. We agreed that they would advertise for a candidate who was suitably qualified as an agricultural engineer and give him a crash course at the factory, and that I would employ him in Agripac for an initial two-year period. So Peter Baker joined our staff.

This was not one of my most successful ventures. We imported five tractors at first and then discovered that we could sell them only by giving generous credit terms. Even then, the sales were widely spaced around Ecuador so that each time we had to service them, Peter had to travel for hours. Spares were a constant problem as we inevitably did not have what was required in the country. Angry customers demanded instant solutions to their problems or they would return the tractors. If we avoided this, we had to accept delayed payments of the already long credits, meanwhile flying in parts at great expense. Morale at British Leyland was then in a sorry state and the tractors were shoddily built and the parts service slow. Then, as we were coming to terms with all this, Leyland sold the tractor division to Marshalls and the confusion worsened. Peter, who had to take the brunt of all this, got fed up and returned to England after only a year.

We managed to replace him with Peter Ryvar, one of the few men I have had to look up to physically because he was six foot five tall. Again, he was contracted in England and again he had to learn Spanish. He struggled on and we sold perhaps thirty tractors over a three-year period. Then Marshalls sold the line again to Theakston Brothers, which went bust, I think, and that was that for the Leyland tractor. However, Peter was full of enthusiasm and enjoyed Ecuador so we changed from tractors to Leyland trucks and bus chassis. This went on for a few years but the business was a capital-intensive and was draining cash from the principal agrochemicals line.

Finally, I had had enough of it and sold the line, which by that time was a separate company called Trace Cia Ltda, to Peter and a few others. It survived another two years before succumbing to an Ecuadorian economic crisis. It then closed and Peter, by this time married to an Ecuadorian lady, Evi, returned to England. Apart from sprayers, which are directly needed for chemical application, this ended my short-lived affair with machinery. I have never had any affinity for it and have little interest in cars or engines, except as a means of transport, the bonnet remaining firmly closed.

Shortly after our return from England in September 1975, Ceci went to see a gynaecologist, Dr Guillermo Wagner, and returned with the joyful news that we were to become parents in February of the following year. Well, February came and went and Ceci grew larger and larger and still there was nothing. I remembered a bitch owned by my mother which was subject to false pregnancies and rather thought that the same thing had happened in this case. We made repeated trips to Dr Wagner, who kept saying that all was well and she would give birth soon. Finally, towards the end of March, he decided that, because Ceci was small and the baby had grown quite large, he would do a Caesarean section.

The day was fixed for the 25th March and Ceci went into the operating theatre at eight am. Now, I do not smoke but another anxious father offered me a cigarette and I must have finished a packet of them while pacing up and down the corridor. One hour, two hours — something must have gone wrong. Ceci had perhaps died on the table, the child was still-born or whatever. Finally Guillermo appeared and, seeing me somewhat distraught, said that all was well. He thought that I had already been told that I had a son as he was delivering two simultaneously and had been held up. Ceci would have to stay and rest before I could see her but if I would like to see my son he was in the babies' ward. Would I? Off we went together and I saw Nick, all $9\frac{1}{2}$ pounds of him. He looked very well as babies do after Caesareans, not having had to struggle out in the normal way. I was allowed only a few minutes with him and could not see Ceci.

So I did the next best thing and went to a bar down the road and had a couple of large whiskies, even though it was only ten o'clock. I rather foolishly announced to everyone in the bar that I was a father, which cost me a packet in drinks for them! But it was a moment of supreme happiness. When I returned to the clinic, Ceci was back in her room and rather crossly asked why I was not waiting for her. Still, it was a great day. I returned to the office to catch up and tell the news to all the gang. That evening, as is the custom in Ecuador, everyone turned up at the clinic with flowers. Drinks were poured and toasts were drunk in a babble of noise around the bed where poor Ceci was lying in pain from the operation and was forbidden to talk by the doctor because it would give her wind. It is a strange custom when compared to the strict discipline, visiting hours and silence imposed in a British hospital but the Ecuadorians would not have it any other way. After two days, she was discharged and, taking Nick and as many of the flowers as remained alive, we headed back to our flat where we had a nanny, Olga, waiting for us. She, good soul, took Nick in her charge and we could relax.

I was very careful to register Nick's birth both with the registration office in Guayaquil as an Ecuadorian citizen and with the British Embassy in Quito as a Briton. Ceci and I had both agreed on the name Nicholas but for his baptism he collected three more names: Robert as a family tradition (I am Colin Robert); Louis for Don Louis and Gerald for Father. We included them all just in case we never had another son, which is the case, so it was just as well.

1976 was a most eventful year for Agripac. Sales and profits were spread across a wider range of products, but more than seventy per cent still depended on Gramoxone, our star herbicide which was growing fast. We had a monopoly because ICI's patent was still valid in Ecuador but this was to end the following year. We had also heard of generic paraquats made in Taiwan, which were entering world markets wherever they could and seriously undermining Gramoxone sales. This was a cloud on the horizon which rapidly grew bigger. In March, we discovered that Fabian Plaza, a farmer who had been an excellent customer of ours, had imported Taiwanese product at half the price. What to do? Ecuadorian law is very slow and cumbersome and it would have taken so long to start a legal action that the patent would be long expired by the time we received a sentence. No, we had to stop it then and there or others in the agrochemical business would follow suit.

I went to talk to the culprit but got nowhere. He knew as well as us that we had not much legal remedy. He offered to desist if we would share our Gramoxone business with him. No deal. So he showed us the door. We tried to have the product seized at the port but we were never quick enough to catch it. We chased it around the country but as soon as we had a court order to enter a warehouse, it moved on. Meanwhile, it was being sold to all our customers and we could hardly sue them and damage future relations. It was a time of great anguish as the cornerstone of Agripac appeared to be built on quicksand.

Mac complained to John Robinson at ICI but he could give no comfort. 'It's happening all over the world,' he said. 'We will just have to live with it and come to a market-sharing agreement with the competition.' Mac was not convinced. His business was in plastics and industrial chemicals, where customers had no loyalty to brands and would change suppliers to save five per cent in cost. He grew depressed about the future of Agripac and his investment in it. This led to a series of rows between us as I maintained the confidence of youth. I thought that something was bound to turn up, and his experience suggested that we were bound to lose the market. This argument came to a head in May, with Mac saying that he wanted to sell his shares in Agripac and would give me first option. If I could not come up with the cash, he would find another buyer. Once again a crisis, once again an opportunity. But was I sure I really wanted to go down this road?

This would mean total commitment to Agripac and Ecuador because, if I were to buy out Mac, I could no longer hide my shareholding in the company. ICI would have to give its approval and know who owned the company or the franchise might be lost. I would have to resign from ICI and risk everything on my own ability to steer Agripac through this crisis, pay Mac out and survive. I asked Ceci what to do. She said: 'You make up your own mind. I am with you either way.' This was very good of her but not helpful. Perhaps she knew me better than I knew myself and sensed that I had to make the decision alone.

Two years previously, we had bought a piece of land in an industrial area outside Guayaquil by the River Daule. Having built a wall around it and a large warehouse (as the warehouse with our offices in Luis Urdaneta Street had long since become too small), I had made a garden. Because we lived in a flat, our only plants were in pots so this garden by the warehouse, which was a separate company called Celtec, was our weekend retreat. Here, we would invite our friends for a barbecue and Snoopy could run loose. It was to Celtec now that I went to ponder our future and, as it was Sunday, I was alone apart from the guard at the gate. The issue was straightforward. I could raise the necessary capital with the help of new shareholders and bank loans and make my life in Ecuador. Or I could sell my shares to Mac or someone else, return to ICI with my capital and continue my career.

I had been in Ecuador for four years and on several occasions John Robinson had suggested that, in the interest of my career, I should be moved back to England. I had even been offered a job as a sales manager for the York area. Each time I had rather guiltily put him off, saying that there were urgent reasons to keep me in Ecuador. Good reasons there were: I was making money very handily while still keeping my career options open. Now the moment of truth had arrived. I suppose my decision was never in doubt but it was hard to cut the umbilical cord to Mother ICI, my safe salary, pension and prospects. I occasionally wonder how far I might have progressed if had I stayed: senior

The Agripac total staff in 1980 (about 75)

manager, director, chairman? Jenkins, my old friend and 'world sales manager' before his retirement, had always said that I was a maverick and not a team player and that is true. I dislike meetings, committees and the endless budgeting and planning that is part of the modern, large company. Although these have recently come to Agripac, most of my career has been guided by instinct and 'seat-of-the-pants' judgement. As I sat in the garden, I thought: 'If I leave now, I will never see this garden mature.' That decided me.

I returned home to Ceci and began calling on people the following day. I went to Miguel Babra, the manager of the Bank of Guayaquil, for advice. He was a good friend and knew Agripac well (it is one of my sayings that you open your affairs totally to only two people — your priest and your banker!). He said that the buyout could not go ahead entirely on bank loans. This would be too much in relation to the earning power of the company, and I would have to take in another shareholder or two. My first reaction was of disappointment. I had wanted to go it alone but US$400,000 was a lot of money to find.

Some years previously, Uncle Jimmy Clark of Johannesburg had clapped me on the shoulder in an avuncular way and said: 'If you ever need help in business, lad, give me a call.' Well, what better moment. I wrote a long letter to him and followed it up with a telegram. Could he possibly lend me US$150,000 or take a stake for that amount in Agripac? He replied at once — 'Err, no!' South

Africa had strict capital controls and, anyway, this was an awful lot of money. No, it would not be a good idea to fly over to see him but good luck in the venture. Well, I suppose this was fair enough. Nephews with little track record and an excess of enthusiasm asking for large amounts of money are probably usually turned down. Jimmy died in 1998 aged ninety-two and I saw him only one more time, when I visited South Africa on business four years ago. Neither of us mentioned that we might have been partners but his refusal was probably for the best as an overseas partnership is unwieldy and would have slowed down decision-making.

That particular door having closed, I approached Don Louis who, having watched the company grow, saw its potential and agreed to come in with me for a twenty-five per cent stake. With loans taken out in my name, my holding had increased to seventy per cent and the other five per cent was supplied by Mario Ramos, who was my administrative manager. He mortgaged his house to raise the funds and Don Louis raised a loan on his farm. So we had all the pieces in place and were ready to sign. However, ICI had to be informed. I was due to go on holiday to England in June and agreed with Mac that we visit Fernhurst together and see John Robinson and Gerry Jenkins. This we did and, after overcoming their initial surprise, they accepted the change. Gerry said that in his long career he had never come across an employee who had become an ICI agent. Although this was rare at the time, it has since become more common as sales personnel have been removed from the payroll and made distributors in several countries, albeit on a much smaller scale than Agripac.

That chore over, I was free to go back to Ferngill where I had left Ceci and Nick with a Norland nanny, whom we had contracted for the six weeks we were to be in England. This was not a success. This good lady was in her late fifties and of 'the old school'. She was in charge, Baby was securely wrapped up to make him feel safe and put in his pram in the garden for much of the day. His parents were permitted to go near him only at certain times as Baby could sense the presence of his mother and would cry to get attention. In fact, Nick was off limits to us! Well, this did not go down at all well with Ceci, who being Latin American and a new mother, wanted a great deal more contact with her baby than the little allowed by the nanny. I thought her system splendid as Nick was well cared for and quiet and I could get on with other things. But if I thought I was going to win this one, I was sadly mistaken. The Norland nanny lasted only one week of the six contracted before, with profuse apologies and most of her six weeks' pay, I had to end the arrangement. We then found someone else more to Ceci's liking and, having established that we could have complete access to our son, we promptly abandoned him and headed for Berlin.

I had just received the representation of Schering Agrochemicals for Agripac and had been invited by its regional manager, Fernando Tramontini, to its head office and research station in Berlin. We flew there from London and were met at the airport by Fernando and driven to the Hamburg Hotel in West Berlin. From there, I went off to the company's offices while Ceci was taken to the zoo by Fernando's wife. The Schering offices were on the edge of West Berlin and the research station grounds were bordered by the Berlin Wall, complete with watch towers, searchlights and guards — all rather intimidating. We had the following day free so Ceci and I took a bus tour of East Berlin, going through the Brandenburg Gate and Checkpoint Charlie. The bus was searched thoroughly by East German guards and then we were allowed to proceed.

Immediately through the gate, the environment changed tremendously. We left the skyscrapers, modern offices and shops with their lights and neon signs behind and stepped into a world I associated with wartime newsreels. The buildings, although handsome, were sometimes drab and grey. The older ones even had bullet holes in them still (thirty-one years after the war had finished!). The new constructions were line after line of drab high-rise workers' flats with no attempt at landscaping or gardening around them. The people dressed in sombre clothes of wartime style, the women in headscarves, and people kept their heads down as they passed each other — a chilling spectacle. The bus was an official tour so we were taken to see a museum in a badly mauled but attractive old building, then on to the highlight of the tour: the monument to the unknown Russian soldier, a gigantic obelisk with an eternal flame guarded by Russian soldiers. This clearly must have been a centre of pilgrimage for every patriotic East German! Mercifully the tour was relatively short. After an even longer search of the bus at the gate, when dogs were sent under it in case some misguided soul should attempt to leave the workers' paradise, we were out and thankfully back to cheerful West Berlin.

That night, we again met our Schering friends and, just to prove that the East German characterisation of the West as decadent was totally false, they took us to a transvestite show. I thought it was excellent with an imitation of Liza Minelli's song 'Come To The Cabaret' and an almost complete striptease, which left me guessing (to this day) whether the dancer was male or female. It was not entirely to Ceci's taste — she sided with East German opinion!

Not that Ceci is prudish about striptease shows. We returned from Berlin by way of Paris, where we went to the Crazy Horse with our good friends, Jean Pierre Banzet and Alain Graillot of Procida, a French agrochemical company. However, this was definitely the real McCoy as the girls wore nothing but feathers on their heads and a smile. Paris excels in girlie shows and over the years we have seen several of them, including the Lido and the Moulin Rouge. This time, we stayed at the Hotel Westminster in la Rue de l'Opera. It was an excellent hotel but we discovered that French room staff do not knock before entering. We were caught *in flagrante delicto*, causing Cecilia to make a dash for the bathroom while I reached for a pillow!

My French connection with Procida was now well established and Jean Pierre Banzet would stay with us on his visits to Guayaquil and, of course, cook dinner. He is an excellent cook. When I visited Paris on my own to see Procida for the first time, he had apologised that his flat was very small but said that he would put me up in a hotel nearby. He collected me from the airport and, being in a rush, dropped me off outside a small hotel with instructions to meet him around the corner at Harry's bar, 'cinq Rue Danue'. I went into the hotel and it was terrible. A slovenly proprietor with a cigarette in her mouth reached down one of the twenty or so keys and told me to follow her. I picked up my bag and did so, all the way up to the attic, where she showed me into a tiny room with a roof window. What purported to be a bathroom was fitted inside a piece of furniture the size of a wardrobe. The carpet was threadbare and everything musty. Well, there was nothing for it but to sleep there that night.

I changed and walked to Harry's bar. This was a great place; it was the meeting place for the local rugby club and Jean Pierre was a keen player. We had a great evening there, marred only by the Frenchman's habit of talking only in French with his mates with no attempt at translation. I found one or two of them who would talk to me in English on and off, but I missed eighty per cent of what was said. My O-level French did not run to much conversation and, anyway, this went back fifteen years. I did convey my dissatisfaction with the hotel to Jean Pierre, who looked surprised as his secretary had booked and recommended it. When we talked to her the following day, we found that it had all been a mistake and Jean Pierre had taken me to the wrong hotel. Anyway, with a Gallic shrug he said: 'It's cheap so you are saving money.' That, I replied, was not the point. As the new majority owner of Agripac, I could easily afford a decent hotel and I am sure that, in my annoyance, I laid it on a bit thick my newfound status. I said that I would not stay there another night, even if it did cost only £20.

Jean Pierre, somewhat miffed, said that he did know a better hotel but that it might cost a little more. 'That's fine,' I said. 'I'll take a taxi there right away and see you later.' He hailed a taxi and gave the driver the name of the hotel. As I got in, I just caught the twinkle in his eye and wondered what was in store for me. I soon found out! I was booked into the Hotel Plaza Athene, one of the best and most expensive hotels in Paris. As the uniformed porter opened the taxi door, I knew my bluff had been called but I was damned if I would give him satisfaction. It is not the sort of place that advertises its prices but, as I went to the marble reception desk across the marble hall, I had a pretty good idea. The room was gorgeous, the bathroom sumptuous and larger than the bedroom of my previous hotel. Everything was perfect except that I was alone and this sort of setting should have been shared with Ceci. As to the price — well, by adding the equivalent of £20 to £300 and dividing by two, I was not too far out for a good Paris hotel for two nights.

Jean Pierre then had a live-in girlfriend called Annie, a flaming redhead with a temper to match and the two would row terribly. However, at this moment peace reigned and I mentioned to Jean Pierre that I would like to buy some lingerie (oh, foolish male) for Ceci. He sent me with Annie, who spoke no

English, to the Rue de l'Opera, where we were to find it. Of course, by the time I got there, I was having second thoughts but it was too late.

Annie explained what was wanted to the shop manager and she beamed at me and asked the size. I indicated in sign language that Ceci was quite petite and we sorted the panties out. The trouble was the bra. I did not know the size so started indicating with my hands more or less what I thought. Madame quite understood my problem and, calling her shopgirls together, asked me to indicate which of them was the nearest in shape to Ceci. The girls all thought that it was a great joke, as did Annie, and the laughter was taken up by other customers. I was in a panic and hastily pointed to one slim girl, but I was not to be let off so easily. She was given a range of bras to model (over her sweater, I hasten to add) and there appeared to be dozens of options to choose from. Eventually a decision was made for me by Madame and Annie and I paid and bolted from the shop. My ordeal was not yet over, though, as Annie insisted on retelling the tale to their group of friends at dinner that night. Of course, when I finally gave Ceci the wretched bras, they did not fit anyway. The panties were OK.

The holiday over we flew back to Ecuador and I walked straight into a crisis in Agripac. Mario Ramos had been left in charge and, in his efficient way, had done a good job but a fight had broken out between he and Marco Camposano, who by now had become sales manager. There was bad blood between them and one would have to go. Mario was the more senior, and valuable, of the two so I had to fire Marco. Firing is never easy and I have always hated doing it. It is especially difficult when the person involved has done nothing to warrant it but it has to be done for the good of the team. Marco did not accept my reasoning and we parted on bad terms. He nursed his resentment for many years afterward and, try as I might, he would not make friends but spoke badly of Agripac and myself. Tragically he was murdered some fifteen years later, while resisting thieves who were trying to steal his car. I was always sorry that we had not been able to make it up. You impugn Latin self-esteem at your peril.

Now I needed to find a new sales manager. This was done very swiftly and in an odd way. I was in the Phoenix Club telling someone of Marco's departure and he said brightly: 'We have a new member who is looking for a job. He is called Giles Harrison.' And so I met Giles. He is an Englishman who had been working in Peru, prospecting for gold. He had married Lily, a Peruvian lady, and come to Ecuador. We talked and I remember asking him if he had any sales experience. 'None.' 'Did he know anything about the agrochemical business?' 'Nothing', he replied. 'Good you are hired,' was my reply. It was not quite as simple as that of course. We had talked several times and he had impressed me with his enthusiasm and energy. His Spanish was perfect, far superior to mine, and he spoke fluent German, as the army had posted his father to Austria after the war and he had gone to Austrian schools. Not that we needed German in our work, but it impressed me that he could speak it. So

Giles started with Agripac. From the first day, he was a great success and established excellent relationships both with the salesmen and with the customers. Sales really took off.

So 1976 drew to a close. It had been a great year. What had started as a threat to Agripac with Fabian Plaza's paraquat import had stimulated Mac to sell out. I had left ICI's employment and become majority shareholder in my own company. The paraquat threat had not materialised and sales of Gramoxone and a host of new products had taken Agripac forward. In fact, the three-year credit terms agreed with Mac to pay for his shares were not necessary. We paid in less than two years. And I had a son.

Christmas that year brought another resident to our flat. Rocio, Ceci's sister, had been to a boarding school in San Miguel in the highlands but now, at fifteen, she was to finish her schooling in Guayaquil and came to live with us. So, after being a bachelor three years previously, I now had a family of three.

The year 1977 began well too. Having acquired the company, Mario and I turned our thoughts to permanent premises for it. Until this time, we had been still in our plywood offices inside the warehouse in Luis Urdaneta Street. In Ecuador, property does not normally change hands through estate agents, which hardly exist. Usually, the seller hangs a 'For Sale' sign outside his property. This appeared on an old villa just around the corner from our offices in Cordova Street. Mario and I knocked on the door and were rather surprised when it was opened by a nun!

This was the house of the congregation of Las Siervas de Maria, a Spanish order of nuns whose mission was to help people to die — that is to say, to ease their passage into the next world (not poison them!). We spoke to the mother superior and she explained that her little group of sixteen nuns was growing and the house was not now large enough for them. They had been donated a piece of land in a suburban area and, with the money they received from selling this house, they could build their new convent, which would take about eighteen months. Our hopes rather collapsed at the thought of waiting so long. We had envisioned moving in the following week. Anyway, the mother superior said that she would show us the house and hoped that we would be prepared to wait. It is a lovely house. Standing in a small walled garden, it has a pillared portico and further pillars in the hall with high-ceilinged rooms and a beautiful, curved staircase with a wrought-iron balustrade. Of course, once we had seen it, we could not resist it and from that day on thought of it as Agripac House. The good mother told us the price they wanted for it — US$240, 000 which, of course, was far more than we had budgeted to pay. But after a visit to the Bank of Guayaquil, we had arranged a mortgage.

Then we went to see the nuns' lawyer. We were assured that he was such a good Christian that he never charged them anything for his services. Well, the whole deal very nearly fell apart when he announced what his fees for the transaction would be. 'No', I said, 'we are paying our lawyer, Alfredo Ledesma, to handle our side and we understand that you don't charge the nuns.' 'I don't charge the nuns', he said, 'but someone has to pay my fees or you'll not get the house.' So with bad grace and after negotiations that would not have disgraced a Turkish carpet salesman, we agreed his price and so paid double legal fees.

But we had the house and in only eighteen months we would move in. Cordova Street is in downtown Guayaquil and it is on the edge of the financial area, where we wanted to be. With all the bureaucracy and paperwork involved in importing, it is convenient to be close to the central and commercial banks, so a messenger can make several trips to and fro in a morning if the papers are not in order.

From signing for Agripac House until the day we moved in, I became the nuns' unofficial clerk of works at their building site. I would pass by every day, push the foreman to work faster and relay any detail that needed resolving to the mother superior. That construction really moved on. I was a real pest to all concerned with my one object of taking possession as early as possible.

The great day came at last and we lent trucks and people to help the good nuns to move. When all were gone and the mother superior was handing over the keys, I asked her, half in jest, to leave us the blessing on the house. 'Oh, I'll do that my son,' she said. 'We are very grateful for all you've done for us.' But having possession did not mean that we could move in at once. To house the nuns, the large rooms had been divided up and upstairs was a warren of little rooms. The wiring and plumbing had not had attention for years and the roof leaked in places. My friend, Luigi Rivas, was an architect and I called him in to do the necessary as quickly as possible. He did work fast but I could not wait and was soon installed in my office despite having workmen all around. What bliss – a permanent house for the company and the place where I have spent most of my time during the last twenty-three years, to date.

In the courtyard behind the house, there was a garage. It was in rather poor repair but would serve us as a small warehouse and, by putting a counter at the front, a shop. As the years went by, the garage disappeared and we built a five-storey building which connected with the house. Later still, the three-floor building next door came up for sale and we bought and remodelled it, adding a fourth floor to form an office complex around a patio. Here, several cars can be parked as well as allowing customers' trucks to pull off the street while they are picking up products from the shop.

BOLIVIA

THE IDEA CAME FROM Alain Graillot during a visit here. Alain had replaced Jean Pierre Banzet as the representative of Procida SA. Over dinner at our flat one night, he mentioned the tremendous potential for Bolivia and suggested he and I should look at the possibility of setting up a company like Agripac there. He had set the ball rolling and I asked ICI what the situation was in Bolivia. I was told that it did have an agent, but that the arrangement was very unsatisfactory and it was thinking of changing if it could find someone reliable. Could I have it? Yes, if I set up an organisation and agreed to certain sales targets. I talked it over with Mario and convinced him that we should go and take a look. Thus it was that on the 2nd May, 1977 we stepped off the plane at El Alto airport in La Paz. El Alto is well named as it is a huge treeless expanse above the city of La Paz, which is bordered by Lake Titicaca and stands at 13,000 feet above sea level. This altitude is much worse than that of Quito and provokes severe headaches in most travellers, which can be helped by drinking the 'mate de coca'. This is an infusion of coca leaves, which is mildly narcotic and is sold quite legally in Bolivia (but beware of taking it into the United States!)

We took a taxi down the hill into La Paz, which, at 12,000 feet, is the highest capital in the world. To my mind, it is not an attractive city, being a mix of old and modern building but does not have the colonial charm of Quito. The population is mainly Indians, who are short and square with broad, red faces and the women wear bowler-type hats of various colours. I have often wondered where these came from — whether they were brought from Europe or whether the early twentieth-century British habit of wearing the bowler hat came from Bolivia. Come to think of it bowler/Bolivia? There could be a clue there. Mother's family were hatters from Denton, Manchester, but there are not many of them left to ask now and the factory closed many years ago.

We spent one night in La Paz and a day wandering around the centre of town, taking a professional interest in the agrochemical stores. They looked very sad and poor — not much business doing up here.

My one and only contact in Bolivia was my old mate of Harper Adams days, Winston Suarez, and so we went looking for him. I had lost all contact but remembered that he came from Santa Cruz. So we flew there from La Paz. You usually fly in Bolivia as the roads are dreadful and I think it was a two-day journey between these cities in those days. Santa Cruz is much more attractive than La Paz. It is curiously built with a small central plaza and a series of ring roads, forming concentric circles. There were at least four of these and each was paved with concrete setts, which is for ease of maintenance, I think.

There was a new hotel, Los Tajibos, which was of the Holiday Inn chain, and we based ourselves there while we tried to find Winston. It was not as hard as it might have seemed as the family was very well known. We soon discovered that Winston was by now a lecturer in animal husbandry at the University of Trinidad, a small town in the Beni province. There was no telephone but contact could be made by radio so we went along to the Beni radio office and duly called him. After eleven years we spoke again in the stilted radio fashion — one talking while the other listened with frequent 'over' punctuations. He agreed to fly into Santa Cruz the next day and we met again. In fact, he was Doctor Winston Suarez now as he had gone on from Harper Adams to Texas A and M University and gained his PhD.

He was interested in our proposal and I pushed ahead, full of enthusiasm although I could see that he and Mario were never going to hit it off completely. Winston had always been a joker and, while I was enthusing on the wonders of our agrochemical world, his levity and sarcasm did not sit well with Mario. But I had known Winston of old and we had shared many a happy time together.

Although he had inherited a cattle farm in the Beni, he did not have any spare capital for the project. It was agreed that Agripac would put up the money and take eighty per cent of the company, while Winston would take twenty per cent and agree to run it for a low salary for the first years. He would come to Ecuador to learn the trade later in the year and then we would import the first products and start Agripac Bolivia Cia Ltda.

That was the start of the venture and Mario and I returned to Ecuador. I was bursting with excitement about the new project, Mario rather quieter. Some years before, an American company, Grace and Co, had set up businesses all over Latin America, selling fertilisers and farmers' goods. I imagined that this would be the start of something similar for Agripac. Ecuador, Bolivia, Paraguay, Peru — who knew how big we could grow. Nor was I put off when I told my plans to a Frederick Goldbaum, a banker in Guayaquil who told me to be very careful in Bolivia because he had set up a venture there may years before and lost everything. 'Bolivia is the country of the future,' I said. 'And always will be!' he replied.

By the end of the year, Agripac Bolivia had an office in Santa Cruz and Winston had taken on a secretary, Wilma, and three salesmen. Gramoxone arrived from ICI Brazil and we began to sell quite well. David Lloyd Williams of ICI came out to visit us and plans were made to expand the line of products, although he and Winston irritated each other and I found myself playing the role of peacemaker.

Winston and I travelled to Cochabamba, La Paz and even to the Beni, that vast lonely province, larger than Ecuador, where there is hardly a road and the ranchers all have huge farms with five hectares of land per head of cattle. Everyone is a pilot and flying is the only means of transport bar horses. We visited it in the wet season, flying from Santa Cruz by jet (Lloyd Aereo Boliviana) to Trinidad and there taking an air taxi for an hour or so to Santa Ana, where several of Winston's many brothers had farms. The idea was to go to Winston's farm but we never arrived.

There was a party in his parental home and his brothers and sisters were present, a bit of a family reunion. The whisky flowed and the day passed and we got no further. After spending the night there and with dreadful hangovers, we were taken by Winston's brother, Huasca, over the flooded fields nearby on a hydrofoil at tremendous speed, turning so violently that I was almost sick and several small fishes were washed into the boat. At last this torture ended and we returned to Santa Ana just in time to catch the small plane back to Trinidad. When we looked down, we saw that the flooding was so great that the original line of the rivers could be seen only by the trees along the banks. This was an abnormally wet year but it went a long way towards explaining why so much land was needed for each head of cattle.

The trip to see a ranch in the Beni had been aborted as Winston had sidetracked us towards his social life but we did make it on another occasion. Winston's wife, Graciela, is the daughter of a wealthy man called Satorri, who was a great friend of the then dictator and now constitutional president, Hugo Banzer, and was mayor of Cochabamba at one time. Satorri owned a huge spread in the Beni: no one would say just how big it was, but in that context huge probably meant 100,000 hectares. He had invited Winston and I to visit and we cheerfully hired a small one-engine air taxi in Santa Cruz.

The pilot did not give us much confidence — he thought he knew the Satorri place and he and Winston had briefly run their fingers over a large map on the office wall. Then we set off. It was a fairly long flight of about one and a half hours, said the pilot. We flew on and on, the one and a half hours came and went. The cloud grew lower and we had to fly beneath it to identify features. To my eye, there was nothing to distinguish where we were at all: just land and rivers with their borders of trees and occasional groups of cattle. The clouds came down further and we came down further until we were only a few hundred feet above the ground, which was luckily quite flat. The pilot kept a wary eye on his fuel gauge and announced that, if we did not see the farm within the next ten minutes, we would have to go back to Santa Cruz.

Then we did see a farmstead whose tin roof sparkled in a ray of sun passing through the cloud. Winston recognised it and we landed thankfully. Senor Satorri came out to the landing strip to meet us and we went to his house for lunch. When he heard our story and the way we had travelled, he was furious both with Winston (with whom relations were somewhat strained even on a good day) and the pilot. 'Stupid idiots', he said, 'you came cross-country in a single-engine plane, not on any recognised air route and without registering your journey at Santa Cruz airport. If the engine had failed, you would never have been found again.' Apparently, this had happened the year before and only recently had bits of the plane and a few of its occupants' bones been found by a cowboy.

The pilot, duly chastened, left after lunch and we stayed on with Satorri's offer of flying us to Triniday the following day, where we would take the regular Lloyd Aereo Flight to Cochabamba. After lunch, we took horses and rode for several hours, looking at the cattle. I got on well with the old man but it was obvious that Winston did not. I did not think he considered Winston much of a catch for his daughter. They had met and married while Winston was studying in Texas. Winston's jovial character had a streak of despotism and he sometimes treated Graciela very badly — so much so that there were times when it was difficult for me to put up with it as a house guest.

Winston's family owned lots of ranches in the Beni. All his brothers and sisters had one or two but, as he was the youngest, his share was the most modest. The family history was fascinating. At the beginning of the twentieth century, Bolivia had practically been owned by four families. One was Simon Patino, the tin king who owned most of the mines around Oruro and was fabulously wealthy; one was a Suarez, who owned all the land in the Beni, and I have forgotten the other two. During the rubber boom in Brazil, before the British planted it in Malaya, the Brazilians had tried to annex the Beni and Suarez had raised an army at his own expense and defended it. But careless management, good living, numerous offspring, both legitimate and illegitimate, and finally the land reform laws had reduced the fortune to today's level. Although not inconsiderable in terms of land, it did not provide much income.

The problem is the lack of roads due to the annual flooding of rivers leading from the Andes to the Amazon thousands of miles away. Because the land is flat, the rivers curve and snake through it looking for gradient. Heavy rain just cannot run off before the rivers burst their banks. Roads have to be built on large dykes at great expense if they are to survive. There were few crops to transport but plenty of cattle. The answer was to build a slaughterhouse on each ranch and fly the meat to La Paz, Cochabamba or Santa Cruz in ancient DC-3 planes. This was expensive and so the rancher earned very little for his beef.

One of Winston's half-brothers, however, had taken steps to improve his fortune. This was the notorious Roberto Suarez, who was known as the King of Cocaine. He had built up such a fortune in cocaine trading that he once offered the Bolivian government a deal whereby he would pay off the national debt (of some $3 billion) in exchange for immunity from prosecution for himself and his son. Of course, this was a wild exaggeration of his wealth and the offer was not accepted, anyway. He was eventually caught and spent eight years in prison, being released in 1996. We met him only once at a family party to which Winston had invited Ceci and I. Although hugely wealthy, he did not appear to help any of his brothers, least of all Winston, who was permanently hard up.

We flew from Trinidad to Cochabamba, which stands at a higher elevation than Santa Cruz but is much lower than La Paz and has an agreeable climate. We stayed in a hotel and our wives, Ceci and Graciela, flew in from Santa Cruz to join us. The girls had become good friends and we made a very jolly group. While we were waiting in the lobby of the hotel, there was a great commotion when a man who had just entered rushed at a woman who had come downstairs and attacked her, punching and kicking her. Winston and I pounced on the man while the woman picked herself up and beat a very hasty retreat. The man was furious with us crying: 'Es mi mujer y tengo todo derecho de castigarla!'(It's my wife and I have every right to punish her.) It appears that he had caught her with another man in the hotel; although we did not see the other party, who must have escaped another way. Winston, being Latin American, instantly apologised to the man and quite understood the situation so we let him get up and go. But by that time the wife had at least got a decent start on him!

We lunched with Graciela's parents in their large house and then wandered around the street markets where the coca leaves are sold. These look like ordinary leaves and are packed in wickerwork baskets and piled up in the market. Coca is a part of the life and tradition of the Bolivian Indians which goes back to before the Spanish Conquest. In fact, in colonial days it was one of the most profitable concessions available to the Spanish. The coca leaves are chewed with a piece of chalk and the mild narcotic enables the Indians to work for long periods in the mines or at high-altitude farms without food or sleep. Of course, this comes at a price to the body and reduces life expectancy to some forty years. The government of Bolivia has a great dilemma over coca. It is a staple for the indigenous people but is also the base from which cocaine is extracted, and this is illegal. The United States spends a great deal of time and money trying unsuccessfully to eradicate the cocaine trade but still has to tolerate the growing of coca. At the time of writing, there are riots in Bolivia against the government's plan to eradicate the coca plantations in a programme financed by the USA.

The finances of Bolivia were relatively stable when we started there in 1977. There was free exchange with twenty Bolivian pesos to the dollar. Then hyperinflation set in and, within a period of three or four years, the dollar came to cost over 500,000 pesos. The government printed ever more bank notes but not very large ones. At the height of the problem, there were still 100 peso notes in circulation, not individually but shrink-wrapped in blocks the size of bricks. Cash collections and the buying of dollars to pay for imports became a logistical nightmare. We would price the Gramoxone in dollars and if payment were in pesos, it would be at the exchange rate of that moment as it changed by the minute. The customer would turn up at the shop with a pick-up truck full of sacks of bank notes. These blocks of bank notes would be counted and weighed (they were never opened) and then the operation would be repeated in a bank where dollars were bought.

Bolivia's credit lines were all cancelled at this time and it became a cash economy but, as the drugs business is inevitably a cash one, Bolivia had plenty of dollar bank notes. Everyone knew that they came from an illegal source but it was the only foreign exchange that was available. The government added to the difficulties by restricting the amount of US bank notes that a traveller was allowed to carry out of the country but, given that the banks had no way of transmitting money, the only way to pay for imports was in cash. On many occasions, Winston had to travel to Brazil with a considerable amount of dollar notes hidden on him to pay ICI Brazil.

I also did this once, suffering agonies of suspense when the customs officers checked my suitcase and briefcase. Luckily, there was no body check as I was wearing it like a girdle. Having reached ICI Brazil and feeling that I had risked a great deal in order to pay on time, I was somewhat miffed by the reaction of the chief accountant who received the cash. 'If there are any counterfeit bills, here you are responsible,' he said. I replied: 'Anyone trying to pass counterfeit notes in Bolivia would have a very short life expectancy indeed!'

Cochabamba airport is dangerous to get into and out of. Planes taking off have to bank very sharply before they gain much altitude to avoid the mountains which are at the end of the runway and, indeed, all around it. Because roads were so poor at that time, Lloyd Aereo Boliviano was rather like a bus service. It would fly internationally from, say, Lima to La Paz with people in business suits. These got out and the plane filled with Indians in their traditional clothes, clutching baskets of eggs, live chickens and other goods, who flew on to Cochabamba or Santa Cruz.

I made one return flight from Santa Cruz via Cochabamba to La Paz and on to Lima with Ceci. Having reached Cochabamba, we were asked to stay on the plane while it collected passengers and cargo. This worried us. Looking out of the window, we saw ground staff rolling barrel after barrel up a plank and into the hold. There were an awful lot of them and we worried about the weight. Eventually, the plane took off and banked steeply but did not appear to be gaining any height. As the mountains grew near, we began to sweat. The pilot was clearly giving all the throttle he could and the engines vibrated frightfully but we were still below the mountain tops. Ceci and I held hands tightly and I heard her saying her prayers while we both thought of our three small children, now about to be orphaned. Then, miraculously, we just cleared the mountain and were away. We agreed that from then on I would do the Bolivian run alone. Ceci never went again. I think I went to Bolivia fourteen times over a ten-year period.

The business had been exciting at first and had even been profitable for one or two years, but when you are building a business there is never any payout. Profits are all reinvested. The inflation put a great strain on the nerves of both of us as did Winston upon mine. Winston could be a most amusing friend or could be impossible. He would sometimes upset customers by his attitude and at other times fall prey to suppliers' salesmen, buying large quantities of unsaleable stock. I think that they must have played on his machismo, suggesting that he was not a good enough businessman to sell whatever amount of product. Of course, he fell for it time and again.

He would not tell me about these wonders over the phone and each time I visited I would expect the worst, and it would be so. Time and again, I would make a plan with him to stick to Gramoxone and a few other ICI products. Time and again, I would find his warehouse full of other products but no Gramoxone. Where was it? Well, we were a bit behind with payments to ICI and they would not ship more until payment was forthcoming. Where had the money gone from the last Gramoxone sales? To buy this wonderful new soya herbicide. But this had never been sold in Bolivia before! No, but he had got a good price and was sure we could move it. How much had he bought? Just $25,000 worth. $25,000 worth of something completely unknown!

I would spend two to three weeks on each visit, normally with Winston and Graciela and their four daughters. Each visit meant fire-fighting: finding out what he had done wrong and trying to put it right, which included introducing more capital and guaranteeing the credit personally so that the suppliers would keep supplying.

Despite all these problems, the company began to do better. Then Winston took another tack and on each visit he would belabour me with the injustice of our agreement. He was working all the hours that God gave, admittedly for a salary, but he had only twenty per cent of the company and I had eighty. Over a period of time, I weakened and agreed to give him a fifty-fifty arrangement, hoping that this would stimulate him to make some profit. Despite this agreement, for which he was initially grateful, he returned to the old refrain. By this time, I was growing tired of his management style and the continuous problems in Agripac Boliviana. As Mario had lost all interest in the venture and had left me to it, I agreed to sell Winston another thirty per cent and keep just twenty with the proviso that I also withdrew my guarantees to suppliers and banks. He did pay for these shares over a period of time.

The last time I saw Winston was in Santiago, Chile in April 1987. We had been invited by Nelson Echeverria of Stauffer Chemical, whom we represented in Ecuador and whom we were considering for Bolivia. Winston was to come with Graciela but he arrived alone. We had a very pleasant three days visiting farms with Nelson and even went to the Concha y Toro wineries, where Nelson knew the owners, lunching with them before flying south to Puerto Mont. But Winston was irritable and on the last day it came out that Graciela had thrown him out of the house. Winston had always been a playboy and had numerous girlfriends and finally Graciela could stand it no longer. She had money of her own and the house was hers.

With this, Winston rather went to pieces. Back in Bolivia, he phoned me to say that the company could not go on any longer; he was in debt and would have to wind it up. He asked me to make over my twenty per cent to him so that he could represent one hundred per cent at the winding-up for tax reasons. I was very sorry that Agripac Boliviana was to finish but had no inclination to go there one more time and bail it out. So I signed over my shares to Winston and wrote off the loss to experience.

It was some six months later that I heard from ICI that Winston, far from closing down the company, had sold it at a good price to a Frenchman, Bertrand du Lassus. I meet Bertrand each year now at the Zeneca (successor to ICI) partnership-distributor conference and hear about the progress of Agripac Boliviana, which is going from strength to strength. That was definitely one that got away! The words of the late Frederick Goldbaum come back to haunt me. Winston tried to call me once or twice since then but I would not take the call. That particular friendship of twenty-three years was dead.

Bertrand du Lassus and I have become good friends and a couple of years ago, after one Zeneca conference in Madrid, he invited a few of the delegates to return home via Toulouse to stay in his mother's chateau for a night. Well, the word 'chateau' covers a great range of house sizes in France and we boarded a minibus at Toulouse airport not knowing what to expect. After an hour's drive into the Pyrenees mountains, we came to a park and gatehouse. Gates opened, we drove up the drive around the lake, and wow! It was pure Disney, the Magic Kingdom — a chateau as they all should be with turrets and towers, a high, pitched black roof on white stone walls and its own chapel standing in formal gardens. Bertrand's mother came out to meet us and, when we hurriedly asked him how we should address her, he said casually 'Oh, Madame La Baroness'. It appeared that our pal was Monsieur le Baron of the Chateau Valmirande. It was a latter-day chateau, built at the end of the nineteenth century by Bertrand's great-uncle, who was a very successful banker. It had passed to his grandfather and father and he, in turn, would one day inherit it. The fortune, however, had long gone and it was a great burden to keep up. On the provision that it was opened to the public occasionally, the French government helped with some of the expenses. Bertrand, determined that a fresh family fortune was necessary to ensure his enjoyment of it, had opted to go to Bolivia and had started several successful business ventures there.

We had a most delightful stay in the chateau for a night together with John and Peggy Greaves, Bob and Mabel McIntosh and Raul and Paz Nogeira. We had lunch served in the garden, including an entire barbecued lamb cooked by an Algerian, which was exquisite. Then madame showed us around the garden and grounds, which included a lake and lovely restored stables. That evening we were taken to the cellars to choose the dinner wine by Bertrand and were amazed by the wonderful collection he had dating back to the beginning of the century. The following morning, the minibus took us on a tour of the surrounding countryside to see a tiny church dating from Roman times and a much larger one standing nobly on a hilltop which was dedicated to St Bertrand, I think. Then, sadly, Ceci and I had to leave to catch our flight to Teesside via Amsterdam.

Agripac Boliviana had originally been formed from an idea put forward by Alain Graillot. He had wanted to take a share in the company but, as Winston had been against it, I had had to put him off tactfully. He was certainly well out of it as I had lost quite a lot of money on the venture. Several years later, Alain and his wife Elizabeth decided to leave Procida and buy a vineyard near Hermitage on the Rhone. This time, he asked me to go in with him and I have always regretted saying no. At the time, I was investing heavily in Tupgill, which left me no spare capital, so I missed being a small part in his very successful wine venture. Ceci and I have been to visit them in Hermitage several times and always return with a case of their wine. It would be nice to be able to tell my friends: 'This rather attractive little wine comes from my vineyard in Hermitage.' Alain's wines are now well known and, when staying at Paris for our silver wedding last year, we had dinner with the Graillots at the lovely restaurant Laurent in the Avenue Gabriel. Alain's wines were on the wine list there and he was warmly welcomed by the owner. Alain now wears the badge of honour of the wine grower, hands blackened by the grapes.

MAPAN

As well as seeing the start of the Bolivian venture, 1977 also saw my debut as a farmer. At school my sole ambition had been to be a farmer. As this was impossible, I had gone into commerce but the pull was still there. I had been with Ceci on many occasions to Guarumal, the 3,000-hectare cattle and banana farm which belonged to Don Louis. He lived there for most of the week in a large, two-storey wooden house with a balcony which ran three sides around it and overlooked the River Babahoyo. It was 100 kilometres from Guayaquil and could be reached by an unmade road in the dry season or at any time by motorboat up the river from Guayaquil.

When I mentioned that I was thinking of buying a farm to Don Louis, he said: 'Why don't we go into partnership on a 700-hectare part of Guarumal called Mapan. You can run it as I've got more than enough to do here.' As he was over seventy years old at the time, that seemed a fair statement.

I was fascinated. I knew Mapan and it was mostly 'banco': that is to say, a metre or so higher than the 'bajo' or lower flooded land of that area. Bananas had already been planted on part of it and it was the closest area of Guarumal to the road, which was being improved to take traffic all the year round. It was all run as one farm and, because the fences were very poor, the cattle wandered where they pleased. In fact, Guarumal was pretty dilapidated. My first memory of it was a ride on the narrow-gauge railway which was used to transport the bananas to the packing house in 1973. This had by now been sold for scrap metal and the banana plantation was overgrown with weeds. Don Louis had been a pioneer in bringing the Cavendish variety of banana to Ecuador many years earlier when the previous variety, Gros Michele, had been wiped out by Panama disease. He had planted several hundred hectares and installed the railway but old age, bad temper and poor labour relations had soured him and he mainly ran cattle now.

We came to an agreement as to the value of the land and the 500 head of cattle to stock it with initially and formed a company, Mapan SA. When I first started to run the farm, as he had suggested, I saw that it was not going to be easy to work with him. The first example of this was the day when we picked out the 500 cattle. I had asked Leo Carofilis, one of the Agripac agronomists, to help me to select the cattle. Don Louis had said 'Pick just what you like.' So we did. After a few hours sitting on the corral fence selecting this one and rejecting the following ten, Don Louis stormed off in a huff. We were taking the best, he complained. Hurriedly, we finished the selection, taking some inferior stock to placate him.

I used to go to the farm every weekend and, though I passed the days in Mapan, renovating the banana plantation, repairing the packing station and building fences, I would sleep in his house in Guarumal. He enjoyed having company and we would talk over a bottle of wine at dinner. The house had no electric light and, although it was difficult to read by their light, the oil lamps made an attractive atmosphere. There was a chap called Juan, who was cook, secretary, paymaster and general dogs-body. Don Louis would call 'Juan' loudly in a hoarse voice every few minutes and ask him to get this, do that, serve dinner or whatever and Juan the good-natured never complained.

While I stayed in Guarumal, we got on pretty well. He would tell stories of France and his family; how his illustrious forebear had been a general with Napoleon and that his name is engraved on the Arc de Triomphe (it is — I have seen it). Don Louis had been a colonel in the French army in the Second World War and had seen his brother killed alongside him, before he was taken prisoner. After the war, he had left France for his mother's inheritance in Ecuador and had rarely returned. He had been married twice: first to a French lady with whom he had had twins, Philippe and Beatriz. After divorcing, he had married again to an American but they could not decide whether to live in Ecuador or the States and that marriage had ended. Philippe lived in Mexico and, curiously, while I was working there in 1971 I met and went out for a short time with a Swiss au pair, Elizabeth, who was working for Philippe. She told me of his father, the count, and his huge farm in Ecuador.

Although I enjoyed Don Louis's company, I felt that I would rather be in charge in my own house than forever a guest in his. Mapan had a very small wooden cabin opposite the packing station that Don Louis had built years before but which now stood empty. It was here that I decided to hang my saddle, and I used it for my weekend stays. In fact, saddle should be taken literally as the cattle were worked with horses and along with the cattle had come a number of horses and vaqueros. In fact, the handover of former Guarumal employees to Mapan had been made very informally. One day they had worked there: now they worked here. They accepted the situation with a certain amount of reserve because, under Ecuadorian law, they should have been compensated for their previous years of service on changing jobs. Don Louis had cunningly escaped from this obligation but for me it was a time bomb, which would explode years in the future.

Mapan then became my all-absorbing interest and pastime when I was not working for Agripac. On Saturday morning I would get up early and, taking Snoopy with me, head for Mapan. I had an American Ford Granada car which was rather too luxurious for farm use but, once I arrived at Mapan, the car remained parked until I left again on Sunday afternoon. All internal transport was on horseback. I had disliked horses as a child when all family conversation had revolved around them and both my sisters rode better than I did. My latent interest had been rekindled in Malaysia and now I was an enthusiast. The cowboy horses were rather small (about fourteen hands), so I bought one that was a cross between a racehorse and a local mare and which was taller. The horse would be saddled and waiting when I arrived and I would ride off, accompanied by five vaqueros with Snoopy running behind.

The first task was to separate our newly branded cattle from those of Guarumal. They had always run together before and saw no reason why they should be separated from former friends now. We had miles of fencing to build or repair and Julio Vera, a foreman I had inherited, undertook this task with a gang of daily labourers. The vaqueros would repair gaps in the barbed wire fences when they had to but did not take kindly to getting off their horses for long. They were small men with rather bandy legs but their artistry with cattle was wonderful to see. Carlos Rizzo was head vaquero. He had grown from boy to man at Guarumal and Don Louis had recommended him to me.

The cattle would be separated from the herd by the vaqueros galloping among them, turning them this way and that. When a group of ours had been collected which included one or two from Guarumal, the final separation would be made in a gateway, letting ours pass and turning back the others. Occasionally, we would come across a cow or calf with a wound which needed attention. The vaqueros would untie their lassos and dash after the animal which, seeing itself as the object of their unwelcome attentions, would hive off at speed. In the mad chase, the vaqueros would lose their hats but never their prey. Firstly, they would get a noose around its neck and, winding the lasso around the pommel of the wooden saddle, would stop the animal in its tracks. The lasso would burn into the pommel with the friction. Then a second vaquero would throw a loop of his lasso on to the ground behind the circling beast and pull tight as soon as it stepped into it. The cow would be caught by the neck and back legs would fall over. While the first two vaqueros kept the lassos taut, a third would dismount his horse and retie the lasso on the back legs so that the animal could be later released from horseback.

The main problems to be cured were wounds, which would attract blowflies and become full of maggots within a day. These had to be scraped out of the wound, which sometimes involved prodding deeply into it to remove them all. Then an insecticide and wound dressing would be applied, the lasso taken off the head and, once all were back on their horses, the noose around the back legs was released and the animal got up. It was of great importance to be back in the saddle by this time as an angry cow with long horns can be quite formidable.

Don Louis had neglected his cattle in recent years and, although these had once been of recognisable breeds — Brahman, Brangus and the local Criollo (descended from cattle introduced by the Spanish settlers) — now all were mixed. Worse, as there was no breeding policy, they had cross-bred and sons mated with mothers, bringing out undesirable traits such as dwarfism. When I referred to Don Louis's herd while talking to George Neal, another cattleman, he said: 'That's not a herd: it's a zoo!'

With the unbounded enthusiasm of a new cattleman, I was going to sort this out and do it well. Having put the fences in order with the cattle more or less on the right side of them, the next job was to divide the herd up into breeding groups and young cattle. In Ecuador calves are usually weaned at six months old. Then the young heifers are kept in one field until they are of a size to put to the bull, normally at two years old. The young bulls are reared apart until twenty-four to thirty months when, at about 1,000 pounds live weight, they go for slaughter. There is no need of housing or feeding apart from grass.

To enable the working of the herd, we needed a corral and we built this of thick stakes set into the ground and crossed with bamboo poles, which are very strong and slightly flexible, so preventing injuries as cattle are crushed together. We removed and sold all the old stock bulls and bought new ones from recognised Brahman breeders, especially from Peter Bohman, an Ecuadorian of Swedish descent who regularly wins the top prizes at the cattleman's show. I went for a simple policy of breeding white Brahmans as they are known as the kings of the tropics, and are tolerant to drought and flooding, easy calvers and good mothers. My herd was now organised and on its way to improvement.

The pastures, however, were a disaster. Overgrazing had caused large areas to be all weeds and even where there was grass, it was of a local variety called gramalote of the paspalum family. This is practically useless for fattening cattle, but at least it was edible and could keep the herd going. So the first priority was weed control and, as it happened, that was my business. Mapan borrowed money from the Banco de Fomento, the government land bank, and bought three Leyland tractors from Trace Ltd, together with ploughs, harrows and a sprayer. With Agripac's selective herbicides, we set to work to spray those areas which could be saved and plough those that could not. Gramalote is a terrible grass to get rid of as it recovers with the yearly rains and can populate a field again in no time. We found that the solution was to plant a cash crop, which allowed us to keep attacking it for a whole year before putting the field back to grass. We grew rice, maize, soya beans, sorghum and even sunflowers over the years as we worked our way around the farm. The crops were not tremendously successful as, for all the agronomists we employed at Agripac, we still appeared to lack expertise. But they at least paid for the cost of changing the pastures.

On the slightly higher 'bancos' we planted African star grass by vegetative propagation. A team of twenty people walked across the ploughed field, making a groove with their machetes and pushing in a piece of grass. This was very quick and it took at once, leaving a good pasture in three months. In the lower 'baja' areas, which flooded every year, we killed the weeds with herbicides and propagated the better local water grasses in the same way.

Over a period of three years, Mapan began to look better. We had healthy fat cattle in good pastures; the banana plantation had been renovated; and we had contracted the production with Standard Fruit Co, which gave me loans to rebuild the packing shed, put in an irrigation system and build drains around the whole plantation. Then, in 1981, I moved out of the wooden cabin and into the large concrete and brick house with a red-tiled roof, which had been

The Mapan house, 1985.

built on the farm by my architect friend, Luigi Rivas. It is a lovely house standing on pillars. There is no ground floor, only a first floor and a partial mezzanine forms a second. A balcony runs around two sides where I spend most of my time. It has five bedrooms and four bathrooms, a kitchen with maids' quarters behind and sitting and dining rooms — altogether over the top, as Don Louis angrily pointed out! He had been unhappy with the amount of money that I had borrowed to re-equip Mapan. Although pleased with the results, he was doubtful that we would ever get out of debt again. Now the house, which I had financed personally and which he had watched being built over eighteen months, was the focus of discord.

 He would not even step inside it. From then on, we did not meet at all but he would send me messages via Julio Vera that this, that or the other was being done wrongly and would ruin the farm. There were also occasional letters full of venom claiming that Mapan had always given him a good income before but that now he got nothing out of it. I tactlessly replied that this was because he had reduced it to an almost abandoned state by not reinvesting anything and that the value would be recovered one day when he sold his half to me. He replied that he never would! Relations deteriorated further when I became fed up with his cross-bred bulls jumping over my new fences and crossing with my cows. We put these animals out 100 times and always they returned. When I complained to Don Louis, he simply said that this was nature's way. He could not, or would not, move his bulls into another area away from Mapan. My patience snapped. 'Castrate the next bulls that are seen on our side,' I said to Rizzo. So he did castrate two and returned them in their neutered condition.

When Don Louis heard of this, he was so furious that it might have been him and not the scrub bulls that had been so abused. He sent threats that he would have the law on us. Hurriedly, I consulted Alfredo Ledesma, my old friend and Agripac lawyer. Although he advised me not to do it again in his cautious way, he could not find that there was much legal redress unless the bulls in question had been pure and their breeding value reduced, which was not the case. I had, on the other hand, a claim that my cows were being impregnated by the scruffy bulls in question.

Shortly afterwards, there was another incident relating to boundaries. My cowboys told me that Don Louis's men had taken down a short stretch of fence on the boundary between us as it was in the wrong place, and had put it up farther inside Mapan. The area lost was less than a hectare but it annoyed me as he had marked out the limits of Mapan four years previously, and now wanted to change them arbitrarily. I put the fence back where it had been with my lads. The following day, he and his men, accompanied by the local sheriff, removed it again. By now, seeing that the law was involved, and knowing Don Louis's reputation as a fighter and his close contacts with the police, I decided to leave well alone. I thought that now we were even. I had castrated the bulls: he had taken a piece of land. But it was not to be.

Don Louis was a twenty-five per cent shareholder and director in Agripac and, as we were not on speaking terms, I wrote to him, suggesting that I buy him out of both Agripac and Mapan. In a fury, he replied that Agripac was not his business and that he had only come in to help me when I needed capital. If that was the way I felt, our lawyers could negotiate a price and he would sell. As to Mapan, never, as this was part of his inheritance, which had passed to him through his mother and had belonged to his family in an unbroken line since the Spanish Conquest. Seeing that this was an emotional issue, I replied that I would return Mapan to him in part-payment for the Agripac shares. But that was not what he wanted at all. Over the last few years, he had sold Santa Rita, another 3,000-hectare spread nearby, which had also been handed down to him. No, he wanted a fight. He had taken possession of his farms using armed force after the war and had withstood a strike by his workers in which at least one man had been shot dead. He had also continued a never-ending war with local rustlers, who were a great problem, sitting out all night with guns to try and intercept them. But mostly that war was carried on through the police and the courts, accusing this or that man of being involved and having them arrested and thrown in jail for a few months.

However, he was distracted from his fight with me as Guarumal was invaded by 150 local people. This was quite a common occurrence at the time as the land reform was in force. The law stated that if land were not at least eighty per cent used for farming, it could be confiscated and divided up among the labour force. This eighty per cent rule was broadly interpreted as referring to land being cultivated, pastures being planted or improved, cattle being reared and so on. However, plaintiff, judge and jury were all one, the land reform director, and there was no appeal. The best defence was either to work the land intensively or to buy the 'inefectibilidad', a document which stated that a farm could not be confiscated as a business plan for its development was in hand. This was really a protection racket through which a lot of money changed hands.

At that time, Guarumal had its 'inefectibilidad' but other forces were at work. Given the military government's left-wing tendencies, it was an each-way bet that an invasion would be successful. Certain people made a great deal of money by forming pre-cooperatives of local people, who would each pay a certain amount with the promise of obtaining the land of a neighbouring farm. During a weekend when the owner was away, they would rush into the farm and start building houses on it. This is what happened to Guarumal, just over the fence from Mapan. It had become known that relations between Don Louis and myself were bad and they calculated (correctly) that we would not work together to see them off. My worry was that they would spread into Mapan and we hired guards to patrol the fence. Meanwhile, Don Louis was improving his already good contacts with the military government and police. The invaders had been there for a month or so when, one dawn, Don Louis appeared with a regiment of paratroopers which, it seemed, needed that part of Guarumal for training exercises. The people were moved off at gunpoint and the rustic houses all burned. This ended the invasion and the military retired soon afterwards. However, one more nail had been hammered into the coffin of my relations with Don Louis. I had done nothing to support him at this time.

In June 1980, we completed the sale of Don Louis's shares in Agripac. Until this time, Mario Ramos had a five per cent share in the company and I had seventy per cent, with Don Louis holding the balance of twenty-five. Mario made a strong case for being allowed to increase his holding to fifteen per cent and he wanted to introduce his cousin by marriage, Ivan Noboa, our Quito manager, who was to put up about two per cent. This left me with eighty-three percent. Don Louis had bought in for $200,000 and sold out for $600,000 four years later, as well as receiving dividends throughout, but his pride was hurt and he would not even shake hands on the deal. Several people warned me to careful as I had made a bad enemy. But how can you be careful? I just had to wait for events to take their course and the time bomb exploded seven years later.

Meanwhile, back in June 1977, Ceci, Nick (aged fifteen months) and I were off to England. I had always wanted to try a sea voyage on a large ship, so what better than the *QE2*? We flew to New York and stayed in the Hilton hotel in Manhattan, while we spent a couple of days shopping. In the evenings, we went out to a show or dinner, leaving Nick with a baby-sitter provided by the hotel. On Monday the 6th June, we boarded the great liner. It was all very civilised, our luggage being taken on the dockside and labelled while we were shown to our cabin. We were travelling first class but at the lower end of the tariff band. The cabin was pleasant, although quite small. The ship sailed in the late afternoon and we watched Manhattan pass from the deck. When we emerged from the river into the sea, there was some movement but we soon became used to it and changed into evening clothes for dinner. There was a baby-sitting service on board so we cheerfully left Nick and went to the dining room. The food was excellent, the wines of the best and the service superb. We would go to the casino or to dance after dinner and there were several shows. During the daytime, we would wander around the ship but, as it was early season, there were cold mists off Newfoundland making sunbathing impossible. The sea, however, was mercifully calm and my stomach remained subdued. I have recently seen the film *Titanic*, where the heroine leans into the wind at the prow of the ship. You could certainly have done that on the *QE2* for, at thirty knots, the slipstream at the prow was tremendous. The journey lasted four days and five nights and we were strangely sad to leave the ship when we arrived at Southampton.

We had not met any people on board whom we knew but had made a few acquaintances. On the last day, we took Nick into the dining room for lunch and all sorts of people came over to say hello. They explained that, seeing we two young people alone together, they had thought we must be on honeymoon and had left us in peace. But now, with Nick there, they saw that we were not honeymooners! The ship arrived in Southampton at midnight but we did not disembark until after breakfast the following morning — again very civilised. I had ordered a Volvo hire car in which we drove up to Yorkshire.

After Mother had died, Father moved permanently to Tupgill with Do, so Ferngill was now ours and we began to think of renovating it. I had met Malcolm Tempest a year or so previously when I had thought of setting up a business with Malcolm Scott, a solicitor in Leyburn, to buy and renovate cottages. That had come to nothing but I was impressed with Malcolm, who was an artist as well as an architect. He would explain his ideas in drawings and pictures and I had always been captivated by how he saw potential to improve buildings.

I called him now and we walked around Ferngill, thinking aloud just what we wanted to achieve. Ferngill had four downstairs rooms in line from south to north: sitting room, dining room, maid's parlour and kitchen. There were two principal bedrooms and two small bedrooms, the latter served by a servants' staircase by the kitchen. Then there was a lean-to scullery, coal shed and small yard. The garage stood a little way away and was a converted army shed of Second World War vintage. There was also a corrugated iron barn and eight dilapidated wooden stables, next to which were Father's vegetable garden and greenhouse.

Malcolm returned the following day with a helper and a tape measure. We were coming to the end of our holiday so we had asked him to hurry and give us some ideas before we left for Ecuador. On our last day there, Malcolm appeared again with drawings and plans, which we accepted at once. The sitting and dining rooms were to be joined to make a large sitting room. A new hall was formed with the front door, from which a circular stair led upstairs and a new dining room with large, brick open fireplace and exposed beams was built out into the garden to the right of the house. A master bedroom and bathroom were above these and a garage was added at the back. The outside of the house, which was of rendered brick, would be given a new skin of second-hand West Riding sandstone, which would cover the new part too, making it all homogenous. It would take more than a year to build so we decided then and there that we would come to England for Christmas in 1978.

BRITISH CALEDONIAN

I HAD BEEN IN CONTACT with British Caledonian since early 1977 when I had heard that it was looking for an agent in Ecuador. Until then, B-Cal had been flying from London Gatwick to Caracas and Bogota. Now it wanted to extend the route to Guayaquil and Lima, returning from Lima, via Quito, Bogota and Caracas.

In September, I visited its offices in Bogota to talk to the Colombian manager, Carlos Cervantes, and his assistant, Carlos Navarro. He agreed that we could become B-Cal agents if we formed a separate company from Agripac, because an agrochemical company was thought unsuitable to represent an airline, and if we opened sales offices in Guayaquil and Quito. We needed a minimum of three people in each office and suitable, smart surroundings to impress the flying public. We all became very excited about this venture and set to with a will. Tony Pannel of British Caledonian in Gatwick came to Ecuador to help us to set up. We took on two girls: Isabel Bascunan, who was Chilean but lived in Quito, and Silvia de Witmer in Guayaquil. They were taken to Colombia for training and to get their uniforms. We found separate offices from Agripac in both cities and one or two office staff for each. Ceci was interested in helping on a part-time basis and did so in Guayaquil. We formed the company Rexel Ltd to handle the line and by the end of October, we were all ready to go.

The first B-Cal flight came into Guayaquil on the 31st October, following a cocktail party to launch the venture the night before which featured a Scottish pipe band. It marched the whole length of Guayaquil's main street, the Nueve de Octubre, and caused a sensation. We had got all the travel agents together for the launch and raffled some free tickets on the first flight. We also made a list of important potential customers in Guayaquil and Quito and gave them free tickets to London and back. It all seemed very extravagant but the cost was minimal as the plane would have been rather empty on a new route anyway, so what was worth a lot to the customer had only a marginal cost to the airline. Despite all the give-aways, the venture was not a success initially. Lufthansa, Air France, KLM and Iberia all flew from Ecuador to Europe directly. Then both Braniff and Ecuatoriana daily services flew from both Guayaquil and Quito to Miami, where British Airways connected to London. In all, there was excess capacity. We had a small budget for publicity and concentrated on keeping the travel agents sweet. Some specialised in sending groups of children to Bournemouth or Brighton for English courses and these were especially useful for putting behinds on seats.

Despite all our efforts, at the end of the first year of operation Ecuador had not contributed much to B-Cal's traffic. It had, of course, gained the other countries on the route but we had a quota to fill and were not reaching it. We had offices on the first floor of a building in Guayaquil and on a quiet back street in Quito. Tony objected to this, saying that airline offices should be on the ground floor on a main street. Fine, I agreed, but let's look at the economics of the operation. As general sales agent, I earned a commission of three per cent on sales and this did not cover half the costs of maintaining the offices, staff and all. The travel agents, on the other hand, could handle all the airlines and they earned up to thirteen per cent commission. 'Well', said Tony, 'if you make a loss, we will make up the difference for the first year or so.' I was not convinced that if we spent more on offices, we would necessarily increase the revenue. After all, the travel agents provided most of our customers so it did not matter much that we were out of sight. In fact, as soon as we had taken possession of Agripac House, I closed the separate Guayaquil office and moved Rexel (and B-Cal) into it.

And so we went on year after year, improving the number of passengers a little but falling short of budget figures and declaring a loss for Rexel. In fact, the only 'profit' I gained from this business was my free first-class tickets when I went on leave with Ceci and the family once a year. Even then, my tickets were standby and I used to wait anxiously in the days before the flight to hear whether there was a full load and I would be downgraded or left altogether. This never happened but I am the most nervous of travellers, and like to have everything planned in detail months before the journey, so this element of uncertainty did not suit me at all. B-Cal owned the Copthorne Hotel near Crawley and I managed to have a night there included in my freebies, before hiring a car and driving to Yorkshire. I remember watching the rice harvest in Mapan at the time, with the Leyland tractors working and Agripac trucks taking away the rice, when a B-Cal plane went over. We were directly under the flight path and I thought 'This is my empire.'

That part of it was not to last. In April 1982, General Galtieri invaded the Falkland Islands and B-Cal flights were prevented from going from London to Buenos Aires. They were also unable to fly across Argentinian air space to Santiago in Chile. These were the most profitable routes for the company and without them, B-Cal found it difficult to support its Andean routes. It withdrew from Ecuador and Peru and some time later retired altogether from Latin America, handing over to British Airways which today flies as far as Bogota, but not Ecuador. So ended my short career as an airline agent but it was an opportunity to see behind the scenes. Each time I fly today I can appreciate all it takes to get passengers from A to B.

1977–79

The year 1977 was one of hyperactivity. I travelled to Costa Rica, Bolivia (twice), Colombia, New York, England and finally Tobago. The last journey was at the invitation of ICI, to attend a regional conference where I was to give a paper on the Ecuadorian banana industry. I was very excited about going to this event as it was the first time that I would see all my old colleagues in my new role as agent — showing off, I suppose. Ceci and I flew to Caracas and stayed a night there at a hotel near the airport, before flying to Trinidad the following afternoon. We arrived at the airport of Port of Spain only to discover, as did many other passengers, that we needed a visa to get in. After an interminable wait, an official was finally found to issue the necessary visas then and there, but they could be paid for only in British West Indian dollars. There was no bank at the airport and so we could not buy local currency. We proffered our US dollars in vain. More hours passed, until eventually it was agreed that we could pay in US dollars at an outlandish exchange rate. By this time, we were all too tired to argue and paid. The British have a lot to answer for for setting up such a stubborn and inflexible bureaucracy!

Finally, freed from the airport, we were put up at the Belair hotel near the airport, which was dreadful but served for a night's sleep before we could take the early morning flight to Tobago. Here, things improved no end and we cheered up to see the lovely hotel on a golf course where the conference was to take place. It was fun meeting all my old chums such as Tom Frears, John Robinson, Mike Chambers, Richard Smith and David Blows again and for the first time Bob McIntosh, an Australian who had set up Southern Cross Agencies Inc in Panama and, like me, was an ICI agent. Bob and I have become good friends and visit each other's businesses to compare notes. I found out later that David Blows had secretly set up the business with Bob while he was in Central America and sold out to him years later, when he left ICI and returned to Australia. So perhaps I was not quite as unique as I thought, and David had done the same before me.

My paper was duly and nervously presented to the conference without making any great impact, but I gained quite a lot from listening to the other papers there. As the only wife present, it was arranged that Ceci should go to Bird Island nearby which she did, joining a honeymoon couple, the Wilsons, who appeared to welcome her presence. All four of us dined together one evening. The last night there was the gala dinner and afterwards there was one of the funniest speeches I have ever heard by Richard Smith. Richard had been at Cambridge with the Monty Python crowd and they had performed together at the Footlights theatre. I often wonder why Richard had not made his name with them. He was an excellent raconteur. He left ICI soon afterwards and set up his own consultancy and visited Ecuador once some years ago.

Before 1977 was out, I had acquired the presidency of the Phoenix Club. Today it seems laughable that there should have been competition for the job, which is a pretty thankless one, but there was that year. I had been nominated and was not opposed until a day or so before the election when Roger Barker, who was assistant manager with Lloyds Bank (then the Bank of London and South America) in Guayaquil, was also nominated. Roger was a good pal and canvassed amusingly with a huge rosette like Screaming Lord Such of the Raving Loony Party but I will admit that I was a bit put out that he had stood against me. I was all the more determined to win, which I did.

However, my triumph was cut short. Just after the election, we were given notice to quit the Fiori building in Pedro Carbo Street, where the club had been for the last thirty-one years as it was to be redeveloped as a bank. This meant a great deal of work, which I certainly did not need, to find new premises within three months. The Phoenix elects a president and committee annually but the president has to do all the work. I had to search all over town for a suitable building that would be large enough for our parties but not cost too much in rent as, like most clubs in Ecuador, we were habitually hard up. Collecting the monthly dues and bar bills from our members was a full-time job. For many members, the Phoenix Club was right at the end of the priority list for payment and if they were at all short that month, it did not get paid. Our dilemma was that if we pushed too hard for payment, they would be offended and resign (without paying), which made the situation worse as we needed 200 members to make a viable club. Numbers were already falling from the original 300 and, by moving premises, we were bound to lose some members. Eventually we found a two-storey building at the corner of the streets Quito and Nueve de Octubre, of which we rented the upper floor. It was a maze of small rooms but we opened them up and it suited our purposes. However, in the end we stayed there for only a couple of years because the members tended to have their cars stolen, this being a rather less salubrious location than our previous one.

Before we left our old premises in the Fiori building, we organised one last party there for Hallowe'en. This was not usually celebrated in Ecuador at that time and doing so in fancy dress, as we did, was even more uncommon. Perhaps the Latin Americans are not quite so prepared to make fools of themselves as the British. Ceci went as a pregnant nun (although she was not pregnant at the time) and I as a monk, in an old standby outfit that was easily slipped on over the clothes. It was a great event and noteworthy for some of the costumes. Julian Sedgwick had come in drag but, as his car would not start, he had to take a taxi. He was rather late to arrive, explaining that the taxis would pull up and then, taking one look at him, would accelerate away again before he could convince the driver that he was only going to a fancy dress party. Peter Baker had a worse experience. He had come as a baby, with only an outsized nappy held up with a huge safety pin and a baby's bottle hung around his neck. As it was a very warm night, he thought that he would risk it, as he was not going to get cold. He was on his way, driving down the main street of Guayaquil, the Nueve de Octubre which is always full of people day and night, when he had a flat tyre. It is all very well being dressed in a nappy within your own group but changing a wheel in the street is a different matter. A crowd immediately gathered around him and he caused quite a sensation. He later reported that no Grand Prix car ever had its wheel changed faster!

The year 1978 began with a change of secretary for Agripac. I have had only four secretaries over the last twenty-nine years. The first, Patricia Aguirre, lasted for two years and then left after a row with Mario while I was on holiday. Mercy de La Mota came next but left for family reasons after three years, which led to Letty Martinetti joining us in February of that year. Letty was a divorcee with two little girls. She was a great character and friend and organised my office, the company, Ceci, our home and everything else. An awful lot of people want to gain access to the president of a company: employees wanting loans, customers wanting discounts, charity workers wanting donations, disgruntled debtors (or creditors) wanting to make their voice heard at the top, beggars from the street and even an occasional lady of the street! Letty was the barrier through which they had to pass and not many passed whom I did not want to see. On one famous occasion, just after I had become honorary British consul in Guayaquil and during the Falklands war, the Argentinian residents in Guayaquil came en masse to the consulate. They demanded to be given the Union Jack so that they could burn it in front of the press. I was away at the time but Letty came to the door and said that they would take the flag over her dead body. However, the crowd was good natured so it just made a formal protest and left.

Letty was an excellent mother and brought up her girls well but their father, although not supporting them in any way, kept demanding access to them and treated Letty with violence if she opposed him. Eventually, she decided to get away from him completely and, having a friend who lived in Utah, she decided to leave Ecuador and take her girls to Salt Lake City. We were very sad to see her go in September 1984 as we had grown very fond of her and the children. Six months went by before I rang her to see how she was doing. She was depressed as she missed Ecuador and her friends but wrote us a letter the next day, saying how much the phone call had cheered her up and that she was going to take a course in real estate to become an agent. By the time, I received the letter she was dead. She had been killed when a truck ran through a red light and hit her car. As is the custom in Ecuador, the family insisted on having her body embalmed and returned to Guayaquil where I saw it for the last time in an open coffin in the church at the funeral service. People filed past, gazing at her. I could not do it.

My fourth and present secretary is none other than Rocio, Ceci's sister. She finished school in Guayaquil, then did a course in English before going to Brighton for three months to perfect it. On her return, she worked for another company in Guayaquil, then in several capacities for Agripac and, when Letty left, she took her position.

Diana, our second child, was born in September 1978, once again in the Clinica Gil in downtown Guayaquil and once again by Caesarean section. This does have several advantages, one of which is that you can choose the date of birth up to a point. Diana was ready to come into the world and doctor Guillermo Wagner had offered us either the twenty-second or the twenty-third.

Ceci wanted the twenty-second so that her star sign would be Virgo. She was a good size at eight pounds fourteen ounces, but not as big as Nick had been. We took her back to our flat, which by now was a rented one on the ground floor of a house in Urdesa, a residential suburb. The address was Mirtus and Ficus, a cross-reference of two streets. We had been sad to leave the twelfth floor of the Simon Bolivar building but the owner had returned from the States and wanted it back. The new place was large and comfortable and had a small piece of garden.

We had by now acquired a second beagle, a bitch called Lafitte, or Fitty to the family — a silly name for a dog. Ceci and I had been to the USA on holiday and, returning through Miami, we passed a pet shop called Dr Pet. On an impulse, we went in and ordered a beagle to be sent on to us in Guayaquil. That night, the last of the holiday, we ate out in style at the Forge restaurant in Miami Beach. We were trying to think of a name and got nowhere so I picked up the bottle of wine and said: 'We'll call her Chateau Lafitte.' The 'Chateau' was lost but Lafitte remained. Don Louis said that it was ridiculous to give a French surname to a puppy but it stayed.

Both Snoopy and Fitty would sleep in our bedroom, he on the bed and she beneath it. In fact, Snoopy slept between us and, should we turn towards each other in the night, he would growl at us. It is a wonder that we started a family at all! The dogs would occasionally want to go out into the garden in the night. If they scratched at the door, I would get up sleepily and open the French windows into the garden and rather than wait for them, return to bed. This happened one night followed, an hour or so later, by a scream from Ceci. I put on the light and she was sitting up in bed shaking; a rat had walked over her! By this time, the dogs had the scent of it and were dashing about the room. The rat got between the two mattresses: Ceci was standing on one chair and I, showing great courage, was on another. Something had to be done. I woke up the maid and between us we raised the top mattress, the rat bolted and Fitty caught it. We never left the French windows open again.

Diana has not yet forgiven us for abandoning her for her first Christmas, however much we try to explain that at three months old she missed nothing. But, rightly or wrongly, that is what we did. Having vivid memories of our first overseas trip with Nick at that age, there was no way that we wanted to do it again. So poor Diana was left with her nanny when Ceci, Nick and I took the B-Cal flight to the UK on the 13th December.

We arrived at Ferngill and went from room to room, admiring the newly refurbished and enlarged house. Malcolm and Elaine had arranged everything to be ready for us, right down to curtains, carpets, towels, sheets and even flowers. My parents' furniture had returned from store and there were the remains of many different tea and dinner services of Mother's, which would do to start with. The house was still drying out and the central heating was on full all the time that we were home, but it was still rather cold. We lit fires in both the sitting room and dining room, only to discover that they smoked badly. But no matter — we were going to enjoy Christmas. It was to be a big occasion as Jane and Peter were to come over from South Africa with their children, Peter and Penny. I had not seen them since they were very small and they were now teenagers. Also Kate, who had married Kit Wildman in 1967 but was by now divorced, came with her daughter, Emilie, who was my goddaughter and eleven at that time. As we were in Ferngill and Do and Father in Tupgill, we arranged for my sisters and their families to stay in Greystones, one of our rental cottages in Middleham.

We all met just before Christmas and I introduced Ceci and Nick to the rest of the family. Christmas came and we had the traditional lunch at Tupgill, and only Mother was missing. With New Year approaching, the weather turned colder and it began to snow heavily. The ground froze and with it the Ferngill water pipes, which had recently been laid across the garden. Snow storms took the telephone wires down and the BBC television service went on strike. The night before New Year, Ceci and I were invited to Peter Walton's party at his farm near Middleham. We had an excellent time but when we emerged, it was into a blizzard. We drove slowly back through Middleham, over the moor past Pinkers Pond and reached the Tupgill drive, but there we got stuck in a snowdrift. There was nothing for it but to walk the half mile back to Ferngill. It was bitterly cold. We clung together and pushed on, with our light evening shoes sodden and our coats providing little warmth until, after falling a dozen times, we reached the house and experienced the agony of hands, feet and ears thawing out.

New Year's Eve was spent in Ferngill with just Ceci and Nick. The snow of the previous day had totally buried the car so we could not even get down to Middleham to see the family. We had had dinner with Do and Dad but they planned to turn in early so there we were on our own: no television, no phone, a smoking chimney and Ceci in floods of tears. We then promised ourselves that future Christmases and New Years would be spent in Ecuador where the weather allows for beach parties and the level of conviviality is so much greater than in Britain.

But we had all come together at Tupgill for another reason: the old folks were failing. Father had cancer and did not have much longer to live — in fact this was to be his last Christmas. Do lived for another thirteen years but was going blind by this time.

We saw Father for the last time the following summer, when he was bedridden in Tupgill. Many of his old friends came to say goodbye to him including Willie Carson, the then champion jockey who had started his career with Father. Willie is about my age and I remember him coming to Thorngill as an apprentice jockey when he was fifteen. To begin with he was just one of the many apprentices, but gradually his name was mentioned more and more by Father as his exceptional ability as a jockey became apparent. His first win was at Catterick Race Course on a horse owned by Mother called Pinkers Pond. He went on to win several other races and eventually Father felt that his career would be better served in Newmarket, where there were superior horses and more opportunity. So Willie moved to Uncle Sam and on to fame and fortune. It was kind of him to come and visit the dying man and they chatted about the old days. Father was deeply moved by the visit.

We had returned to Ecuador after our summer holiday in August and the end came in November. Jane had come over from South Africa and Kate from Bournemouth, and they were with him when he died. I had left it too late and arrived a couple of days afterwards. The funeral was held at Coverham church, which is only a mile from Tupgill. Although we had got out of the habit of regular churchgoing, Coverham church had seen many Armstrong events including our baptisms, the grandparents' funerals and both Jane and Kate's weddings. Now we gathered for Father's funeral. It was a freezing day with a fierce wind and, as we stood around the grave with his brother Sam and old friends of the British Legion, all bareheaded and throwing poppies on the coffin, I wondered how many of them would survive this day. Do could not face the funeral so afterwards we invited the guests to Ferngill for a whisky to sustain them.

When they had finally gone, Michael Hutchinson, our family solicitor, stayed for a while and read us the will because we were all to disperse the following day. Father left all three of us the same amount, about £20,000, after making gifts to Doug Weatherill and others. My share was to include his interest in Ripon Race Company, of which he had been a director for some thirty years and his father had been chairman. But he warned me never to own a racehorse as he had seen many good men lose their fortunes that way. So in the course of the following year, Michael Hutchinson, who was also the managing director of the racecourse and a large shareholder, invited me to become a director.

As to the stipulation of never owning a racehorse, I am afraid that I defied that rule when I bought Balcash, a four-year-old gelding, in 1986. Miss Acacia and Miss Saman (named after tropical trees) followed in subsequent years, all trained at Tupgill by Bill Stubbs. Although they were placed occasionally, I never won a race so perhaps the parental curse was on the venture. When Miss Saman fell in a hurdle race, broke a leg and had to be shot I got out of the racing game. However, I still keep the colours registered. These go back to 1885 when old Bob first registered them with the Jockey Club: cerise (cherry), white sleeves and cerise cap. Father had duly inherited them but as he did not want me to own a racehorse, he gave them to Cousin Robert, who was training at Newmarket. I felt that I had a right to them and approached Robert, who agreed that I could have a variation on them, with the cap quartered cerise and white to differentiate, and he would have the originals.

I was in England for only a few days for the funeral but it gave me a chance to inspect the work in hand at Tupgill stables. Ferngill had been completed the year before and now it was time to make a start on the ruin that was the stableyard. I had initially invested in three rental cottages in England for holiday lets but these had not proved to be a success. So they were sold that year and from then on, I would concentrate all my efforts and capital on the Tupgill estate. The first job that needed doing was to start clearing away the remains of the army huts, which still stood rotting where they had been built forty years before. Some of them were in the main stable yard so, after moving them, we were able to put in foundations on which to build eight new wooden stables. Then we began to repair the roofs on the old stone stables and change the rotting doors. From this, we moved on to the cottages, which had stood empty for many years, and gave them a complete overhaul.

One of these, Arch Cottage, was needed to house a couple who would look after Do now that she was alone: a man to do the gardening and his wife to cook. These were Brian and Kath Morris, who came with their two-year-old son Leo. Both Brian and Kath were rather bohemian; Brian wore earrings and Kath gipsy-like clothes. Little Leo seldom had his curly red hair cut and was sometimes mistaken for a little girl. However, the arrangement worked very well for several years until Brian died of cancer. Kath stayed on until Do herself died and her cooking was excellent. Leo being of Nick's age, they played together, grew up together and have become the best of friends ever since. Today, Leo is an executive with a wine company and living in Brighton.

One of the jobs that Brian undertook was the planting of a wood as a windbreak in a small field to the west of Tupgill Stables. This field contained several Nissen huts of army vintage, which Do had used to keep chickens in over the years. There was also a midden of horse manure, which would be spread all over the yards in a strong wind. It was for this reason that I thought of making a windbreak. We decided on conifers as they would give winter protection too. The little field was cleared of the buildings and midden, rotavated and planted in the autumn of 1979. We called it the Nicholas Wood. On my visits each summer, I would rush to see how the trees were growing and for the first two years, was very disappointed when I could not see trees for grass and nettles. We bought a strimmer and strimmed away, trying to give them light to grow. We lost a lot and were forever replacing them. But, little by little, the battle was won and the trees grew above the grass level and then to head level. As they were densely planted, they soon blocked the view across the field and the lines strimmed up and down the rows gave it the feel of a maze. This was fun for the children and we heightened the effect by strimming not in straight lines, but by snaking about the field, and would play hide and seek there.

At the far end of the field, we had a favourite spot where, on a clear day, we could see all the way down Coverdale, across the Vale of York and as far as the white horse carved into the hillside by Sutton Bank, a view of some thirty miles. One day, I called Malcolm into this area and suggested that it would make a lovely walled garden and that we could put a viewing place at the far end and perhaps even a grotto. We discussed this latter idea and it proves the point that a single word can mean very different things to two people. I had in mind what is sometimes seen on the roadside in Ecuador: a little, rustic stone cave in which there is an icon, normally a doll-sized image of a saint or virgin in a glass case. The Spanish word 'gruta' means grotto and covers this sort of thing. Malcolm, on the other hand, had in mind Welbeck Abbey and the famous reclusive Duke of Portland, who tunnelled extensively under his park. I found out the misunderstanding only when, after giving the go-ahead, I had returned to Ecuador. Elaine rang me one day in a panic. 'Malcolm has an enormous digger and is twenty feet down already and still going. What do I do?' Well, that was how it all began — what is today the Forbidden Corner.

ECUADOR 1980

THE YEAR 1980 SAW the end of the military dictatorship in Ecuador after eight years and Jaime Roldos was elected as a constitutional president. The original military dictator of 1972, General Guillermo Rodriguez Lara, nicknamed Bombita (little bomb) as he was tiny and rather fat, had been quite a benevolent ruler. His government (not fortuitously) had coincided with Ecuador's petroleum boom, when the economy had grown very fast. In fact, the *Financial Times* had published an article about its fifteen per cent growth rate maintained for several years, the highest in the world at the time. But however much revenue the country had, it was never enough and, as borrowing was easy, the present-day burden of the national debt began. In 1976, Bombita was replaced in another military coup by a triumvirate of senior officers from the three armed services. They continued the profligate spending, especially on arms.

Ecuador had a long-standing border dispute with its southern neighbour, Peru. This dated from 1941, when Peru invaded Ecuador and cut about a third of its territory off. The part lost was mostly on the Amazonian side of the country, which is a vast tract of rain forest and rivers with practically no roads and inhabited by Indian peoples. A peace treaty (the treaty of Rio de Janeiro) defining the new border was agreed in 1942 and sponsored by the United States, Brazil, Argentina and Chile. However, some forty miles of this border could not be mapped as it ran along a mountain range which was covered by permanent low cloud. Several planes were lost in the attempt before it was abandoned and a vague written description substituted in the treaty text. Over subsequent years, this undefined area witnessed border clashes between troops of the two countries and provided a reason for the military of both sides to help themselves to the national revenues very freely in the sacred name of the patria.

In 1977, the triumvirate had bought a squadron of Jaguar fighters from the British government and with it came Sandy Aitken and his wife Ella. Sandy had been in the air force and at the time was a test pilot for British Aerospace, which built the Jaguar and he was here to teach the Ecuadorian pilots to fly them. We soon became good friends and as the couple enjoyed riding, they often came to Mapan. Sandy soon became a great favourite with the Ecuadorian air force officers including an eccentric colonel named Frank Vargas. They were sad to see him go in 1981, when his contract ended and he returned to British Aerospace in England. In 1987, the Jaguar squadron celebrated its tenth birthday and Sandy and a fellow pilot, Derek Reed, were invited to attend. We too were happy to see Sandy again and, as they arrived on a Saturday, I picked them up and we went to Mapan for the weekend.

The following Monday, they went to the Taura air force base for the ceremony but it was completely sealed off by heavily armed troops and they were turned back and had to return to Guayaquil. Leon Febres-Cordero was then president and during the previous year, he had had increasingly bad relations with the commander of the air force, the now general Frank Vargas, who was known as loco (crazy) Frank. Febres-Cordero had tried to discipline him on several occasions but could not because the air force stayed loyal to its commander. This became an impasse, which was broken when the president used the army to arrest Frank in a scrap which cost several lives. Frank was imprisoned in Quito but the air force was furious. On the day of the tenth anniversary of the Jaguar squadron, Febres-Cordero was the guest of honour and flew into the Taura base early for the ceremony. He was immediately kidnapped by the parachute regiment and his two bodyguards shot and killed. A state of emergency was called and the airport surrounded by the army. The conditions for the president's release were a pardon for Frank Vargas and immunity for the parachute regiment. Later that day, these conditions were agreed. Frank Vargas retired from the air force and went into politics, eventually becoming a minister in another but short-lived government. Sandy and Derek never managed to see their old friends and returned to England.

By this time, my life had fallen into the routine of weekdays in Agripac and weekends on the farm. The Mapan house was now complete and Ceci set to making the garden. We had planted rows of oil palm trees there even before building the house to make shady walks and these were now ten feet tall. Between them and in front of the house, we planted lawns and put in flowering bushes and trees: hibiscus, barcelonesas, red acacias, jacarandas, tulip trees and robles as well as the powerfully scented cananga, the country girls' perfume.

While Ceci gardened, I would ride around the farm on my horse, taking Snoopy and Fitty with me. I preferred an English saddle and had brought several over from a saddler in Bedale in Yorkshire. With my escort of vaqueros, I would tour the work in hand: the soya being grown in this field, the rice in that, the pastures planted here, the fences mended there. The bananas were by now totally rehabilitated and producing well. They were harvested for three or four days each week all the year round, being cut on their stems which were then hung on cable ways and pulled in a train of thirty or so to the packing station. Once there, the hands are separated from the stems and go through a water bath before being packed into boxes and into a truck to be taken to the port of Guayaquil and loaded aboard the refrigerated reefer ships.

Bananas need water in large amounts and must be irrigated throughout the dry season. To do this, we drilled a borehole 110 metres deep and crossed two underground rivers, which provided ample water. These rivers run at about seventy metres below the surface and, as Mapan stands only ten metres above sea level, they must discharge into the sea several miles from the coast. In the

Colin (on Piolin) and Ceci, 1982

The oldest cowboy on Mapan — Albino Franco — with the mares and foals

Mapan's Brahman cattle

wet season, bananas require good drainage and huge pumps with pipes up to thirty inches in diameter are used to drain the canals surrounding the plantation. The banana grower lives with the worry of his pumps operating both inwards and outwards, as any failure here has immediate consequences for production. We had about ninety hectares of bananas and ninety people to work them. But although bananas provided the bulk of the income for Mapan, my chief love and interest was the cattle.

The previous year, we had heard that the government had introduced water buffalo to the Oriente (Amazon) provinces of the country and that there were auctions of stock from time to time. Each buyer was supposed to take only three animals, two females and a male, so I sent two people over and bought six. Then there was a problem with the Ministry of Agriculture, as the buffaloes were not allowed to leave the Oriente. This was resolved when we claimed to be an experimental farm and so the first buffaloes came to Mapan. A year later, we had a call from the ministry to say that, among our six buffaloes, there was one cow of the original import, which should not have been sold. It would send us a heifer as replacement but wanted its cow back. No problem, we said, and the heifer arrived. What impressed both the vaqueros and myself was the way that the old cow recognised her former handler. He took off his shirt and waved it under her nose and she followed him into the truck without being roped.

Buffaloes are more intelligent than cattle and, if handled from calves, can be trained to pull carts or ploughs. In Asia, children ride on their backs. We did not handle ours much and they became very independent. We did milk one once to see what the milk was like; it is pure white, as neither milk nor fat has yellow pigmentation, and contains twice the solids and fat of cows' milk. The Italians use it to make mozzarella cheese. But generally, we kept the herd for meat production. The meat is similar to normal beef when the animal is killed young but very tough from old beasts. The cows can live for more than thirty years and generally give birth to a calf each year although the gestation period is eleven months as with a mare (compared to nine months in cows). The females become very aggressive when a calf is born and we have had vaqueros on horseback thrown to the ground by a surprise attack. The stock bulls also become aggressive with each other and with any young males and will chase them for miles from the breeding herd. It is quite common to find young bulls wandering around on their own, too frightened to return.

The other characteristic of buffaloes is that they move about at night and, as they have very thick hides and large curved horns, a barbed-wire fence is no obstacle to them. We try to keep them towards the centre of the farm for, if they get into the neighbours' rice or maize crops, there will be expensive damages to pay. In banana plantations, they can be even worse as they take delight in shredding the banana trees with their horns until not one plant is left standing, rather as though a whirlwind had hit that area. Today, the buffalo herd has stabilised at 100 or so — one stock bull, forty cows and their progeny.

The nicest time of the year at Mapan must be the months of October and November. It is then that the naturally flowering trees are at their best, the pale pink of robles, the cream turning to orange of Fernan Sanchez, the yellow of the buttercup tree, the orange Palo Prieto and misty blue Pechiche. Also the mangos, which although once planted by the hand of man, have become as large as oaks and produce small mangoes which we pick and suck as we ride.

The only thing to spoil the pleasure of that happy period was that Snoopy died. Ceci was out of the house and the maid rang the office to say that I should come home quickly as Snoopy was dying. I rushed back, hoping that it was an exaggeration and that he was only ill. But he was dead when I arrived. As far as we could see, he had eaten something poisonous in the street. I was distraught. I had loved Snoopy far too much. I did not know where Ceci was but I needed to do something to relieve my grief, so I put the body in my car and drove to Mapan. I had the gardener dig a grave and, just as I was placing Snoopy in it, Ceci arrived so we completed the job together. Some years later, Fitty also went to our pet cemetery. Jazz, the third beagle that we acquired that year, was stolen while still a young dog and never heard of again. We now have two more, Charlie and Phoebe. But, fond of them as I am, there is none to compare with Snoopy.

I have mentioned the problem of rustlers in Guarumal. It was a constant threat for Mapan too and we had armed night guards who rode around the cattle. We have had occasional losses but normally these occur when the guard who should have been on duty is seen drinking in the local cantina.

We once had an attempt on the house too. We had a guard who would sleep inside the house during the week when we were not there. He was armed with a two-two rifle. One night, he heard a noise at the door and, peeping through the kitchen window which overlooks the front door, he saw three armed men trying to force it. He fired and wounded one of them and they ran off. The following day, the farm foreman, Diego Cano, called me on the phone to say that the police had located a man in the local clinic with a bullet wound in his back. Should he press charges? Yes was my first reaction. But, Diego said, if the man died, our guard would have to go to jail, perhaps for years. I asked what the alternative was. He replied that the man in question had told the police that he had wounded himself — in the back — while cleaning his gun. So we let it go at that. He did recover and, seeing that we were watching his progress and would accuse him when we thought that he was out of danger, he did a flit from the clinic and we never heard of him again. Although incidents like this are rare, I sleep at Mapan with a loaded revolver to hand, trusting that my faithful hounds will hear an intruder in time to alert me.

The spring of 1981 brought two pieces of good news: Ceci was pregnant again and we were invited to the royal garden party in July. These two events clashed in Ceci's case as the baby was due in August and there was no way that she could travel in July. She was furious but there was nothing for it; I would have to attend alone. I wondered if this invitation predicted anything else. I had long wanted to be British consul in Guayaquil, and in 1973 had suggested to the then ambassador Peter Mennell that I could help Kingsley Fox as vice-consul. He said that there was already a vice-consul but that I should wait and would maybe take the consul's job when Kingsley left the country. I rang Brian Toseland at the embassy but he poured cold water on the idea. We have a quota of invitations, he said, and just thought you might like to go.

I flew to London the day before the event and stayed at the Atheneum Hotel in Picadilly, as we normally did when in London. Then I headed for Moss Bros in Covent Garden to get a morning suit and grey top hat.

Back in the hotel, I changed but after one look in the mirror I thought that I could not walk out of the hotel like that as people would stare at me. I crept down to the hall and asked the porter to get me a taxi. 'The palace is only across the park, sir,' he said. 'You can easily walk it.' 'I feel such a fool,' I replied. 'You look fine, sir, there are plenty of others going to the palace. Just walk along with them.' I looked across the road and, sure enough, there were others in similar outfits. I joined one middle-aged lady, who turned out to be an American, and asked if I could walk with her. 'Delighted', she said 'this must be your first time. I've been twice before.' So, feeling a bit more comfortable, we entered the palace gates together and, with an increasing crowd of guests, crossed the square, went through the inner courtyard and into the palace itself.

Here, I gazed for a while at the pictures and in so doing lost my lady escort. So I joined the throng and went out into the gardens at the back. There are some 7,000 people at a garden party, or at least there seemed to be that many. The garden is huge but it was well peopled with morning suits, uniforms of all sorts and clergy; the ladies in their finery with hats and gloves. Not knowing anyone and wishing desperately that Ceci had been with me, I wandered off on my own, down the lawn to the lake at the end where a band was playing, then back up the lawn to the marquees where I had a cup of tea and a sandwich. Finally, her majesty appeared with assorted members of the royal family and the crowd formed a corridor down which she came, stopping occasionally to talk to one or two people. As I was late to form up, I was some five rows back and in no way could I have been addressed but, being tall, I did see what was going on. When the queen reached the end of the line, she retired with her retinue to a roped-off area to have her tea. The rest of us milled about until she finished and withdrew, which was the signal for us to go too.

On the way out, a photographer offered to take my photo. Great, I thought, as no cameras had been allowed inside. Just as he took it, two large policeman grabbed him. 'Did he ask you for any money, sir?' asked one. 'No', I said. In fact, he had asked for my address, which I had given him. 'I'll send the photo on,' he said as he was led away. I do not know what local rules he had broken by taking photos commercially outside the palace but he was as good as his word and the photo arrived. I sent him the money but the photo is not very flattering. I look somewhat Mafioso, all moustache and eyebrows under the topper.

That evening, I met up with Hans Schuback, who happened to be in London, and we went out on the town. The next day we drove to Yorkshire and he stayed with me in Ferngill for a few days. One of those days was remarkable because it featured the royal wedding of Prince Charles and Princess Diana. BBC television reported the whole event and Hans and I, still in our pyjamas and with a hangover from the night before, watched it from 10am to 5pm and drank a bottle of port to celebrate.

Do was now alone as Father had died almost two years previously and I found that I was trying to fill his place by visiting her every day at about five in the afternoon. We would have two gin and tonics together, never more, never less, and I would tell her of my doings of the day. She really looked forward to my coming to see her and I felt rather guilty on the days I could not go. Her sight was almost gone and she had started her long series of 'Country Cousins', those good middle-aged ladies who would live in with an old person for a week at a time, help them and give them company. Elaine ran a rota of them with one week on and two or three off to suit them. We soon got to know them and had our favourites, the chief of whom was former nursing sister Jeanne Turner, who had also nursed Father.

Do was especially fond of Jeanne and I am sure that she was grateful to all of them. For my part, I preferred those who would treat her as an adult and converse normally rather than resorting to the nannying baby talk so many use for the very old and very young. If I reach this point, no doubt I will have to accept it with good grace!

The sad day came when I had to say goodbye to Do and in those days, it was for a whole year. She was then eighty-four and neither of us knew if we would meet again. I left in a rush because doctor Wagner had told Ceci that Alexandra would be born on the 14th August. I got back to Guayaquil on the 13th and was there for the birth. That is to say, I was outside the operating room — I never had the courage to watch a birth. Alex was somewhat smaller than Nick or Diana but a healthy child and we carried her back to our flat in Mirtos y Ficus in triumph to show to her brother and sister.

By this time, Nick was five and, having graduated from 'Los Pajaritos' play school, had become a student of the Inter American Academy. This was the American school in its second reincarnation. The original school had been founded many years previously and, in order to grow, had opened up to non-English speaking Ecuadorian children. But the day came when the parents of these children dominated the school and the English-speaking section was closed. This was the year before Nick was enrolled. The school almost had to start again with grade one, just one class, using rented rooms in the American Cultural Association, coincidentally next to Agripac's offices in Cordova Street. The following year, they had grade one and two and so on, the school expanding by one grade each year to accommodate the initial students. After Cordova Street, it rented a large house in the suburb of Urdesa and eventually bought premises in Puerto Azul on the outskirts of the city. During this time, my three children attended the school and I had to put hand to pocket quite regularly for all the fundraising events that were held. Ceci and I wanted the children to have an education in English and the Inter American was the only school to do so in Guayaquil. It had one other great advantage: it worked to the American year with the long holidays in the summer. Our friends who had their children in other Guayaquil schools, including the German school, had the long holidays from January to April which fitted in with the beach season here but ruled out European holidays.

I had always had the idea that Nick would go to an English public school and had no hesitation in putting his name down for Sedbergh's junior house, Cressbrook, for when he was eleven. When I was at Rossall School, Sedbergh regularly beat us at rugby and cricket and I liked its situation in a small market town, whereas Rossall was practically absorbed in the suburbs of Blackpool and Fleetwood. I had expected opposition from Ceci, as most of her friends were dead set against boarding schools but she supported me. Eventually not only Nick but Diana and Alex went to boarding school, the girls to St Anne's in Windermere.

It was soon after Alex was born that I had a call from Kingsley Fox, asking me to meet him. He had decided to take early retirement from his job in Ecuador and return to England. He had suggested my name as his replacement as consul in Guayaquil and to the ambassador, Adrian Buxton, who had accepted it. Would I like the job? Yes, I would like it very much indeed. Kingsley was due to leave in December and before then, he would find a few minutes to fill me in on the job. Well, a few minutes were all I had. He had been understandably busy with his own arrangements and leaving parties after eleven years in Ecuador. On the 9th December, he came to my office with his driver, carrying several boxes. 'Here are the files: read them and you'll see how things are done. Here's the Union Jack to fly outside your office and one for covering the coffin at a funeral. This is the plaque with the coat of arms to fix outside the building. Here is the seal. Would you mind signing for all these now as I'm off to the airport.'

When he had gone, Letty and I started to read the files and forms in the boxes. She needed to know them even more than I did as the consular secretary does nine-tenths of the work. In fact, she went to the embassy in Quito the following week for some training. For my part, I received a visit from Adrian Buxton, when he presented me with my formal letter of appointment written on vellum. The official Ecuadorian exequatur signed by the then president of the republic, Oswaldo Hurtado, was dated the 29th January, 1982. Hurtado had been vice-president to Jaime Roldos and succeeded him when the former was killed in an air accident in 1981.

My appointment as consul coincided with our moving into our own apartment on the sixth floor of the Monterrico building in the hills above Urdesa.

We had been shown plans for this flat before the building was more than one storey high. Each floor had two flats but we bought the whole floor and were able to reposition the internal walls. It made a great place with 400 metres of space from which we made four bedrooms, four bathrooms, two sitting rooms, a dining room, kitchen and two maid's rooms as well as one for the dogs. The building backed on to the hill and was, in fact, cut out of the hill so that at the front our balcony gave views over the city while at the back it is at road level on a rather steep hill. We had two garages leading off this road. We were very happy here for the last seventeen years with lots of Christmas party photos to mark the passage of time.

It was, therefore, with mixed feelings that on the 4th December, 1998, I watched the furniture, pictures, clothes and assorted junk that we had collected over the years being carried out and loaded on to a truck. For today, we move to our new house further outside the city. When we moved in, it was a quiet residential area with little traffic. Now the world and his dog have come crowding in. There is a meat restaurant just up the hill (occasionally useful) and a tyre warehouse just below us. The road that we overlook is sprinkled with chemists, a pet shop, a mobile phone shop, an antique shop and more. The traffic up the hill is continuous and makes getting in and out of the garages hazardous. But still...well, we have moved now.

In all the excitement of 1981, have I forgotten to mention Agripac? That year, sales exceeded $10 million for the first time.

Among the first consular duties of the new year are the protocol visits. All the consuls in Guayaquil, and there are sixty or so counting consuls general, consuls and vice-consuls (Xavier Velasquez MBE was British vice-consul for fifteen years, having started with Kingsley Fox and continued with me) are summoned to call upon the governor of Guayas province, the mayor of Guayaquil, the provincial prefect and the archbishop. The format is the same. We shuffle into a large state room in each organisation, the great man comes in and we shake hands. Then the dean of the consular corps reads an address and the other party replies, champagne is served and, with another handshake all round, we leave. Each visit takes about half an hour. These are normally annual events but, should a governor change during the year and there have been years with three or four governors, then we are all summoned again.

The large majority of consuls are Ecuadorians of note who offer their services and offices for the benefit of nationals of the country they represent. These are honorary positions and unpaid. They do it for the prestige of membership of the consular corps and a few fringe benefits such as consular car plates and permission to receive passengers in the airport. The United States and most South American countries maintain a professional consular office with career diplomats, because of the much heavier workload they have, with many more nationals in Ecuador.

My letter of appointment was as follows:

By me, Adrian Clarence Buxton, Her Britannic Majesty's Ambassador residing at Quito.

Be it known to all to whom these presents shall come that, by virtue of the Powers vested in me by Her Majesty's Commission, I do hereby constitute and appoint Colin Robert Armstrong to be Honorary British Consul at Guayaquil with full power and authority, under the superintendence of Her Britannic Majesty's Consul at Quito by all lawful means, to aid and protect Her Majesty's subjects trading in, visiting, or residing in Guayaquil.

Witness my hand and seal of office at Quito this the tenth day of December 1981.

So Letty and I set out to aid and protect her majesty's subjects. The first two who presented themselves at our door were really Australians. Letty came charging into my office with a beaming face and said: 'Colin, you've got to see this.' Two tanned Australian chaps were shown in. In fact, all they were wearing were their tans and brief swimming trunks. They had been visiting the beach resort of Playas and, deciding on a swim, had left their rucksacks, passports, money, clothes, watches and all on the beach and gone into the sea. When they came out, everything had disappeared. They had managed to hitchhike to Guayaquil, trying to ignore the amused stares of passers-by but at least the climate was suitable for their (lack of) dress. I sent home for some clothes and lent them the 'phone to get in touch with their families in Australia and obtain funds. The embassy issued emergency passports so, within a week or so, they were back on the road — our very first satisfied customers. Today, the Australians have their own consulate here but we still cover a multitude of Commonwealth countries which do not.

My first visiting VIP was Sir Peter Rees (now Lord Rees), who was then minister for trade. The ambassador, Adrian Buxton, had called to say that the minister and his party of businessmen had a free day on a Sunday in Guayaquil and how about taking them to Mapan. I rang up half a dozen English businessmen to come along with their wives. These included Nigel Simpson of the Bank of London and South America (Lloyds), Richard Pearse of Finansa, Giles Harrison and Simon de Montfort. Simon is an interesting chap, born in Ceylon and whose father was a tea planter. Having obtained degrees at both Oxford and London universities, he came to Ecuador with a British aid forestry programme. When this finished, he stayed on and made his business growing and drying marigold flowers, which are subsequently processed to extract the carotene used as a natural colorant in the food industry. I refer to Simon as my 'educated friend' and he kindly helps me out on these sorts of occasion.

We had organised a minibus from Guayaquil to Mapan for the visitors and both Adrian Buxton and Sir Peter brought their wives. After lunch, Sir Peter spotted the croquet set and suggested a game, so we made up two teams and away we went. Sir Peter and his wife were playing together and we of the other team very soon saw that we were badly outclassed. In fact, it was a total walk-over. Only after the game, did they admit to being members of Hurlingham where they played regularly.

Sometimes problems present themselves in a totally innocent form. When David Bolton came to see me one day, his request seemed quite straightforward. He had been employed on a contract in Ecuador by a British company and, a month before he was due to leave the country, his car had been stolen. The terms of the insurance policy stated that sixty days must elapse after the event and, should the car not appear by then, the money would be paid. As David was now leaving, he asked if he could sign over the insurance form to me so that I could forward the sterling proceeds of the payout. What could be easier, of course I would be delighted to help.

There were only three days to go before the scheduled payment day when I had a call from an insurance investigator. The car had been seen in Guayaquil and he had made a citizen's arrest of the driver. The car was now in the police station and if I would accompany him there with David's documents, I could collect it. An Ecuadorian police station is always very crowded with people, there to report thefts, to visit prisoners or to make complaints. Whatever the nature of your business, the bureaucratic procedures are slow and one is passed from desk to desk or told to take a seat while one wait one's turn, or better still, returns tomorrow. My guide, the insurance inspector, did seem to know his way about and we moved more quickly than most but nothing in that place moves quickly. After an hour or so, we saw a lieutenant who knew of the case and we all padded out into the yard where the car was identified. It was a sleek, black Japanese car of a sporting model and appeared to be in good condition.

'Where do I sign?' I asked. 'I'll take it right away.' But it was not to be so easy; there were checks to be made on the case and protocols to fulfil. Could I come back tomorrow?

I did so and still it seemed that the paperwork was more than could possibly be handled in such a short time. Well, come back in another two days' time, we agreed. I turned up for the third time and this time I was shown into the captain's office. 'Ah, Senor Consul', he said 'you have come for the car but we have a small problem. There is another man who is claiming that it is his car.' 'That's impossible,' I said. 'I have copies of the car's import papers in David Bolton's name.' 'Yes', he replied, 'but the other party has a matricula for the car issued in Loja (a town in the extreme south of Ecuador) last month, and that is an original document.' When I heard this, my confidence faded. In Ecuador, as in most of Latin America, there is an exaggerated regard for the written word and an 'original' outranks a 'copy' any time. The originals of David's documents had been inside the car when it was stolen. This is normal as the traffic police want to inspect original documents at all times, which often leads to the absurd situation in which car and documents are stolen together. We could have obtained new originals of the import papers from the Central Bank but this can take some time.

The captain suggested that I return the following day, when the other claimant would be present and the issue could be sorted out. I was by now becoming fed up of the whole job. I had wasted hours of time and it looked as if I was neither going to recover the car nor the insurance cash for David. That evening, I retold the tale at dinner with our good friends, the Hardings. Trevor is British and met and married Rosi in London before coming to Ecuador, where he was now farming and trading in coffee. Trevor said that he knew David's car and if we recovered it, he would be delighted to buy it. I said that I doubted if we would, given the appearance of the other claimant from Loja. Rosi said that her father, Don Guillermo Borja, a prominent banana grower, was a great friend of the police colonel in charge of the station and would ask him to intervene to see that our case had a fair hearing.

The following day, we finally got the car. It happened like this: I arrived at the police station and was immediately shown into a large room, which was crowded with people. There always seem to be a lot of unnecessary people about, who have nothing better to do than to listen to what is going on. I was on my own as my new-found friend, the insurance inspector, having found the car and thereby saved the insurance company from paying out, had disappeared from the scene. The captain was sitting at a desk in the centre of the room with the other man to one side of him and I was offered a seat in front of them. Then we went through the ritual of showing the documents again, my copies against his originals. There was much nodding of heads in agreement when my rival expostulated his position. He had bought the car in good faith from a man who had had good title to it. Mr David Bolton had obviously sold the car and reported it stolen. I fought back, saying that, on the contrary, David was an executive of an important British company and a very honourable man who would not stoop to such practice. But time was passing and the opinion of the room seemed to be going against me. The other claimant, whoever he was, was obviously well known there and I was resigned to failing my first job as consul of helping David to recover his property.

Then the door opened, everyone sprang to attention and in walked the colonel with Don Guillermo Borja and his son-in-law, Trevor Harding. I was introduced to the colonel and my spirits soared, the fifth cavalry had ridden to my aid, the case was as good as won. But wait — the colonel and my rival were embracing like long-lost friends! Now what would happen? The evidence was shown to the colonel all over again, with both sides having made a personal plea for the verdict. Mine was short and to the point, my rival's seemed to take hours. At the end, the colonel said he needed time to consider his verdict and, as he stood up, so did we and followed him out of the room. Trevor, Don Guillermo and I went off to discuss the issue. Apparently, my rival was a car dealer from Loja who was well known in Guayaquil too. He maintained that he had bought the car in good faith but the question remained as to whether whoever had sold it had good title to it. The colonel took into account that a foreign national and a consul were involved and that, on balance, our case was stronger. He ruled in our favour, Trevor bought the car, I sent the money to David and the case was closed satisfactorily. However, it had taken a great deal of my time and did serve to show me the rather meagre limits to my consular power.

Power as such may have been in short supply but a consul does have a certain social standing in the community, and a good way to improve the standing of one's country is to hold a party on the national day. For most of my consular colleagues, this is their independence day; normally from Spain in the case of the majority of Latin American, from Britain in the case of the USA. Britain is a strange case. We celebrate the official queen's birthday either in April or in June, depending on the country. The date is flexible too. I do it on the second Saturday in June, which I believe to be the correct date, but the embassy in Quito does it on a mid-week day early in June. In Britain it is not even a holiday and is marked only by the trooping of the colour. I am afraid this all comes of not having a written constitution.

In Kingsley Fox's day, the queen's birthday had been celebrated with a modest cocktail for a few Britons in his flat. When I took over, we moved the venue to the Phoenix Club. This had moved once again to the fourth floor of the Gonzalez Rubio building in Pichincha and Elizalde streets, just a block away from the Malecon and from where the club had originally been in the Fiori building. The address where I had taken the Phoenix (Quito and Nueve de Octubre streets) had not been a success and we had lost members. My presidency ended rather weakly and Andres Argudo (the former Life manager and now the owner of his own agrochemical business, Fitosan Ltda) moved the club again. This time, we were able to purchase the freehold of the premises, which allowed us to invest in improving the club facilities.

We held my first queen's birthday party here in 1983. We did not celebrate one in 1982 it was not considered appropriate during the Falklands War. The Ecuadorian government, along with most of Latin America, had taken a pro-Argentinian position, or rather an anti-colonial one. But the general feeling among Guayaquil residents whom I knew was pro-British. The Argentinians are not popular with the rest of Latin America because they have a very high proportion of European immigrants (mainly Italian and Spanish) and consider themselves European, tending to look down on other multi-ethnic countries. In May 1982, I had been in Bolivia, which had a right-wing military government and was sending arms and support to Argentina. In a taxi, Winston had rather naughtily said to the driver: 'This is the British consul in Guayaquil.' The driver turned, smiled and said: 'Give those SOBs a real beating!'

The guest list for the cocktail party is made up of the British living in my parish, which covers all of coastal Ecuador although we number only about 170 including children. Then we invite dignitaries such as the governor of the province, mayor, prefect, archbishop, local military and police commanders and consuls of other countries. Dignitaries and consuls receive an enormous number of invitations each month so the people who come to your 'do' demonstrate your and your country's standing in the community. My first attempt was quite modest. The Phoenix can accommodate perhaps 100 people and we gave preference to the British. I have always made a point of making a speech and drinking a health to her majesty. I feel that this at least distinguishes the occasion from the many different cocktail parties one attends. Surprisingly, only a few other consuls do this and normally there is no focus to the event. However, I will admit to being outgunned (literally) by the Mexican consul, Carlos Nunez, who shouts 'Viva Mexico carajo' and fires six shots from his pistol into the air. Fortunately the party is held in the garden!

For subsequent queen's birthdays, we much improved the occasion by using Mapan as a venue. Mapan lends itself ideally to this with its large house as a backdrop and it has wide lawns and flowering plants and trees. We had recently seen the film *Out Of Africa*, where there is a garden party scene and so stipulated that the guests should wear white clothes and a hat. This is quite easy for men in Ecuador, as the traditional suit of the tropics is white, and the guayabera and cottona, decorated white shirts worn outside the trousers, are popular. Panama hats are, of course, made in Ecuador so are readily available. The ladies always rise the to occasion and have great fun organising their outfits. In fact, once when we could not hold the party in Mapan for climatic reasons, one matron took me to task as she had already bought her hat and there was no other occasion to use it!

The distance of ninety kilometres from Guayaquil is a bit of a problem but friends share cars, with one non-drinker to drive them home, the wealthy bringing their drivers. Once the police decided to put a speed trap on the road to the farm on the morning of the party. After they had caught a dozen cars all filled with people in white clutching their hats, they asked: 'What's going on?'

The 2000 Q.B.P. showing the crowd dressed in white with hats.

On hearing that it was the British consul's party, they laughed and said they had thought it was a funeral, when people wear white too.

For many years, the catering for the event was done by a very fat man called Gordo Daniel, who ran a restaurant in Guayaquil. He would turn up at six in the morning of the day of the event and slowly cook twenty sucking piglets on grills over a charcoal fire. They would be ready for lunch at two o'clock. We hired tables, chairs, waiters and plates and glasses. Ice would be bought in blocks and broken up to cool the beer, wine and soft drinks; glasses washed and the whisky and gin set out. The house was decorated with Union Jacks and the Ecuadorian flag and we were ready.

Often the British ambassador would join us for the day with the military attaché. With Ceci and I, they would stand towards the front of the garden to receive the guests. Rocio, who by this time had succeeded Letty, would be in charge of the guest book so we would later know who had been there.

We averaged about 250 guests and, as the journey was long, they would arrive over a period of two hours for the twelve o' clock start. We shook hands with all the guests, introducing them to the ambassador, and they moved on.

We would stand under a toborochi tree for shade, as it was generally very hot while we were receiving guests. One day, this caused a minor incident. The toborochi is popular with iguanas, which can grow up to three feet long. They apparently pee only once a week but when they do, they do. This happened as the then ambassador, Frank Wheeler, was below in his white suit. There was a moment of consternation, then Frank laughed and we all joined in. Ceci took his jacket to our housekeeper Amarilis for cleaning and, as the ambassador had removed his jacket, so did everyone else and we were much more comfortable.

When we felt that we had a quorum, we would assemble everyone around the flagpole in the lawn and draw important people to the front to make an official party. Then the ambassador would make a speech followed by mine, which would end with a toast to the President of Ecuador, followed by the Ecuadorian national anthem, then a toast to her majesty and the British national anthem. After this, I would invite the guests to eat. One year, in the moment of silence which followed the British anthem, I kept them waiting for a few seconds. Then they heard bagpipes and, looking up to the second-floor balcony of the house, they saw a piper in full uniform, who played *Amazing Grace*. The crowd loved it. The piper Andy Bishopberger, who was Swiss and worked for the Swiss-owned cement plant in Guayaquil. He had always loved the pipes and played with a pipe band in Switzerland. The poor fellow nearly died of heat stroke in his regalia so after two pieces, he changed into lighter Scottish attire and continued to play.

We always tried to provide a show of some sort and, apart from the piper, the best was an Esmeraldeno group of black marimba players and dancers. They performed folk dances involving jealousies over women, which included very realistic machète fights, with the sparks flying as they clashed. However, it was a rather a large group and became somewhat difficult to control. At the end of the party, when the group was getting into its bus to go home, we had to rescue a large turtle and a sloth that it was taking away. Both turtles and sloths (an arboreal animal which hunts at night and sleeps all day, hence slothful!) are quite common on the farm. But it is remarkable that they had found both so close to the house and taken the sloth out of the tree, as these creatures are usually in the higher branches.

The show would be followed by a disc jockey playing music to dance to on the cement floor under the house. Ecuadorians are great dancers and soon the floor would be packed. I am not too keen myself but Ceci had plenty of dancing partners so I was allowed to opt out, as were most of the British. One year, we had a visiting colonel from the Ministry of Defence, whom we had met in Quito at the ambassador's party the week before. Hamon Massey was there in all his guard's uniform splendour and, as he stood six foot six inches tall, he was a very imposing figure. Moreover, he was a very charming person. Ceci immediately invited him to attend our QBP the following week and he accepted. This time, he was wearing a tropical uniform but was no less imposing. When dancing time came, he was the first choice for all the ladies and he did not

ECUADOR 1980

disappoint them. He danced and danced until his uniform was soaked with sweat, then he disappeared upstairs into the house and reappeared in slacks and tee shirt to continue dancing — such are the resources of the guards!

Towards five o'clock, the party would begin to break up and, once again, I would spend a couple of hours shaking hands as people left. Some hands were repeatedly shaken as I had already said goodbye before they were recalled by a group of friends and returned for a final drink. The mosquitoes would come to my aid about dusk at six o'clock and the stragglers would slap their legs and jump about before calling it a day and going home. These were very happy events but found me totally exhausted at the end of the day. We would stay at the farm overnight, with perhaps ambassador Richard and Brigitte Lavers, who became very close friends, and one or two others. Over dinner, we would hold an amusing post mortem on the day.

Mapan has been the scene of many parties and happy times but early in our occupation of it, Ceci felt very uncomfortable. She had trouble sleeping there and once awoke me in a panic to say that she distinctly felt someone breathing heavily in her ear. She had tried to turn to me, asleep on the other side of the bed, but felt paralysed and could not move while this went on. The house, she said, was haunted and should be blessed before she would stay there again. We

H.M.A. Richard Lavers, Brigitte Lavers, Ceci and Colin (and others) at the Queen's Birthday Party in Mapan, 1995.

told Julio Vera and he confirmed the rumours we had heard that there had been a wooden house called la Violetta where a murder had been committed on the site of Mapan. Don Louis had had the old house burned down but obviously the ghost lived on.

We had met an Irish-American priest, Father John Maloney, who was with a missionary group in Ecuador, in the Phoenix Club. So I asked him if he would be kind enough to bless the house for us and at the same time baptise Alex. Poor Alex, her baptism does sound rather an afterthought but we were planning to do it anyway and thought that we might combine both jobs and have a party too. Father Maloney knew his priorities, even if we did not, and the baptism came first. After this, we followed him from room to room while he sprinkled holy water. As they say in Ireland 'It's a miracle, bejesus' because this worked. Ceci has not seen or felt any more ghosts and can sleep safely there.

As a footnote to my description of my early consular days, one day I received instructions to fly the flag at half mast as King Sobhusa Dlamini of Swaziland had died. He was the longest-reigning monarch in the world and the man I had met fifteen years before.

THE NIÑO

Much has been heard recently about the Niño current and the aberrations in world weather patterns that it brings. The Niño current is an annual event for Ecuador and it is only abnormally severe Niños which cause problems. The climate of the Ecuadorian coastal plain is clearly divided into wet and dry seasons. The dry season, which generally runs from May to December, is caused by the cold Humboldt current, which travels north from Antarctica, hugging the coast of South America and causing deserts in Chile and Peru. In December, the Niño (named after the boy-child) pushes in from the western Pacific along the equator and, on reaching the Ecuadorian coast, spreads north and south, forcing the Humboldt out to sea. Then the rising sea temperatures bring heavy rains in the evenings after hot days of clear blue skies.

When the rains began early in September 1982, we farmers were very pleased to see them. The pastures became green and the land was tilled ready for an early season. But the rains grew heavier month by month, until the rivers burst their banks in December and bridges and roads were washed away. Crops were submerged and cattle had to be moved to higher land. I was at Mapan on the 30th December, 1982, inspecting the flooding which I did not think too bad. That night, the river rose and the flood bank broke at Guarumal. The following morning, I woke up to find that the water had risen four feet in the night and had flooded ninety per cent of the farm. The cattle were huddled together on any small area that was above water level. The road out of the farm was likewise underwater and I was told that I would be unable to drive out. But it was New Year's Eve and I was certainly going to try to get back to Ceci and the family in Guayaquil. By this time, I had my first Range Rover, which I had bought second-hand from ambassador John Hickman before he was posted to Chile. I arranged for a farm tractor to follow me until I was clear of the worst and, with low gear and high revs, I ploughed into the flood water. It says a lot for the Range Rover that it got through. The water was lapping over the bonnet and up to the windows, and the car hardly leaked: there was the smallest puddle on the floor at the passenger side. That was the last time I was able to drive into Mapan for three months. The surface of the road had been washed away and trucks ploughing through had rutted the base underwater until it was impassable.

There was little we could do to save parts of the banana plantation, which were waterlogged and would have to be replanted, but the cattle would have to be evacuated before they starved to death. They were collected together and sorted so as not to separate cows from their calves, then about half the herd of 800 head was swum through the flood water and on to the hard surface at the junction of the Babahoyo/Quevedo road. Here, we built a temporary bamboo corral and loading ramp and took some thirty truck-loads of cattle about fifty kilometres to a farm we rented north of Ventanas in the hills. Two vaqueros and four horses were left with them.

For the next three months, I would perform the ceremony of the changing of the guards. I would drive to Babahoyo and meet two of the vaqueros who had come down-river in a canoe with an outboard engine, each bringing his saddle. We would drive to Ventanas, ride around the half of the herd that was there, then return with the two vaqueros of the week before to Babahoyo, leave my car in the town and take the canoe to Mapan. The River Babahoyo meandered a great deal and the journey took over an hour. At the beginning, I found it very interesting, and indeed beautiful, to glide up the river with the sun setting over the sugar plantation and pastures. But the journey became irksome with time. The river was so high that we would have to duck our heads when passing beneath the concrete bridge that joins the road to Mapan. This bridge usually appears ridiculously high over the meagre river but the engineers had calculated for extremes such as this. Then, leaving the main river, now the Pueblo Viejo, the canoe could go into the estero and I could land only a few yards from Mapan house. The house itself was never flooded but parts of the garden were.

We continued to cut and export what remained of the bananas, using large barges that had once been used to take the fruit down to Guayaquil, before loading ships in the river in front of the Malecon. These had been made redundant years earlier when the Guayaquil New Port had opened and all transport was now by truck. Luckily, they had not been broken up but had sat rusting quietly on a slipway until this year of the Niño, when they returned for one last fight like old warriors. In fact, one difficulty had been digging the old river men who had run them previously out of retirement, because the river is treacherous and full of sand banks that, even during floods, could snag a heavily loaded barge.

By April 1983, the rains were ceasing and the waters fell. We had had 6,000 millimetres of rain in a nine-month period, four times the normal rainfall. The countryside eventually dried out and the government repaired the roads and bridges. In fact, it did better than that. The road to Mapan, which had been washed out, was raised two metres and surfaced. Farmers, including ourselves, set to work to build banks of earth, canals, drains and pumps to protect their bananas and more valuable crops.

Although we had to wait fifteen years for them to be tested fully, they did stand up to the next Niño in 1997/8. This one was even longer and heavier than the previous one, lasting eighteen months and producing 9,000 millimetres of rain. This time, the road survived and, although we still had to evacuate some cattle, we could load them directly into trucks on the farm. We came through this trial less damaged than the previous time but, now that the fields are drying up, we face years of work on the pastures. They have been reduced to a mess of dying water hyacinth and weeds, and must be restored to good grassland.

Two years ago, while I was riding around and looking at the cattle, I would point indignantly to a cheeky mimosa weed and a vaquero would dismount from his horse and swipe at it with his machète. If we were to do the same today, we would not ride 500 yards in a day. First, we need an expensive round of herbicides to get the weeds down and the grasses up. I believe that nature cannot stand a void and will fill every space with something. The smart farmer will try to help his friends (the good grasses or crops) against their enemies, the weeds. There is no point in killing weeds and leaving nothing behind, as more weeds will grow. But killing weeds and encouraging grass to spread over the area reduces the light and nourishment available to the weeds. This is why it is important to keep cattle out of the field until the grass has had a chance to recolonise it. This, of course, creates problems when large areas of the farm have been flooded and the cattle are thin and hungry. It is hard to keep them off treated areas long enough to permit recovery. Good fencing is essential and this is the first step towards recovery, which we are making at the time of writing.

TUPGILL 1980-85

THIS WAS A TIME of great activity at Tupgill. I had bought it from Do in 1974 but the expense of the purchase meant that there was nothing left for renovations. Eventually I started to repair the cottages in 1979 and now I moved on to the stables. Unfortunately, when you begin to tackle an old estate, the first expenditure goes, literally, underground. The drains under the stables had long ago ceased to function properly and were, in fact, just a series of unconnected soakaways. This had not been noticed while the cottages and stableboys' accommodation had been empty but now that we were filling up with people again, it became apparent. Indeed, the local authorities condemned the drains. I had earmarked a certain amount of cash for stable improvements but was dismayed to find that it was all to go into drainage and a new septic system.

Malcolm took the necessary measurements and for six months or so afterwards, the resulting trenches resembled the Battle of the Somme. In addition, the culvert which ran down the park from the Ferngill wood to the river had partially collapsed. During heavy rains, water would issue at intervals, pouring down the park and continuing down the road, taking the road surface with it. This culvert had been built a century or more before. It was made of drystone walls and the base and top were flagged. It was about three feet high and two feet wide and had worked well over the years. The damage to its structure had occurred when branches washed down from the wood had become jammed across it, and the resulting water pressure loosened the walls and caused sections to cave in.

Albert Calvert was the building contractor by this time and he looked at the problem and suggested that the upper part of the culvert could be repaired but that the lower part was beyond help and would have to be rebuilt. This would be very expensive, taking many man hours to dismantle the original structure and rebuild it, so we opted for a bypass. This involved taking a concrete pipe of three feet in diameter on a new line and leaving the old culvert line undisturbed, because it continued to perform a service in picking up the water from numerous land drains.

My problems did not finish there because insufficient drinking water came from a spring in the Ferngill wood. Even in grandfather Bob's time water had to be led up from the river in horse-drawn tanks in dry times. Once again, we faced a lot of expenditure to correct this deficiency. Horses consume a great deal of water but today so do people. In Bob's time the stableboys' lavatories were 'long drops' over the midden area and baths would not be taken more

Aerial photo of Tupgill Stables showing how they were in 1970. The army Nissen huts are visible.

often than once a week. Now building regulations required showers, baths, wash basins and lavatories for the houses and flats and also for outside workers.

We studied the flow of the spring but found that we would have to construct very large storage tanks if we were to guarantee a water supply for, say, seventy-five horses and thirty people, which was the theoretical capacity of Tupgill. Ferngill, Ashgill and Thorngill were on the public water supply which came from Pen Hill and down the low moor to Middleham. Father and Uncle Sam had laid the connecting pipe using stable labour in the 1920s. By now, the original one-inch pipes were corroded inside, leaving only a half-inch bore which was completely insufficient. Mother would continually complain that, when horses were watered at Thorngill, her Ferngill supply would dry up.

Recently, the new owner of Thorngill, the Italian marquis Don Enrico Incisa, had laid a new pipe from Thorngill as far as the storage tanks just on our side of the moor wall and this, although improving his supply, worsened that of Ferngill. So we saw that the best solution to the problem would be a larger pipe over the moor, both to the original storage tanks and in a direct line from there to Tupgill. The water authorities would allow the connection but I would have to pay for the new pipe. More buried treasure! To make absolutely sure that Tupgill had good water pressure, we sacrificed one stable and made it into a large water tank with pressure pumps and from there laid new water pipes to the cottages, stables and even to the cattle drinking troughs in nearby fields.

There were two more services that I wanted to improve. Before mains electricity had been installed, Tupgill had had a generator. Afterwards, until the 1980s, all the electricity wires emanated from this building and spread out in a giant cat's cradle to Ashgill, Thorngill, Ferngill and Brecongill. There was a large transformer up a pole in the centre. I was determined to rid myself of all this clutter which spoilt the look of the estate for me. The North Eastern Electricity Board would put the wires underground but the interested party had to pay a 'contribution'. I am sure that this contribution more than paid for the whole exercise as it was quite substantial. When the board workmen came to look at the job and I showed them what I wanted, the foreman shook his head and said: 'You obviously have plenty of money to throw away.' One man's throwing money away is another's gain from an uncluttered view. The transformer proved a problem as it had to go somewhere and I had visions of one solitary post with a large carbuncle on it in the middle of my pristine view. We avoided this by using part of a small stone barn that stood at the corner of a field by Ferngill Lane. The barn's appearance was later enhanced and today

Building of the Fishing Temple.

part of it is the Fishing Temple. I also set about having the telephone wires laid underground, which was much easier and less expensive. I was helped in my tidying-up activities because the electrical services to Brecongill, which passed over our land, were found to be deficient and Sally Hall could not rely on the power for her milking machine. The board re-routed her supply over the low moor and I gleefully removed the posts that had linked her supply to ours.

Services all up to date, I could finally spend money where it showed. We had already renovated Gate Cottage at Tupgill for a Mrs Larder, who rented it. Arch Cottage was improved for Brian, Kath and Leo Morris. Next in line was West House, which for years had been Mrs Weymes's house, until she could no longer cope alone and had left to live with her son, Ernie, and his wife Pat at Ashgill. West House was quite a large cottage but part of the ground floor had been converted at some time to accommodate two stables, leaving very little room downstairs but four bedrooms upstairs. We set about to restore and improve it with Malcolm, turning the stables into a garage and utility room and terracing the garden at the front, which fell away steeply. In fact, the cottage garden had been part of Tupgill House garden and Do had grown vegetables there when she was fitter. Now that she had no use for it, we restored it to West House. A porch on the front door, new windows and doors, and central heating turned it into a really comfortable house and, being in line with Tupgill, it shares the wonderful view across the dale.

Removing the plaster.

In its undress state.

The new look.

Doug and Margaret Weatherill had been farming a small acreage since Doug had ceased to be Father's farm man. They rented a cottage at Ashgill from Ernie Weymes and farmed the twenty acres or so there plus part of the Tupgill land and a piece at Middleham bridge. Now Doug was approaching sixty and had decided to give up farming. I went to see them because we had remained great friends over the years and suggested that they move into West House and that Doug could help around the estate, gardening and bringing the coal in and so on for Do. They liked both the idea and the house and moved in shortly afterwards.

The next job was the stables. The wooden army huts had been removed from the centre of the big yard and Malcolm had levelled the resulting space and laid brick foundations, on which we had erected eight wooden boxes. That was a good start but wherever we looked in the old stone boxes, there was desolation. The doors and windows were rotten. The floors were broken up, the roofs leaked and the roof timbers sagged badly. It was depressing to think that it would be years and tens of thousands of pounds (actually it was hundreds of thousands!) before the old place could be restored to its former glory. Where to start? Malcolm reassured us that it would all be done over time. We had only to begin.

So we started with what was called the Warren, a maze of cage boxes along dark passages with doors that were awkward for horses. Consulting our trainers, Jumbo Wilkinson and Walter Bentley, we found that cage boxes were no longer popular as it was said that viruses could spread more easily between horses. In fact, Newmarket has recently moved towards the American barn-type stables so this argument is suspect. Anyway, this gave us the idea of turning these stables so that they opened outwards. We recovered ten good boxes out of the jumble that was there before.

Then we began doing the same thing in the yard at the back of Tupgill House with the same good results. As we had tenants while all this was going on, we were constantly made aware that the builders were upsetting the horses and this led to a certain amount of friction which poor Elaine had to sort out. Nor could we progress in a straight line as we wanted to, as we were forever being called upon to patch up the unmodernised stables as they would deteriorate and fall to pieces before we reached them. The stables were not the only problem: stable staff was the other. There are several flats above the stable blocks and these were also in disrepair. Under Weatherby's rules, the trainers had to have someone resident at the stables to avoid the risk of the horses being doped. We initially overcame this by allowing a caravan to be parked behind the stables. Then there were no washing facilities so the old army latrines were temporarily and cheaply made suitable for use. This might have been all right for a lad alone but the lad in question acquired a girlfriend so pressure was brought to bear to have a flat renovated for them. We did this but it took time and cost money because we reasoned that we would go around the estate only once, at least in my lifetime, so we would do a quality job.

This attention to quality included using blue Welsh slates on the roofs, cast-iron gutters, downspouts and light brackets, cobbles for the yards, cut stone decorations and wrought-iron gates, which added a great deal to the cost. When the flat was finally ready, painted and heated, we asked both trainers to share it with one lad (or couple) each. This arrangement lasted for six months when there was a disagreement between the lads and an immediate request for a second flat to be made available. Once again, the stable work was deferred for this.

At the same time as we were building, we were planting too. Tree planting is a cyclical event. In the eighteenth and nineteenth centuries, landowners planted trees for pleasure and as a source of future profit. Labour was cheap and spare money could easily be dedicated to it. The twentieth century saw the harvesting of this wealth and, with financial constraints, little new planting was undertaken. Then, in the 1970s and '80s, Dutch elm disease removed millions of trees from the landscape. Bob had not planted trees, Do had put in a few copper beeches and Father some poplars, but this effort had been more than cancelled out by the elm trees lost. I am very fond of trees and set to with a will to repopulate the estate. We had a gardener called David Perkins, who was very knowledgeable about trees, and in the winter months, when Tupgill's garden did not need much attention, he would be asked to plant trees.

Our first small plantation was in the park, where it was strategically placed to block the view of the Coverham dairy (a factory making Wensleydale cheese) from Tupgill House. We then planted Nicholas Wood (named after my son), which was the foundation for the Forbidden Corner. The following year, we fenced off four acres in the Ferngill field and planted Diana Wood (named after my eldest daughter). This was on a rather poor area of hillside where the grass would become brown in summer. It was very steep so I thought that we would lose little grazing land in planting it. It was planted with a mixture of conifers and hardwoods and the following summer, my first action as soon as I arrived at Ferngill was to walk across the field and inspect it.

The weather was hot and dry and disaster had struck — all the little trees were wilting and dying. My niece, Emilie, was staying with us so she and my three little ones were press-ganged to help out. We bought several hundred yards of garden hose and, connecting this to a Ferngill outside tap, attempted to water the trees. It was all rather futile. The pressure at the end of the hose was minimal and the dry, gravelly hill absorbed what water we could give it without much benefit to the trees. I prayed for rain every day but no rain came. We persevered for all the five or six weeks that we were there, which meant giving up practically all our time from early morning to late evening to take turns at the end of the hose. I suppose we saved a few trees but there were heavy losses and a lot of beating up to be done the following winter. Luckily, the next summer was a wet one and, although replacements were needed for several years, we finally won the battle and today have a fine wood.

I was by now hungry for land and had asked Elaine to keep her eyes open for any piece of land for sale within a reasonable distance of Tupgill. In March

1983, she rang to say that there were sixty acres of land at Horsehouse, about four miles from Tupgill, coming up for auction. She and her farmer husband Charles had been to see it and reported that, although steep, it was in good heart but was not worth more than £1,000 an acre. I was very excited by this. Despite being four miles from Tupgill, it was close to a forty-four-acre piece of land owned by Do, which I might reasonably hope to inherit one day. I waited anxiously for Elaine's call but when it came, I heard that we were unsuccessful. Someone else had paid £1,100. However, all was not lost. People had noticed that we were interested in land and we were approached to see if we might like to buy two other pieces. By good luck, these were on either side and adjoining Do's land, and covered fifty-three and seventeen acres.

The larger piece surrounded Deer Close House and I knew it well because, some years previously, it had been owned by Do in partnership with her great friend, Betty Meiklejohn. They had bought the estate and the Horsehouse pub, the Thwaite Arms. Later Betty and her husband, Colonel Ian Meiklejohn, had moved in to Deer Close and eventually gave it to their son Paddy, when he left the fleet air arm. Paddy and I had grown up together and when we were kids, Do would take us to Deer Close where we would shoot pheasants, rabbits and an occasional grouse. Paddy and Do had sold out when he decided to move to a larger farm in Scotland. It was good to have at least part of it back again. This made a block of 110 acres at Horsehouse. Do's land was rented to Clive Weatherall (no relation to Doug) and I also rented out my pieces in the meantime.

The land at Tupgill was also rented out, Doug taking one field and Harry Morris, who farmed the next door Birdridding Farm, the rest. Now Doug was to relinquish his part as he gave up farming and I decided to farm myself. The question was what to farm? I fancied having suckler cows and debated the relative advantages of breeds with Elaine and Charles. My first inclination was to go for Highland cattle, as they are very decorative. Charles said that if it came to a choice between planting trees and rearing Highland cattle, he rather thought that trees grew faster! I then thought of having a pedigree herd of Aberdeen Angus cows. Charles pointed out that I would be better using a Charolais or Limousin bull on Angus to produce a good cross-bred animal. However, I had set my heart on having a homogenous herd of black cattle in England to contrast with the white herd in Ecuador. So pure Angus it would be.

Elaine and Charles began to look around to see where we could buy some initial stock while I talked to Doug to see if he would be prepared, having just given up his own farm, to look after mine. He said that he would but only in the short term, until it built up into a full-time job for a farm man. There were only seventy-two acres of land and some old stone cow sheds available at Tupgill so we set the limit at thirty cows and a stock bull.

The great day arrived on the 26th March, 1984 and my first cattle came to Tupgill. The schoolboy dream of twenty-five years previously had come to pass, for in a way the farm in Ecuador did not count. My vision had been of my own stock at Tupgill. Doug bought a second-hand 1976 model Leyland 245 tractor and, with trailer, sprayers and grass topper, we had the tools for the job. The cattle were registered as pedigree animals, we joined the Aberdeen Angus society and I dreamed of breeding champion stock. This, as we were to find out, was no easy matter and, having bred and sold one or two moderate bulls, we eventually gave up the fight. But in 1984, there appeared no limit to what we could do.

Having started a farm and made good progress on the planting and renovation works, 1985 represented the peak of our activity at Tupgill. To this day, I am amazed at what we accomplished and how much, mainly borrowed, cash was spent. My letters to Elaine and Malcolm Tempest are full of exhortations to obtain plans and quotes and get going! We employed an assortment of building contractors all that year and the next. Albert Calvert had some fifteen men employed; Paul Waterstone six; Denis Fawcett began his fifteen-year stint (to date) walling the fields; Keith Houlston worked with his JCB tractor and Peter Townson was responsible for the planting.

This is what we achieved: the clock tower barn was built (today the entrance to the Forbidden Corner); another barn re-roofed; twenty stables and the crenellated wall by the clock tower built; the lake dug; and the Fishing Temple and its bridge created. The Ferngill and stable gateways were also completed with wrought-iron gates; the circular road laid outside the clock tower and the

The renewed entrance to Tupgill stables.

The building of the clocktower.

The digging of the lake.

The finished Clock Tower.

area landscaped with large trees. Ferngill House car park was made; the barn and wooden stables at Ferngill removed and replaced by the pyramid-roofed building housing the water and oil tanks; old army huts and dangerous buildings removed; and extensive drainage and tree planting carried out all over the estate.

While I was looking at the building work on the stables, the local building inspector arrived. I introduced myself and he said that he had worked as a builder before the last war and had made repairs to Gate Cottage for Grandfather. Old Bob had said: 'Make it a cheap job.' Nellie, rather annoyed, replied: 'I want a first-class job.' 'Yes', said Bob, 'but keep it cheap!'

Malcolm Tempest, as always, was the architect for all this work and he and Elaine kept me informed of progress. That winter was unduly harsh and Elaine's letters appeared to be full of gloom as snow, rain and freezing winds slowed things up. Because the mail was unreliable in Ecuador, we had fallen into the habit of using DHL couriers once a month to convey letters, plans and photographs relating to the work. Otherwise, we would talk on the telephone for an hour or more while I took notes. Both were expensive ways to communicate; today fax serves this purpose and now also e-mail.

The year 1985 was remarkable not only for the building activity but because my land holdings suddenly increased dramatically. Farm land is mostly held for long periods and one can wait a generation or more for a neighbouring farm to come up for sale, so we had extraordinary luck when two farms became available. The first was Birdridding, comprising 103 acres bordering Tupgill across the Middleham to Carlton road. This was owned by Harry Morris and a Mr Dawson in equal shares, with Harry working it. He and Dawson had disagreed about the working of the land and Harry approached me to see if I would be interested in buying Dawson's share while he continued to work it. I was not, but said that I would like to buy it outright and take on Harry and his son Allan to farm Birdridding and Tupgill for me. This was agreed and negotiations took place with Dawson to sell his half, which he eventually did. A trip to my friendly Barclays Bank manager in Leyburn, Len Parry, secured a mortgage and I was very content with my deal.

I now had 175 acres altogether at Tupgill and seventy at Horsehouse — quite enough to make a farming unit. But when your luck is in, it is really in. Not two months later, we were approached by land agents with the offer of the 125-acre West Park farm which lies just over Middleham moor from Tupgill. This had belonged to the Peacock family (descendants of Dobson, the trainer) since the 1920s and now my good friend Lennie Peacock wanted to sell it. Elaine rang me in Guayaquil and said that she felt she ought to let me know for form's sake but she was sure that, after buying Birdridding and the tremendous expense of the work at Tupgill, I would feel unable to make an offer. She had a point in that I was over-extending myself financially and was beginning to lose sleep over the bills. But then I reasoned that, if I did not at least make a bid, I would always regret it, as the land might never come up for sale again in

Ferngill House from the air about 1990.

my lifetime. So I offered the minimum that the agent calculated West Park might go for – and was successful!

Strictly speaking, West Park was not a farm as it contained no buildings and had been let yearly as summer grazing for adjacent farmers. But this did not worry me. I had plans for new buildings to form the farmyard at Birdridding. Once more, I went to Barclays, but this time borrowing was rather less easy as Len, like Elaine, thought that I had over-reached myself. But after I painted a somewhat optimistic picture of future cash flow from Ecuador, he reluctantly consented to a further mortgage and I went ahead. Of course, farms need stock and Harry, Elaine and I went through the figures and decided on buying more suckler cows and sheep. Our pedigree Aberdeen Angus herd was to remain small and future cows would be more commercial cross-bred animals. We bought Angus-Friesian heifers and crossed then with a Blonde d'Aquitaine bull. The sheep were the traditional Masham ewes crossed with a Suffolk tup.

Then, of course, we needed more tractors and machinery, which we bought from Harry's sale. Finally new buildings were built in 1986 when we replaced most of the dilapidated ones at Birdridding with a large 150-cow cubicle house and silo/straw barn.

Aerial photo in 1992 showing the new farm buildings at Birdridding.

How was all this financed? In those days, farm buildings were 60 per cent grant-aided. This period also coincided with a time of extraordinary profitability at Agripac, helped by a weak pound which depreciated from over $2.5 to the pound almost to parity with the dollar (today there are about $1.5 to the pound.) This meant that the dollars I earned went a great deal further than at any time before or since. Luck once again took a hand in bringing together both the opportunity and the means to further my farming ambitions.

With Harry and Allan Morris — both large, powerful men — now working the farm together, Doug transferred to the estate, where there was more than enough to do looking after a huge quantity of newly planted trees, hedges and lawns. Looking at photographs of 1985 today, I see that it marked the turning point from a small, rather bleak farm with racing stables attached to an integrated park. The trees were planted in groups to hide neighbouring stables and houses. The old army parade ground in front of the clock tower was dug up and lawns planted together with twenty-year-old trees supplied by Civic Trees Ltd, which were an instant solution to landscaping. The internal roads were given drains and kerbs, the gateposts refashioned in cut stone and new wrought-iron gates hung. I have mentioned before that Tupgill and Ferngill were criss-crossed with electricity and telephone wires on poles. These were now laid underground. In the case of the electricity supply, we had to look for somewhere to hide a transformer as the pole-mounted one was to go. We solved the problem by using half of the Fishing Temple to screen it.

Malcolm — forever the artist — came up with a bright idea. He said that, rather than putting a keystone on each new building engraved with CRA and the date, we could use the Armstrong crest of an arm and a leg (with its reference, too, to what it had all cost me!) He showed me the crest which he had discovered in a book of heraldry and which is described thus: 'A sinister arm in armour, embowed proper, grasping at the ankle a leg in armour, severed at the thigh, fessways proper'. We agreed to do this and it is now widely displayed in all sorts of ways around the estate. It occurred to me that perhaps I did not have a right to use it but we went ahead, anyway. I had visions of an irate owner of the crest one day demanding that it be chipped off buildings and cut out of iron gates. Eventually in 1991, when I made up my own coat of arms, the Lord Lyon King of Arms (her majesty's authority for such things in Scotland) allowed me the use of the crest so all is now perfectly legal.

While the building work was at a peak in late 1985, we had a fire in one of the hay barns over a stable block which still had to be renovated. This proved both a hindrance and an opportunity. Although we were still very much stretched with the building work in hand, we were forced to have men repair the damaged stables which had been occupied by horses. Luckily, the animals had been rescued in time, even though the fire occurred at night. But where could we put them while work was in progress? A barn was quickly partitioned to make temporary stables and we began to shift the rubble of the fire. We decided that the hay barn above the stables was not a good idea so we converted the space

Statue showing the Armstrong crest.

into accommodation for stable lads and lasses. The stables underneath were completely renovated as they had been boarded inside and, when these partitions had burned, the old stone walls had caved in and become unsafe.

One of the boxes affected had always been known as 'Pretender's box'. It was named after the horse Pretender, which won the Derby in 1869, ridden by John Osborne, the very famous jockey-turned-trainer who owned Ashgill in the late nineteenth century. The owner was Sir Robert Jardine of Jardine Matheson, the Hong Kong trading firm. When we rebuilt the box, we put a plaque on the wall bearing these details. Pretender was the penultimate Middleham-trained horse to win the Derby, the other being Dante, trained by Matt (son of Dobson) Peacock in the 1930s. Matt also had a son, Dick, who followed him as a trainer and Lennie is his widow — the longest-surviving training dynasty in Middleham.

I remember Tupgill as a plastered and whitewashed stable unit with black tar lintels to the doors before the renovation. I prefer stone so, as we worked around the stables, we had the render hacked off and the stone revealed and pointed up. The new stables and barns required a great deal of new stone for, when old stone buildings are demolished, a great deal of the material turns to dust and flakes and cannot be used again. On the various pieces of land we had acquired were numerous ruined barns and walls, which we used as our quarry for stone so, at the same time, we cleaned up these constructions of centuries past. In those times of cheap labour, fields had been very small and were worked by hand. Stone was available locally and drystone walls were the ideal way of dividing fields. The barns were placed in the centre of the fields and hay stored in them with the minimum of haulage. The few cows that each farmer owned would also be wintered in these barns.

But, these days having passed, the barns became redundant as new wooden or metal structures were erected by the farmhouse and fodder was brought in by tractor. The little fields were amalgamated, leaving broken walls to mark the old boundaries. Tupgill had a set of old stone farm buildings comprising cow byre, barns, feed house and piggery, but they had become impracticable as they were too small, and had to be cleaned out by hand rather than with a tractor front-end loader. Moreover, they were in the wrong place. The Birdridding purchase provided the opportunity to pull these down, use the stone and landscape the site. Today, it is occupied by trees in the little valley at the top of Tupgill Park and is a far, far better sight.

At about this time, some of the characters in this story passed away. Uncle Sam died in Newmarket in March 1983; Florrie Hammond, our old daily who had been with my parents and myself for many years, and Charlie Brown, former jockey and later Father's horse box driver also left this world. Both Florrie and Uncle Sam were buried in Coverham churchyard, where my grandparents and father were already interred. The grave markings of my grandparents, which were made of wood, had rotted away over the years. Nellie had wanted these to be made of oak by the firm of Thompsons of Kilburn, which made the oak furniture she adored, each piece marked with a mouse. When Bob told her that it would be better to have a gravestone of granite as the wood would only last forty years, she replied: 'Who on earth will remember us in forty years time!' So one more task of that time was to renew the wood which, together with my cousins and sisters, I replaced it with granite. You see, Nellie, you are still remembered and, through these pages, will be for some time to come.

The land-buying frenzy did not stop at the end of 1985. The deeds had hardly been signed on Birdridding and West Park, when Guy Reed contacted me in early 1986. Guy is the owner of Spigot Lodge, another long-established racing stable over the moor from Tupgill, where Chris Thornton trains for him today. He had made a fortune in the poultry business, before cashing in and dedicating himself to his love of horses. He had bought Spigot Lodge from Sam Hall, who, in turn, had bought it from Colonel Wilfred Lyde, Father's great friend. Wilfred had sold Thorngill to Bob and rejoined his old regiment, the Warwickshire Yeomanry, in 1939. When he returned from the war, he bought Spigot Lodge and trained there until he retired to the nearby village of West Witton in the 1970s.

Racehorses passing the lake.

There was a small farm attached to Spigot Lodge and Guy offered to sell this to me: some thirty acres adjoining West Park. It was perfect for me as the two areas could be worked together, and as the Spigot land extended to the Wensley to Carlton road, it would give me access to both pieces. The West Park land already had a right of way over the Middleham moor but this could be awkward for tractors and trailers in wet weather. So the deal was done. In fact, Guy offered to sell me the indoor riding school in the corner of one field on a purchase and lease-back basis but I felt that this was one step too far. Beyond Tupgill, my interest was only in land.

Then one more piece of the jigsaw fell into place in 1987. Ernie Weymes had trained at Ashgill with his wife Pat for many years, and now felt he would like to release some capital while continuing to train there. Would I be interested in buying Ashgill and leasing it back? This was a very different proposition from the indoor school. Ashgill adjoined Tupgill and, as well as an attractive house, had several cottages, forty stables, barns and other buildings, together with twenty acres of land. Some of the stables were in a rather poor condition but I saw this as a challenge which I would one day take on and rebuild them. In fact, this work was started in 1999 and is now almost completed.

There was also an historical angle to this purchase, which made it more significant. Ashgill was once the home of the great nineteenth-century jockey and trainer John Howe Osborne. Bob had bought it in 1924 for his son Sam, who began training there at the age of twenty-one and did so with great success until he sold it in 1945 and moved to Newmarket. It was then bought by Lord Joicey and rented to Captain Jack Fawcus, with whose children, Charles and Thalia, we played as children. Finally, it was sold again to Ernie. Ashgill stands between Tupgill and the Middleham low moor and, as well as having a right of way along Tupgill drive, it also has a right of way over a track across the moor to Spigot Lodge and Wensley. Thus we had connected up the two parcels of land on each side of the moor with a legal right of way. We could also use this way out of Tupgill when travelling west up Wensleydale. So the Ashgill purchase was very convenient from many points of view. Perhaps one more might be mentioned. When we were landscaping the lake and its surrounds Malcolm and I were only too aware that several neighbouring properties were visible, rather spoiling the effect we wanted to create. The most prominent of all was Ashgill so, now that it was ours, we were able to screen it by planting trees thickly on the steep bank in front of the stables. This has proved very successful and today the buildings are well hidden from the south. We also planted trees between Tupgill and Thorngill and between Tupgill and Brecongill (Sally Hall's stable), which are well on the way to giving similar screening.

HOLIDAYS

I HAD MADE A conscious decision to find a profitable way of spending weekends in my first years in Ecuador. Mapan was a break from the office but also a job, as I ran the farm hands-on for fifteen years. With the foremen reporting directly to me, and a labour force of over 100, there were more than enough problems to fill my so-called free time. Something similar was now happening in England. My holidays were taken up with meetings with Elaine, the bank manager, the accountant, the solicitor, the architect, the builders, the tree planters and so on. It was just a case of change of sink for the housewife. But there were memorable times when we would get away from it all. When the children were small, we would take a nanny to Ferngill with us and she would be left in charge of them while Ceci and I went off to exotic places. Later on, when the children were older, we shared some superb family holidays. But these early ones were for us alone.

Elaine had a friend called Dennis Briggs, who lived in Starbotton (near Kettlewell) and was the manager of Redfern Travel in Bradford. She introduced him to us and we have found him a mine of information over the years. Once we had established that we wanted to avoid package holidays and chain hotels, he put together some delightful journeys for us. The first of these was to Egypt. He did warn us that July was not the best month to go there because of the heat, but in those days we visited England only in summer, so we had no choice but to go then. We flew via Vienna as Austrian Airlines had given us the best deal and stayed at the Bristol Hotel, which is old-world and first class. We were surprised that Vienna was so small (less than 1,000,000 people) as it had been one of the great empire capitals of the world. The airport and city were connected by what appeared to be very minor roads. The Spanish riding school was closed, as was the Opera House, but Schonbrunn, the palace of the emperors, was quite delightful with its huge lawns and gardens.

From Vienna, we went on to Cairo. We arrived in the evening and were very frustrated by the terrible slowness of the immigration and customs desks. We waited for hours to get through. Then we crossed the city by taxi in suffocating heat, surrounded by nauseous smells and with crowds everywhere. By this time, we were beginning to regret having chosen Egypt. The taxi finally reached Giza and the Mena House hotel. This was much better — a very palace of a place. It had been the hunting lodge of a former ruler of Egypt and was the site of a famous meeting between Churchill, Roosevelt and Chiang Kai Chek (the Chinese ruler) during the Second World War. The original part of the hotel has lovely airy rooms with fretwork panels, wooden carving and marble floors. When we were shown to our room, the porter threw open the shutters and there, seemingly at the end of the gardens, were the pyramids, lovely in the moonlight. It was a moment to remember. The following day, we rode around them on a camel, went inside one and then went to the Cairo museum and saw grave relics including Tutankhamun's sarcophagus. We also visited the main mosque, where you paid to have someone change your shoes for slippers on the way in and on the way out paid again to have your shoes back! The streets of Cairo lived up to their first impression of crowds, noise and dirt. The taxi drivers were thieves and would demand outrageous sums for any journey. If the hotel had advised us that it would cost, say, ten Egyptian pounds to go downtown, the taxi driver would demand 100. As you argued with him, a crowd would gather around and, in fear of losing a handbag or wallet, you eventually settled for thirty pounds. This was the most unpleasant aspect of Egypt: not only taxi drivers but camel drivers indulge in this haggling too. They all appear to speak in half a dozen languages and can rip you off in any one of them.

We flew from Cairo up the Nile to Luxor and, looking down, were impressed by the very precise line of green cultivated land on either side of the river. Where the irrigation stopped, the desert began. Luxor was extremely hot, about 40°C, so we did our exploring in the morning or the evening. There was lots to see including The Valley of the Kings and Tutankhamun's tomb found by Howard Carter early this century. It was fascinating to stand inside it and see the freshness of the wall painting, which had been preserved by the extremely dry air. We saw the *son et lumière* show at the Luxor temples and ruins and took a felucca on the Nile. When Ceci let her hand trail in the water, the boatman said that we would be sure to return to Egypt. The sun was setting and the loudspeakers on the mosques were calling the faithful to prayer. The river was wide and calm and the heat had abated as we drifted about. This was the Egypt to remember rather than the horrors of downtown Cairo.

Another year, we had a holiday of a totally different sort. We took the *Royal Scotsman* train from Edinburgh to Aberdeen, Inverness, the Kyle of Lochalsh and back to Edinburgh. The *Royal Scotsman* was made up of carriages from the early part of the century, which were totally refurbished with sleeping cars, a restaurant, sitting room with bar and obviously a kitchen. There were only twenty-one 'guests' and about the same number of staff. I was the only European, given that Ceci is South American and all the rest came from North America. We must have been the youngest by some twenty years but, given our American cousins' love of meeting people and general friendliness, we were soon all one group. Starting with 'Where are ya'll from' (used in the singular as well as plural) we found points of contact and interest.

The train spent the first evening in a station by the Chivas Regal distillery, where we were taken after a splendid dinner on board. We had our tour, sampled the fare and then a piper turned up, which provoked spontaneous dancing. Huyton Hill prep school had given me a good grounding in the 'Gay Gordons' and 'Strip the Willow' so, with a dram or two inside me, off I went with a set here and a circle there. I was quite the life and soul of the party and much appreciated by the blue-, pink- or orange-tinted ladies. Ceci was somewhat surprised by my ability as I am considered a rather useless dancer by my family. On the other hand, scope for the 'Gay Gordons' is somewhat limited in Guayaquil! It was as well that I could oblige as our group was heavily weighted towards the fair sex, who had generally buried their husbands before indulging the insurance cash on a holiday.

We returned to the train to sleep and the next day went on to the Kyle of Lochalsh, where we took a coach over the ferry and visited the MacDonald Centre. In fact, the coach kept reappearing during our trip. It shadowed the train and took us to Cawdor Castle, Blair Athol and the Aberdeen museum of art. We enjoyed the castles and their gardens very much but less so the museum, where there was an exhibition of modern sculpture. I gazed at one piece of scrap iron and wondered who had the cheek to call it art. I was about to ask the man standing next to me when he spoke first. 'What a wonderful interpretation!' he said. I closed my mouth and moved on.

All in all, it was a wonderful three-day trip and we were rather sad to leave the train and our newfound friends. In fact, one couple was due to tour through Yorkshire and we invited them to lunch with us at Ferngill. They came and saw the countryside, then asked us why we had bothered to go to Scotland when we had such beautiful surroundings at home. It was a good point but Scotland had looked beautiful too in wonderful sunshine and the view at Ferngill we have to hand.

We had driven to Edinburgh via Carlisle. From there, we took the A7 and crossed the border. Five miles farther along on the right at Hollows stands Gilnockie Tower, from where Johnnie Armstrong rode out on that fateful day in 1530 to meet his king and his death. We noted the landmark as we were on our way to visit a couple called Ted and Judy Armstrong, who lived near Langholm. While sorting Father's papers after his death, I had come across a membership card of the Armstrong Clan Society presided over by Edward H Armstrong. I wrote to him and became a member. We had corresponded several times and thought we might now meet as I was passing his door. We had tea together and he told us of how he had had the idea of rallying the clan in 1969 when Neil Armstrong had walked on the moon.

At that time, he lived in Surrey but had moved to Langholm to be in real Armstrong territory. He had collected some 1,000 members worldwide and published several newsletters during the year. These contained pages referring to genealogical details. Each member would file his ancestry as far as he could go back and Ted would try to match these up, finding the relationship between one Armstrong and another. He did this for my family, connecting us to a Mrs Caroline Randle in Australia, to whom we are related through Richard the carrier (1744-1840). The fun behind all this mixing and matching was to try to trace a descendant of the chief of clan Armstrong. There had been chiefs until

1603, when the sons of the then chief were either hanged or disappeared during James I's bid to rid himself of these troublesome folk.

Conversation turned to Gilnockie Tower and Ted said that his dream was to acquire it for the clan. Until recently, it had been owned by the Duke of Buccleuch. He had sold it to a Mr Armstrong-Wilson, who had re-roofed, floored and made it habitable as a house, albeit a rather uncomfortable one with five main rooms one above the other and connected by winding stone steps within the width of the walls. It also had a parapet with spectacular views over Eskdale.

We left Ted and Judy and drove to Borthwick Castle at Govebridge, which had become a hotel. This was very imposing and we were given the room where Mary Queen of Scots is said to have slept. We changed for dinner and ate with our host and hostess and six or seven other (American) guests. It was a very pleasant evening in another of Dennis Brigg's special hotels.

Dennis really was an expert at finding these. One year, we went to Florence and stayed at the Michel Angelo; another year we went to Venice and the Hotel Monaco Grancanal; then to the Ciragan at Istanbul, the Gran Bretagne in Athens and the De la Ville in Rome. Each was excellent and made the centre point of a comfortable stay. Generally these were three- or four-day trips. We would arrive in these cities, tour them furiously, with or without a guide but always with a guidebook, and visit the best restaurants and theatres we could find. Then after shopping (the price I had to pay for my sightseeing), we would return to Ferngill. For several years, we fitted these breaks in by sending the children to school after the Easter holidays, flying off for a week, and returning to take them out of school for the weekend, before having a tearful farewell and going back to Ecuador. And this leads on to the trauma of boarding school days.

SCHOOLDAYS

In 1987, Nick was eleven years old and at the Inter American school in Guayaquil. He had passed an exam to gain admission to Malsis preparatory school near Keighley in Yorkshire, with the idea that he should progress from there to Sedbergh after taking the common entrance exam at thirteen. We had all gone back to Ferngill as a family in July but by mid-August Ceci had to return to Guayaquil with the girls as the Inter American school began its year. Nick and I were left together after going with the others to Amsterdam to see them off on the KLM flight to Guayaquil. We had a month before he started school so we used the time to buy his uniform from Rawcliffe's in Bradford and Margaret Weatherill sewed on the name tapes. Then we went down to ICI in Haslemere together and, while Jeff Pullen and I talked business, Sally kindly took Nick to see places of interest.

Then he and I went up to London to see my dear old Uncle Stuart who I had only once visited in all the years since I had stayed with him as a boy of Nick's age at Manor Farm, Rockbourne. He now lived at Harley Gardens and was eighty-one. He received us very well and insisted on cooking us a lunch, which we ate in the kitchen, he wearing his typical blue and white striped butcher's apron while he cooked, exactly as he had done thirty years previously. He told Nick stories of when I was a boy of his age and referred to me as 'little lad from up-dale', who had been sent out to shoot pigeons each day. Uncle Stuart had always been pedantic and was fond of declaiming. I remember him saying: 'If I am spared, I will be eighty-two come Michaelmas.' He liked the sound of it and repeated it several times. Sadly, he was not spared and died suddenly later that year. He had always been our 'bachelor' uncle but, as we found out afterwards, he had married Bobby, the widow of a general, with whom he had been great friends for many years.

Time was now beginning to hang heavy for Nick and I, as the first day of school drew nearer. I tried to cheer him up by taking him shooting rabbits with .22 rifles, which we both enjoyed, but even this eventually lost its appeal and he would grow very quiet. The dreaded day arrived on the 17th September. We drove off from home, Nick with his trunk and tuck box, having said goodbye to Doug and Margaret. It is an hour and a quarter's drive and the silence was oppressive before we were halfway there. My cheerful 'You'll enjoy the rugby' or 'Only six weeks until we see you at half-term' did not have the desired effect. We had visited the school with Ceci at the end of the previous term and met John Clark, the headmaster. Nick had been shown around by two other boys and left them with a cheery 'See you next term.' But that seemed an age away. Now it was for real.

Together with dozens of other parents, I helped Nick to lug his trunk up the stairs and put his tuck box in the right place. Then John Clark summoned another lad to show Nick where tea was being served. He whispered to me: 'I think you should just say a quick goodbye and leave while he is busy.' Nick seemed quite composed so I gave him a quick embrace...and burst into tears! It was not at all the thing for a father to be sobbing like a baby. Nick looked somewhat nonplussed as John Clark led me away crying to my car. What an example! I managed to drive halfway home before stopping at a pub and downing some medicinal whisky, which gave me sustenance to carry on. The road across the moors from Kettlewell to Coverdale is quite narrow and, pulling over to avoid an oncoming caravan, I put a wheel in the ditch and could not get out again. I was supposed to be flying back to Ecuador that night and here I was, stuck on the lonely moor. But Lady Luck, in the guise of Keith Houlston who was working at Tupgill as a contractor, happened by and kindly pulled me out.

We returned to England for the half term and took Nick out. This ended on the fifth of November and we attended a fireworks party at the school. When Nick was safely back among friends, we quietly left.

On the whole, Nick enjoyed his time at Malsis especially in the second year, when he was a senior and in the rugby team. But there were still moments of crisis. The worst part of the school year must be the spring term with its long nights and cold weather. Nick had been out to Ecuador for Christmas and we had put him on the KLM flight for Amsterdam and from there to Leeds as an unaccompanied minor with his tickets in a pouch around his neck. He had a couple of hours to wait for the connection in Amsterdam and found a telephone. However, although it was eight o'clock in the morning in Holland, it was two o'clock in Ecuador. Ceci answered to hear Nick say: 'I miss you, Mummy, and I want to come home.' This must rank as one of the worst moments of our marriage as she accused me of heartlessness, of wilful cruelty, of hating my own children, and of being stupidly British in wanting to send Nick away to school when all her friends and any self-respecting parent said that it was wrong, and so on. Luckily, we called the school later that day. Nick had by now totally cheered up said that he was sorry for upsetting us.

Malsis had a tradition that, at the end of the summer term, senior boys, parents and staff would camp out in a field near Settle before climbing the Three Peaks of Whernside, Pen-y-ghent and Ingleborough, a gruelling twenty-eight mile hike. Nick had phoned to say that all the fathers of his friends were going to do it so I could not let him down. This was May 1988 and the event was in early July. I was not given to indulging in sport of any kind, my only exercise being riding around Mapan at the weekends and the occasional walk with the dogs on a Saturday evening. If I were to enter the Three Peaks walk, I had to do something to improve my fitness. So I bought one of those gadgets that you put in your pocket and which records the distance you walk. Then I made an effort to walk more at Mapan and, having arrived in England a week before the event, carried on my training until I imagined that I was quite fit.

The great day arrived and, as I could not persuade Ceci to come the to the camp, never mind the hike, I set off alone for Malsis, picked up Nick and drove to the camp site. There we met up with Jane Gower and her two sons, James and Matthew, and pitched our tents together. We had met Jane and Peter Gower the previous summer, before Nick started at Malsis. We had asked John Clark whether any other parent lived near us so that we could make contact and Nick would know someone before starting school. He said that, by great coincidence, the Gowers had a house at the pretty village of Scrafton in Coverdale, which is only two miles away from Ferngill. We telephoned them, met and both adults and children have been good friends ever since. Peter was an executive with Shell and the family had moved around the world but had bought and renovated a cottage in Scrafton to have a home and holiday base in the Dales. All the Gowers enjoyed the outdoors and long-distance walking was a regular feature of their lives so the prospect of the Three Peaks challenge did not overwhelm them. Peter was away at this time so Jane came with the boys.

As neither she nor I knew the other parents, we were somewhat left out of their jollifications as they appeared to be whooping it up with wine and drinks on the eve of the struggle. I had great admiration for their apparent stamina as they seemed rather well fed and portly to be seasoned hikers. Breakfast was to be cooked by John Clark at five o'clock and then we were free to break camp, drive to the Three Peaks Cafe in Ribblesdale and, leaving the cars in the car park, go round the course at our own speed. The average time for completing it was eight hours, which would bring us back to the starting point for a mug of tea. Lunch was to be provided at a spot between Pen-y-ghent and Ingleborough.

It proved to be a fine night and the following morning we were among the first away. The day was overcast and it looked as if it might rain so (having become acclimatised to the tropics over the years and thinking it might be cold up there), I put on plenty of clothes and took my walking stick with me. Within minutes of the start, it became apparent that I was going to be a dead weight for the group. Jane was fit, the three boys were fit, I was by no means so. 'Please do go on,' I said. After a polite 'No, no, we'll wait for you' we agreed that Jane and the boys should go on ahead. Nick, who would have liked to continue with them, loyally stayed with Dad. I had climbed many a Lake District mountain while at Huyton Hill but forty years had passed without my trying it again. I had forgotten the effort needed to climb scree runs, the aching knees on almost vertical paths, the wet feet splashing through bogs. My outfit was totally wrong. Far too much clothing was slowly discarded and hung around the waist, the stick was just something more to carry. My boots were flat-soled and no help in gripping the track.

Alex, Diana and Nick plus Charlie – Christmas 1990.

We toiled up Whernside and down again, then tackled the long walk past the Ribblehead Viaduct and up Pen-y-ghent. Boys were racing past us all the while and the Gowers were miles away ahead. But the mystery was the whereabouts of the other fathers, the carousers of the night before? All was revealed at the first checkpoint. There they were, standing by their Volvos, handing out tea, lemonade and chocolate. 'Come on, you're awfully slow', 'You've done nothing yet', 'The worst is still to come' and other cheerful phrases were cast at us!

I was exhausted. Nick and I came down Pen-y-ghent towards the lunch stop and I said to him: 'Well, I've tried but I can't go on. I'm going to opt out after lunch. You can go on with the other boys.' Sore of foot, knee, hip and shoulder and badly winded, I limped into the lunch area and collapsed. We had lunch and I was negotiating a lift back with one of the other (sensible) fathers when a group of boys came over to me. 'Sir, are you going on to Ingleborough? The headmaster says we can't climb it without an adult because it's clouding over. And you are the only adult left.'

Moral pressure indeed, and Nick was looking at me expectantly too. 'Yes, I'm going on' I said. With that, the boys ran off towards the mountain and we did not see them again until we reached the cafe at the end of the day. I fail to see what use I was as an escort but perhaps, being last, I could have picked up any casualties. However, I was clearly the main casualty. Going up and down Ingleborough was a nightmare, the final stretch being across limestone pavements. These are said to be in danger of being destroyed by walkers. The sooner, the better for me — these pavements conspire to twist the ankles of the tired. And boy, was I tired! We made it to the Three Peaks Cafe in a not exactly record-breaking nine and a half hours. Mugs of tea and ham, eggs and chips cheered us up and I drove Nick and some friends back to school for the last few days of term. Then, with eyes like slits, I drove home and lay in a bath of hot water for hours. After this, to Ceci's great amusement, my knees would not even support me.

I vowed never to attempt such a thing again. But stupidly I did so the following year, taking both Nick and Diana. This time, I was at least better kitted out in shorts and trainers. I went on the understanding that, as soon as Diana was tired, and she was only ten years old, we would opt out. The little wretch did not tire and, once again, we finished the course in nine and a half hours!

Diana's school career in England began the following year when she started at St Anne's in Windermere. We had selected this school through recommendations and after visiting it and Casterton near Kirkby Lonsdale. St Anne's had the more pleasant atmosphere of the two and the then headmaster, Michael Hawkins, really impressed us with his approach to the education and wellbeing of the girls.

Poor Diana was once again let down by her parents. Having been abandoned for her first Christmas and left in Ecuador while Ceci, Nick and I went to

Ferngill, she was now left to start school alone as HRH The Princess Royal was visiting Guayaquil and I had to be present as consul. In fact, she was not quite alone as Ana Zelia, the daughter of the Portuguese consul in Guayaquil, was to go to St Anne's as a sixth form pupil. So she stayed with us and the two went to school together after I had left.

Later Alex followed suit and has just left after taking her A-levels. All three of our children have turned out to be athletic. Nick was in Sedbergh's first rugby team, and Diana and Alex played tennis and hockey and won many track events for the school, also competing in county events. Alex became the school sports captain. They must have inherited their sporting abilities from Ceci who is an excellent squash player and Father was squash champion at Rossall and played rugby for Westmorland, so it may have come from him too.

ECUADOR 1986-90

MY PARENTS STARTED the Ferngill guest book when they began their married life there in 1939. Ceci and I have kept up the tradition of asking guests who have spent at least one night there to sign it. In 1986, Peter and Cathy Shane stayed with us. Both Americans, they had met and married in Ecuador.

Peter had played a large part in beginning Ecuador's modern shrimp farming business. He had first worked in fish farming in Chile and then come to Ecuador, setting up the first shrimp larva hatchery with technical advice from French experts. Ecuador had traditionally fished for shrimp in the sea then, when the supply proved insufficient, shrimp farming began by bulldozing areas adjacent to the coast and forming ponds surrounded with earth dykes several metres high. Sea or brackish water would be pumped into these and the shrimp larvae caught in nets on the seashore would be seeded into the ponds. These were then fed balanced diets and the water was fertilised to promote the growth of algae and provide food for the shrimps. After three months, they would be harvested by draining the ponds (at night, when the shrimps are at the surface) through large, hooped nets placed at the water outlets.

This system worked well until there was a shortage of shrimp larvae caught at sea or by the shore. The next step was to set up hatcheries. A gravid (pregnant) mother shrimp can lay up to 200,000 eggs at a time. This is nature's way of ensuring that some survive because a huge percentage of these eggs are eaten by fish in the sea. If the gravid shrimp can be induced to lay her eggs in the protected environment of a hatchery, a very much higher percentage survives and can be sold to shrimp farmers. Today, this technique is well known but this was not the case when Peter introduced it in the 1970s.

By this time, Peter had sold up in Ecuador and was living in Aberdeen from where he traded in fish around the world. Cathy was his second wife and we had become good friends with them both in Ecuador. Now we invited them to stay with us for a couple of days and we went to Ripon races together. Over dinner one evening, we talked of beach houses in Ecuador.

Ceci and I had rented several houses or flats over the years for the beach season, which runs from January to April and coincides with the rainy season when the warm Niño current pushes out the cold Humboldt current and the sea temperature can reach 28°C (compared to, say, 23°C the rest of the year). Peter said that he had not yet sold his beach house at Punta Blanca and asked if we would like to buy it. Yes, we would, as we knew it well. It stood right on the beach and was built of adobe, with huge windows overlooking the sea and a red pantiled roof. We negotiated a price over port and Ceci and I returned to Ecuador very pleased with our deal. But it was not to be. Peter had left power of attorney with a lawyer in Guayaquil and the house, unbeknown to him, had already changed hands. We were not in a position to dispute this so unfortunately we had to think again. We tried to buy a house on the same beach once more but were gazumped.

Then we were lucky at the third attempt. We found a piece of land for sale on the beach not far from Peter's house, contacted the owner, Carlos Francisco Calderon, and bought it. Carlos Francisco is an architect and he offered to build us a house in six months. We agreed the plans and at the end of the said time, it was at least habitable, if not totally finished. Under Ecuadorian law, foreigners are not allowed to own land within a certain distance of the frontier and that includes the seashore. This was not a problem as the house was put in Ceci's name and is, indeed, really hers. She loves the seaside and while I accompany her on alternate weekends, spending the other at Mapan, she always goes, season or no season. We subsequently bought another plot of land behind it and joined the two together in a walled garden. Peter Carlstrom (Sueco), our Swedish friend, built a barbecue and it is a most delightful place where one can escape from Guayaquil. I joke that it is the only one of our four houses where I do not have to work. It is not mine; I do even garden; I am a guest there. We have had many family parties, with the children loving the beach (sadly to the exclusion of the farm) and many new year parties with open-air celebrations and fireworks. Long may it continue.

That was a happy event for 1986: another was much less pleasant. In 1987, Don Louis and I were on bad terms. He had sold out of Agripac and eventually of Mapan, which I had bought from him totally in 1984, with so much cash down and the balance in quarterly payments over three years. He waited until he had collected them all and then he attacked. I was in Ferngill in July of that year when I received a phone call from Michael Atkinson, the British ambassador in Ecuador. 'Colin, I think you should know that I have received a copy of the newspaper *El Clarin* of Babahoyo, which carries an article 'Consul Honorario esta involucrado en delito de abigeato'.' (honorary consul involved in cattle rustling).

The story went on to say that, according to Don Louis de Reiset, a large farmer and French aristocrat well known in the area, Carlos Rizzo and cowboys working for Colin Armstrong had confessed to the police that they were instructed by the said CA to take and castrate two valuable bulls belonging to Count Reiset. These bulls had subsequently disappeared and it is presumed that Colin Armstrong had stolen them. In fact, the reporter went on, perhaps this dreadful man is behind all sorts of cattle stealing in the province. For good measure, he stated that, according to unnamed witnesses, this honorary consul had offended the dignity of the law of Ecuador. He had said that, as consul, he was above the law and could not be brought to book, even if he were accused. Ecuadorian judges had their price and he could easily buy them off. The article concluded by calling for this disreputable foreigner to be punished and then expelled from the country. It was distributed to every member of the consular corps in Guayaquil.

What should I do? Should I cut our holiday short and rush back to Guayaquil to deal with the matter? I had been in Ferngill for only a week or so and I was loath to leave again so soon. I called Alfredo Ledesma for his advice. He offered to investigate, find out which reporter had submitted the article and then help me to compose a reply through the same newspaper. 'Meanwhile', he said 'enjoy your holiday. The whole matter may die down.'

I composed my reply and this was published in the *El Clarin* on the 28th July. It said that Don Louis and I had been partners in Mapan at the supposed time of the crime; that he had waited three years before making the allegations, during which time I had bought and paid for his share of Mapan; and that I had never insulted the Ecuadorian legal system, and so on. I had hoped that the matter would die down but I had hugely underestimated the tenacity of Don Louis.

He had planned his attack carefully. As soon as I had left for England, he had had Carlos Rizzo and three cowboys picked up by the police and taken to the Babahoyo police station. Here, they had been made to make a statement to the effect that I had ordered them to castrate two bulls and, furthermore, to move a fence that he had erected on a disputed part of the border between Mapan and Guarumal. This was the truth as far as it went, but then Don Louis's lawyer embellished the tale by converting the scrub bulls to highly valued pedigree stock. They had found out that the castrating of bulls could be considered only as a civil crime. The bulls were made to disappear so that it became a penal matter. Why anyone would want to first castrate and then steal bulls was never explained but, as I have mentioned before, the written word carries tremendous weight in Ecuador.

So, clutching this scrap of evidence together with the *El Clarin* article (to prove the genuine outrage of the population) Don Louis's lawyer filed a complaint against me in the Babahoyo penal court and I became the defendant in a trial which lasted some three years. Ecuadorian justice is conducted mainly by written disposition and is a very drawn-out affair. The judge receives the demand and notifies the defendant in writing three times. On the third occasion, a date is set to visit the court and make a statement. This is followed by both sides submitting evidence in writing until that period closes and the fiscal, or state prosecutor, decides whether the state has a case. If it does, this weighs heavily with the judge; if not, the case is more open. Finally, the judge makes his decision. The losing side immediately appeals to the higher regional court and if this is lost, it can appeal on a technicality to the Supreme Court in Quito. Hence cases can go on forever. However, there are tricks to every trade and in this case, it is to have the defendant jailed on remand.

This, of course, is punishment before the verdict and Don Louis would use this weapon indiscriminately against people whom he accused, rightly or wrongly, of stealing his cattle. If they were penniless cowboys, he would inevitably get away with it. He tried the same tactics on me and with each disposition to the court, he would ask for my immediate arrest as a dangerous man to be at large. This kept me in a state of nerves, as it was quite possible that the judge might be persuaded to agree and I might have been arrested at any time — not a pleasant prospect.

Alfredo had put together a defence team of Dr Edmundo Duran Diaz, a very well-known lawyer, and Ab Jose Vicente del Pozo, a man of many contacts. He would do the footwork as the case moved first in the Babahoyo and later in the Vinces courts, both at some distance from Guayaquil. The courts had to be checked frequently for any movement of the opposition so that it could be countered. Another trick was to ask the judge for some disposition which had be filed within three days and then make sure that the notification was delayed until after the closing date, so the defendant was in contempt of court and lost the point.

Don Louis started with all the advantages. He was a well-known personality in the area. Because of previous demands against supposed rustlers, he knew the judges and police. He had never lost a case and, because he lived in Guarumal, he was closer to the courts than I was.

We began our defence by asking why it had taken him three years to complain about the castrated animals when everyone on Mapan knew that he had been furious about it the day after the event. We also asked him to demonstrate which breed of pedigree bulls they were supposed to be and where they had been bought. He huffed and blustered but gradually we were winning the day. Then, by sheer chance, rustlers really did break into Guarumal and a butchered cow was discovered. This was what he needed and he opened a second front by denouncing Carlos Rizzo and Colin Armstrong as the possible culprits, because it was plain to see that this was the sort of thing they got up to! A second penal case was opened and, once again, he called for my arrest. There were two cases against me. I was beginning to feel hunted. In fact, I was furious at the injustice of it and at the time wasted in attending to the defence of two cases instead of concentrating on Agripac — not to mention the expense of legal fees and costs.

I said to Edmundo Duran 'I am going to hit back the same way. What can I get him for?' He replied that first we had to win the case against us up to the final instances. Then, if the superior court ruled that it was a case of malicious and unfounded allegations, I could sue Don Louis civilly for a large amount of damages and penally for false accusation. This was what I looked forward to doing but I had to wait three years for a verdict. Meanwhile, Don Louis made sure that Guayaquil society was aware of his accusations. Luckily, over the previous fifteen years, I too had made many social contacts especially as I had been consul for six years. In fact, Don Louis was widely regarded as being somewhat eccentric and his complaints fell on deaf ears.

The great day came when the first case was decided in my favour at the superior court and the accusation was ruled to be wilful and malicious. At once, we filed our cases against him, claiming $3,000,000 in damages as well as the penal case. There was no defence left to him as, with the court's ruling, the case was cut and dried. He immediately changed the ownership of Guarumal to a paper company, supposedly owned by lawyers, to avoid my claiming it. As the penal case drew to a close with the judge about to order his arrest, he made one last attempt at avoiding the outcome. He contacted me through a mutual friend and invited me to meet him at the Union Club, for which he had sponsored me for membership in happier times.

At the meeting, he said that perhaps it had all been a mistake; that we had both been badly advised; and that we should let bygones be bygones. But I was in no mood to accept this and said that the whole business had taken years off my life and cost me a fortune. However, I would drop my cases against him if he would pay my legal costs and publish an apology in *El Clarin*. He was not prepared to accept these conditions. He said that he too had spent a great deal; that we should each pay our own costs; and someone of his standing would never be jailed in Ecuador. 'That we shall see,' I said and we parted.

I had my arrest warrant within a couple of days. But by that time, he had flown to Mexico where his son, Philippe, owns a hotel in Morelia. He stayed there for some two years until the case against him had expired under Ecuadorian law and he could safely return.

We never met again although I saw him in the streets of Guayaquil once or twice. He occasionally went to Guarumal although his grandsons, Henri and Nicholas, were running it now. As they were interested only in banana production, Philippe sold off large parts of it that were unsuited to bananas including, strangely enough, a further 500 hectares to myself for cattle raising. Sadly, Don Louis's lovely, wooden farmhouse burned down at this time, together with all his pictures, furniture and memorabilia. The old man died shortly afterwards and I felt very sorry as, for good or bad, he had played a large part in my story. Ceci was heartbroken that she never had been able to make up with him after everything he had done for her as a young girl — giving her a home, paying for her education and indirectly causing us to meet. He died while we were in England so we did not even have a chance to attend the funeral.

This was a busy period for consular activity. We had had our first British prisoner, John L. He had turned up in Guayaquil and stayed in a small hotel for some weeks, at first paying the bill. Later, with promises to the hotel owner that he was just about to receive an overseas cheque, he obtained credit until finally the owner's patience ran out and he had John thrown in prison for fraud. We had not heard of him until he called for his consul and I went to the prison to visit him.

The Penitenciaria of Guayaquil stands some ten miles out of town on the Daule road, just past our Celtec warehouses. It covers acres of ground and consists of huge courtyards with high walls and guard towers. In the centre of the complex are the prison blocks and staff offices and quarters. Although the complex is dirty, dusty and unpainted, there is a certain liberality to it. The prisoners are locked in their respective pavilions at night but can wander about inside, cook their food, play cards or read. During the daylight hours, apart from the regular roll calls, they wander about the outside courts and play football. It is an easy-going system and bearable — but only if you have money. Everything except the most basic food has to be paid for. On visiting days, relatives bring food and whatever cash they can for their prisoners. The wealthy ones, which include drug traffickers and gangsters, have access to mobile phones, colour televisions, drink and even prostitutes. The poor stay alive, but only just.

According to the consular rules, I should visit British prisoners at least once a quarter. But, as John had no cash (and especially because he was my first prisoner), I would visit him every two or three weeks and take him newspapers, books and cash. This went on for six months or so and it seemed as though John would be there forever. He had been accused but was only on remand. The trial was not progressing at all. The hotel owner calculated, correctly as it turned out, that sooner or later relatives or friends would cough up what John owed to have him released. But it appeared that John had cut himself off from family and friends and wanted us to contact no one. Eventually, with Christmas approaching, the lads at the Phoenix Club had a whip-round and a delegation proposed to the hotel owner that he accept fifty per cent and drop the charges. He finally did so and we freed John. After a welcome-back-to-life party at the Phoenix, he left the country for Peru. He was a strange character when he first went to prison but even stranger when he emerged, seeing the hand of Jesus Christ or the CIA behind everyday events.

We thought that we had seen the last of him but there was a sequel to the story. Some two years later, he appeared in the Phoenix Club with several rather thuggish Americans. He said that he had a good job now. We crowded around to congratulate him. 'Yes', he said, 'We are a team which repossesses ships that have not been fully paid for.' 'How?' we asked. 'Well, we swim up to the ship in the harbour at night, throw the crew overboard and take the ship out.' It sounded like piracy to me. Luckily, his assignment was in Peru so now, for all we know, he is decorating the inside of a Peruvian gaol.

A law has recently been passed in Ecuador whereby, if a remand prisoner has not been convicted within one year, he goes free. I think this is an excellent law because, as in the Bastille before the French Revolution, it used to be quite possible to have poor people shut up for years and never finish the trial. Last year, hundreds of people were released, some of whom had been inside for five years or more. More recently, several Commonwealth and two British prisoners accused of drug trafficking have been released under the new legislation. It has not been proven whether they were guilty or not so they are free. This is an incentive to state prosecutors or private accusers to provide the evidence and obtain a court sentence in less than a year. To facilitate this, there is a move to change from written statements to verbal hearings and thereby speed up the law. This has to be a good thing — I speak from experience.

That year, we had a series of consular guests, who occupied a greater or lesser amount of our time but all of whose visits we enjoyed. The largest group was naval. *HMS Liverpool* (a destroyer) and *Hermione* (a frigate) came to Guayaquil for three days and, together with the military attaché at the British embassy, Group Captain Tony Salter, Roci and I organised the visit.

There were protocol visits by the captain of *HMS Liverpool*, Mike Bracelin, and Commander P W Herington to the governor and mayor; football matches and receptions organised by the Ecuadorian navy. The Phoenix Club, as always for these events, arranged a party for fifty officers and men and recruited fifty ladies to entertain them. The logistics of overseeing a ship's visit included arranging fuel and supplies, local currency (and the changing back of any left over), mail delivery, reception and the organisation of tours to Salinas, Quito or Cuenca. In return, there were cocktail parties and lunches on board which we always enjoyed.

The arrival of the ships was a poignant moment for me as I stood on the dockside with the ambassador, Michael Atkinson, Tony Salter, the port captain and other local officials. Guayaquil port is approached by two channels with an island in the centre. The first we would see of the ships were the superstructures with the white ensigns flying. Then the salute started, with the ships firing twenty-one guns. This was loud but bearable at a distance. What I had not foreseen was the reply from the Ecuadorian navy and its guns, which were positioned just ten yards from us. As I was standing to attention looking quite the part in a white suit and Panama hat, there was no way that I could put my hands over my ears. So I stood it out and was deaf all day!

The ships rounded the island with the sailors lined along the decks and came alongside with wonderful precision. Then the gangplanks were set down and Mike Bracelin came ashore and invited the local authorities aboard. While the ambassador, military attache, port captain and others went to the captain's cabin, I went off with the relevant officer to sort out mundane details regarding cash and mail.

The media were then welcomed aboard and a press conference was held to attract favourable publicity for the visit. It was announced that the ships would be open to the public at certain times, that there would be sporting events with the Ecuadorian navy, and that the crew would entertain thirty children from a Guayaquil orphanage for a tea party.

There were both golfers and squash players aboard and we arranged for them to use the local clubs. We even managed to supply twenty-five girls, whom the chief petty officers had invited on board for their party.

Michael Atkinson held a lunch at a Guayaquil hotel for the captains, officers and local dignitaries, which included the police chief of Guayaquil. We wanted his support, as with over 500 sailors loose on the town, we needed sympathetic treatment from the police. As it turned out, there were no arrests or serious trouble and a good time was had by all.

A delightful visit over and — hopefully — all men back on board, the ships prepared to leave. This was much less formal with just Tony and myself present, except, of course, for the minibuses of girls who had reached the dockside and waved their sad goodbyes to the sailors despite port security.

We had fairly frequent naval visits as the ships would come off Falklands patrol and return via Valparaiso in Chile and Guayaquil, before crossing the Panama Canal, calling at Charleston and sailing home to Portsmouth.

Following *HMS Liverpool* and *Hermione*, we had visits by the frigates *HMS York, Campbeltown, Scylla, Montrose* and *Lancaster*. Each visit was memorable but perhaps the most fun was that of the *Montrose* in May 1996, whose captain was Niall Kilgour, a tremendous character. The ship was a showroom for naval electronic equipment and, to reinforce the campaign, the Ministry of Defence sent out Rear Admiral J F T G (Sam) Salt, CB. Sam had been the captain of *HMS Sheffield*, which was sunk in the Falklands War. He is a most vigorous person and, having completed an arduous day of meetings and visits, he had no hesitation in accepting our offer of dinner that night. This was a lively affair attended by Niall Kilgour and several of his officers, Captain Keith Ridland,

The H.M.S. *Montrose* visit. 2 June 1996.

the defence attache, Ceci and I with a few others in Enrico's, the best Italian restaurant in Guayaquil. When dinner was coming to a close some time after midnight, Gina Schniedwind, a good friend of ours, came over to the table. She said that there was a great party in a friend's house just around the corner and invited us all to come. Sam said 'Let's party' and, rather than wait for the others to move and let him out (as he was in the corner seat), he walked across the table and led us to the door. Where the admiral goes, the navy goes too so we all set off.

The party was in full swing when we arrived and it was past four o'clock when Ceci and I sneaked away, leaving the others to continue. The next morning, we had duties to perform and we looked a sorry crew. I had to collect the mail for the ship from the KLM flight, which arrived at 6.30am. The bag arrived but the customs officials would not release it until, after three hours nursing my hangover, I finally contacted an officer who accepted that, as it was going straight to the ship and so leaving the country again, it could be released.

Niall was to go to Mapan with Chris Bailey but, as I heard later, he was so under the weather that the journey there was full of pit stops. After riding and lunch, he regained his spirits and when we all met up again the next evening both he and Sam were back on good form.

The *Montrose* also had some twenty female officers and crew, the first time I had come across this in her majesty's ships. Everyone appeared to work well together and perhaps the ship was happier for it, although there were strict rules about fraternising aboard ship. It was with genuine regret that we waved them goodbye. Come back any time, *Montrose*.

Other visitors included David Mellor MP, then Home Office minister, Tim Eggar MP and John Selwyn Gummer MP, then minister of state for agriculture. The latter stayed overnight in Mapan. Michael Atkinson, who was then ambassador, called me to say that on the 9th January, 1988, John Gummer would be touring Ecuador and asked us to bring him to Mapan for the night. Certainly, I said. So Ceci and I prepared the house, mowed the lawn, put lots of flowers everywhere and stood by to receive this important personage. He arrived in the late afternoon in a convoy of three Range Rovers with his secretary, Tony Bastia, and Michael Atkinson. The rest of the crew were drivers and policemen.

We welcomed them and, as they were in suits, suggested that they might like to have a bath and change before drinks and dinner. This was January and the beginning of the hot and wet season. The temperature was some 27°C inside the house and the humidity nearly ninety per cent as the clouds gathered for the promised downpour. We have air-conditioning in the bedrooms but not in the high-roofed, airy remainder of the house.

We were not at all sure if protocol demanded that I wear a suit or whether we could get away with shirtsleeves. It was much easier for Ceci as a dress can be as light as you want it to be. I put on my suit, rather hoping my distinguished guests would ask for informality, but not a bit of it. They appeared in suits and ties. Not only was the attire formal, but neither of them appeared to be able to relax at all, even to the extent of using first names — except mine. So we sat having our drinks with the conversations running along the following lines: 'How are you enjoying Ecuador, Minister?' 'Very much, Colin.' 'Which way did you drive down from the Sierra, Ambassador?' 'By the Riobamba route, Colin.' It was clearly going to be a riot with this pair of stuffed shirts! Worse was to follow — the storm broke and it rained furiously, then the electricity was cut off and so the fans stopped working. We opened the French windows on to the verandah and clouds of insects flew in. But the minister and the ambassador did not flinch. In true diplomatic style, they were not going to give in to adversity so they sat and sweated in coat and tie. Tony was somewhat more human and showed genuine distress as the flying bugs landed on his plate. Ceci was very upset as her carefully prepared dinner party was spoilt but I was very relieved when a fairly stressful evening ended.

The next day was better as we put everyone on horseback to see the cattle. Even our guests could not wear suits on horseback and with the suits went a certain degree of formality. There were even jokes and some polite hilarity as John Gummer was helped on to his horse and almost went over the other side. We had brought the buffaloes into a nearby field and these caused great excitement with Tony, who bore the video camera, insisting on dismounting his horse to film them. He very soon scrambled back on again as the buffaloes began to take an interest in him. By lunch time, we were all in a better frame of mind but I cannot say I heard a 'Call me John' at all. After a good lunch and a couple of beers, they were ready to leave. The cars, drivers and police escort had reappeared and Tony was carrying down the ministerial bags, which he placed beside the car to be counted before being put aboard. Jazz, our beagle of the time, wandered by and lifted his leg to the minister's portfolio. Perhaps it was a symbolic act of disdain but I could not let it go by, so I rushed along with my handkerchief and dried it off, hoping that no one had noticed. To be fair, we did receive a very courteous note on House of Commons paper thanking us for the hospitality.

Jazz was our third beagle. Snoopy had died but we still had Lafite (Fitty). Then we bought Jazz after a trip to New Orleans but he was with us for only about two years. At Easter 1988, we were down on the beach in Ceci's house, now named the Mena House after the Giza hotel. The gas cylinder was empty and, to finish cooking dinner, I was instructed to drive to the village of San Pablo and buy some more. It was dark and Jazz must have followed me as he loved travelling in cars and I would stop and pick him up. But I did not see him and when I got back, no one could say where he was. We spent not only that night but all of the Easter weekend looking for him but he was never seen again. We supposed someone had picked him up off the road and kept him. We advertised in the press, offered a reward, followed up dozens of false leads but heard nothing. It was a great loss as we were very fond of him.

When we finally gave up the search, we were all very depressed. So I faxed Elaine and, as a surprise for everyone, asked her to find a beagle dog puppy which we could bring back with us from England that summer. Thus Charlie came into our lives. Elaine appeared with him one day and we all fell in love with this gorgeous puppy, all paws and ears and with a wonderful appetite and an endless capacity to pee! Amarilis went to England with us that year and the duties of feeding and mopping up after Charlie fell to her. She did this with good grace and the two bonded immediately. Diana, then ten years old, fancied herself as an animal trainer and would encourage Charlie to launch himself off tables into her arms or on to cushions. We later learned that we should not have put this sort of stress on to a puppy's legs but Charlie survived.

As Ceci and the girls had already gone back to Ecuador while I waited to take Nick to Malsis, and Charlie still needed injections and certificates, he travelled back to Ecuador with me. We flew from Newcastle to Amsterdam and I have never before or since been at the centre of so much female adulation as every hostess there ever was crowded around his flying cage in Newcastle airport. He could not travel in the cabin with me but had to go into a pressurised hold with the other pets. I heard him barking as he was transferred to the Guayaquil KLM flight in Amsterdam but could not obtain access to him. In Caracas, however, we had an hour's stop-over and I was allowed to walk him on the tarmac. Finally, we reached Guayaquil and, armed with many pieces of paper, I was fully prepared for officialdom as Jazz had been held up for hours in customs. But this time I was smarter; I took him out of the travelling box and walked him on a lead through customs and no one asked for the papers.

So Charlie came to Ecuador and has been the centre of family life for the last twelve years. The children are now grown up but still send their love to Charlie when they ring, fax or email. He is growing old now and the once dark black-and-tan coat is turning greyer. He can no longer follow me around the farm behind the horse and, indeed, lags somewhat when I walk him around it. But his appetite is still there and he is the biggest thief of food in the canine world. He has been known to pull tablecloths until the food falls off the table. The family rule is that if you stand up from the table, you should push your chair in or Charlie will bound up and scoff everything. He will eat until he cannot stand and then lies helplessly with a belly like a football. But that is Charlie and we love him.

This period was a very active one for Agripac. When Don Louis had withdrawn from the presidency after selling his shares, I assumed that position and Mario Ramos, who had been administrative manager, would now become general manager. Giles Harrison was sales manager; Victor Hugo Quimi (who had obtained his PhD in London) was technical manager; and we had recently recruited Chris Bailey, an Englishman who was married to Marna, an Ecuadorian lady, to administer imports while Johnny Coloma managed the credit department. However, all was not well with our team. Giles had been with the company for eleven years and, although very competent, his forceful personality led to increasing conflict with Mario. This came to a head when Mario discovered that Giles had invested in an outside company that had potential conflicts of interest with Agripac. I unwillingly had to ask for Giles's resignation. He had contributed a very great deal towards the success of Agripac and I hope that I was fair in his pay-off settlement. However, he bore a grudge and I did not talk to him again after he left the company.

Only three months later, he suffered a stroke, which has left him seriously handicapped. He returned to England and is now in sheltered housing near Oxford, where his mother lives. His wife Lilly, who is Peruvian, stayed on in Guayaquil and, with Giles's brother Nicholas, runs the British Garage, a car repair shop which is very well thought of. Their two children, Romily and Nicolette, are now at university, which is a great credit to Lilly. Poor Giles — he was a man of huge talent and energy, fluent in three languages and a workaholic, but he was overweight, smoked three packs a day and drank endless cups of coffee. His body finally could not take the strain.

With Giles gone, Victor Hugo Quimi took on the sales management and Jaime Aragundi the technical management. There was a financial crisis (as there is today) when a fifty-kilometre length of the oil pipeline, which runs from the Amazon over the mountains and down to the port of Esmeraldas, was broken by an earthquake. This interrupted the flow of oil for six months and with it seventy per cent of the country's export revenue. The sucre, which stood at 200 to the dollar in September 1987, had reached 400 by March of the following year. The then President of Ecuador, Leon Febres Cordero, reacted in a high-handed way and decreed that the exchange rate should be 270 sucres, not 400. Furthermore, all importers were ordered to reduce their prices at once to reflect this arbitrary level. Through the chamber of commerce we collectively refused to do this. Until foreign exchange was available to us at the government rate, we were not prepared to obey and sell at a loss. The governor of Guayas at the time was Jaime Nebot (today the Mayor of Guayaquil and twice presidential candidate). He summoned the leading businessmen of the city to a meeting to discuss the issue. They turned up and were all thrown in gaol!

Mario, as general manager of Agripac and a director of the chamber of commerce, received a summons to attend, which was brought by an official from the governor's office and four policemen. Suspecting what was about to happen, he left his office through the connecting door to mine and thence through another office to a window, where our lads had left a ladder. He climbed down to the patio and there put on an Agripac tee shirt and cap, lifted some boxes on his shoulder, took them to a truck parked on the road outside and was away. Meanwhile, policemen were standing outside his office and mine while the officials set off to obtain a search warrant. I had called Alfredo Ledesma. When he arrived and after some debate, he said that I should leave too as, if they could not arrest the general manager, they would go for the president of the company, even though I was also the British consul. I therefore walked out past the policemen and worked from different parts of the city for the next two weeks, going to my office only after dark. The precautions were wise as I later heard that Nebot had said: 'Consul or not, arrest him.'

But the affair blew over shortly afterwards as the Central Bank began to issue dollars at the official rate and we, in turn, lowered our prices. However, it had been a nasty moment. I obtained a small revenge some years later when Nebot was campaigning to become president of Ecuador. He sent a delegation to my office to seek a political contribution and I told the story of my near-arrest. I said that I was afraid that I could not contribute as I had already made a donation to his rival for office, Sixto Duran Ballen, who luckily won.

This time also saw the start of the shrimp products line for Agripac. The shrimp business was growing fast and, following Peter Shane's first larva hatchery, there were now perhaps thirty in operation. A product called artemia is used to feed these almost invisible shrimp larvae. Artemia consists of brine eggs, which are harvested in several parts of the world but the most important source is Great Salt Lake in Utah. These brine eggs or cysts are in suspended animation and can be packed in cans for up to several years. When they are exposed to water, they hatch and the shrimp larvae feed on these even smaller larvae. This is a natural product and, although widely used, there are circumstances when a more complete balanced diet is necessary. Dr David Jones of Bangor University perfected a micro-encapsulated diet, which was then manufactured under the Frippak brand by Thomas's, the pet food division of the Mars corporation, in its Bradford factory.

As consul, I had been visited by a Mars executive, Ram Mylvaganam, a British national of Sri Lankan origin, for advice on choosing an agency in Ecuador. During our conversation, I became interested in the possibilities of the line and suggested that Agripac form an aquaculture division. He agreed with the, by now usual, suggestion that the company send an expert to set it up. Ram suggested that I visit the Bradford factory while I was in Britain later that year, and we later took on the line.

It has been very successful for us and some twelve per cent of our sales came from this sector in 1998. Not only do we sell Frippak and Artemia to shrimp hatcheries, but we also sell other products for the 250,000 acres now dedicated to shrimp ponds up and down the Ecuadorian coast. These include fertilisers and wheat-based diets as well as medicated feeds. We have been helped tremendously by the marine biologists sent out by Mars. First Danny Fegan, then Roy Buddle contributed their expertise as the line needed a great deal of technical help in the early days. Today our own manager, Javier Lavayen, runs the line very successfully.

Ecuador's shrimp industry has been hard hit in the last two years by a virus called white spot, which has reduced production by some seventy per cent. However, it is thought that this problem will be overcome, as it has been in Thailand and Indonesia, and production should then recover to its former levels by the year 2002.

Not that the Frippak brand stayed with Thomas's for long. In the manner of large corporations, Mars decided that Frippak was not a core business for them and sold it to the French group, Sanofi. Along with the brand went my pals, Ram and Roy. Ram, however, was perhaps too successful in negotiating his contract with Sanofi when it was discovered that he was paid more than his superior. So Ram left and today runs a very successful venture capital concern from his home at Linton near Wetherby in Yorkshire. Ram is a terrific businessman who speaks five languages, including Japanese, and deserves his success.

Roy, however, stayed the course and when the Frippak line was, in turn, sold to Inve, a private Belgian company owned by Flor Indigne, he too moved with it. But there the connection was broken as, after a difference of opinion with the Inve US manager, Howard Newman, Roy left and went to the States, until recently working for Continental Grain. He then moved to Rome with Isabel, his Ecuadorian wife (whom he married while living in the country) to market wines for a Bulgarian company. Roy, Isabel and their children have now returned to live in Ecuador. We keep in touch with Roy, Ram and their families as we do with so many friends who started as business contacts and whose careers have, in many cases, taken them elsewhere in the world.

The business world is increasingly becoming a kaleidoscope as companies buy each other, merge, de-merge, create new entities or even fold. Few, if any, of those we represented in the seventies exist in the same form today. ICI became Zeneca and recently Syngenta; British Leyland tractors became Marshalls then died; Union Carbide Agrochemicals was taken over by Rhone Poulenc, which became Aventis on merging with Hoechst; Cooper Pegler Sprayers, formally of Burgess Hill, Surrey, now belongs to Hardi of Denmark. Meanwhile, Petoseed of California is now part of Seminis, the largest vegetable seed company in the world and owned by Mexican interests; Chevron Chemicals passed to the Japanese Tomen and Zeneca's seed business merged in an Anglo-Dutch company, Advanta (now, in turn, sold to Dow Elanco). A whole string of computer-generated words has become prominent in the last few years: Zeneca, Advanta, Aventis, Seminis and others in the agrochemical world like Novatis (Ciba and Sandoz) and Agrevo (Hoechst and Schering). The most recent of all is Syngenta, which is a fusion of the agrochemical interests of Novatis and Zeneca.

Before unloading its seeds interest on to Advanta, ICI (as it was then) was an aggressive buyer of seeds companies in the USA. The slogan in the eighties was 'Forget chemicals; all the added value is going to come from seeds.' This policy has, in fact, shown itself to be correct following Monsanto's terrific success with genetically modified seeds despite serious reservations in Europe.

ICI had already bought Garst Seeds and went on to purchase Continental Seeds, the seed business of Continental Grain (today part of Conagra). In Ecuador, Contisem was the local business of Continental seeds. It was very small and had no plant and equipment — only registered brands and a year or two of sales experience in Ecuador. John Greaves, who had by now taken over from John Robinson as the senior marketing manager for Latin America at ICI, contacted me to see if Agripac would like to buy Contisem from ICI. Yes, I said, and bought it for $30,000.

This was the moment when we moved into the grain seed business. We had handled Petoseed for fifteen years but it specialised in tomato and vegetable seeds, which we imported in cans from the USA and more recently from Chile as well.

There is a great difference between grain crops and vegetables as the volume of the former is so much larger that the seeds must be multiplied locally. This means that there must be an infrastructure of drying, storing and processing equipment. We had none. Contisem had developed one maize hybrid called Pacific, which it had multiplied on a small scale for the previous two years by contracting acreage with farmers and using the facilities of the government research institute, INIAP, to process the seed. Pacific yielded over five tons of grain per hectare compared to an average of three tons for the local INIAP varieties commonly grown. It was clearly a winner and we wanted to expand production as quickly as we could. Contisem's manager, Alfredo Garcia, was a seedsman of great experience.

We would use INIAP for one more season's production but would then have to find an alternative as its capacity was limited and, as it was developing a hybrid maize of its own, there would be a conflict of interests. The cost of investing in a new plant was high but we had to do something quickly. Then an idea occurred to me. I rang Simon de Montfort, whom you will recall from Sir Peter Rees's visit. He lived in Colon in the province of Manabi, some two and half hours from Guayaquil, where he grew some 300 hectares of marigolds on contract with small farmers. The dried flowers were then sent to Quito to supply an extraction plant, producing carotene as a natural colorant.

Simon's business involved drying the flowers and I had once visited his factory and was very impressed with his dryers, which he had designed and built himself. I explained my plan to him and, after some hesitation, he thought that it was a great idea. My suggestion was that we should go into partnership, with him supplying the infrastructure and us the processing machinery, and that he should organise the nearby farmers to multiply the maize. We began the first year with some 100 hectares, which produced 300 tons of seed. This was cleaned, sorted, treated with fungicides, packed in Agripac bags and then returned to us for sale to farmers.

The farmers in Manabi are mostly small growers with between one and ten hectares. As it is a very dry province, it is essential that they have access to irrigation water. Proman, Simon's company, would provide the basic seed, fertiliser and chemicals and supervise the crop from start to finish. The farmer would supply his land and labour and obtain a premium price for his product over the commercial market price. However, there were rules to be followed. The crop is a hybrid and must not be allowed to pollinate itself. Three rows of female lines are planted, followed by one row of the male. The female rows are then 'detassled' by removing the male pollen stalks and so can only be pollinated by the males. Of course, the whole field must be at a certain distance from another maize crop to avoid contamination from it. ICI would send us the male and female base stock from Brazil and, apart from buying this, we agreed to pay it royalties on all the new crop we produced.

Pacific was the market leader in hybrid maize for many years. More recently, both Dekalb and Pioneer (the world's largest seed producer) have taken some market share from us, but now we have an even more productive hybrid called Brazilia, which can produce up to eight tons a hectare. This is somewhat more difficult to multiply successfully but it is now in its third year and we are hoping for great things. We have already raised the farmers' average yield from three to five tons and if we can further increase this to eight, we will indeed justify our presence in Ecuador and all the hard work which has gone into building the seeds business. Maize has been particularly successful as hybridisation has improved yields drastically. This is not so with rice and soya beans, which are open-pollinated and where there is less to be gained from breeding. However, we also multiply these and supply a selection of seeds to our farmers.

Now that we stocked seeds, we were able to make up a package of products and differentiate ourselves from the competition. It was a logical progression to eventually supply fertilisers too, and give farmers credit until the harvest. This, in turn, led to our buying a grain-drying and storage facility, so that we could receive the harvest in kind. Then, after recovering our outstanding credits, we negotiated the crop with agroindustries that need raw materials of maize, soya or rice. That is where we are today — but we are running ahead of the story.

We had our most prestigious visitor of all, HRH the Princess Royal, in 1989. As I have mentioned earlier, Diana was abandoned to enter St Anne's School for her first term without her father in September. Michael Atkinson had left as ambassador and Frank Wheeler had just arrived a month before the visit. We had been given several months' warning and before I went on leave to Ferngill, Roci and I had drawn up our guest list for the lunch to be held at the Union Club. It was to be the British community's invitation with a subscription lunch to which we invited selected guests and some members of the Consular Corps — a total of 120 people.

The great day arrived and promptly at ten o'clock on the morning of Friday, the 8th September, the queen's flight from Quito touched down in Guayaquil airport, where we were lined up to receive Her Royal Highness. She wore a white dress and was accompanied by ambassador Frank Wheeler, Lt Col Peter Gibbs, her private secretary, and Mrs Carew Pole, her lady-in-waiting, with two British policemen. The reception committee included the lady mayoress of Guayaquil, Elsa Bucaram, and the governor of Guayas, Rafael Guerrero, who were political opponents, and between them (to prevent fisticuffs?) was myself. The mayoress presented the keys of the city and the rest of us shook hands, then the princess was swept away in a cavalcade of cars to visit the

Colin greeting HRH The Princess Royal at Guayaquil airport. Elsa Bucaram, Mayoress of Guayaquil next to Colin.

Dolorosa Clinic in a slum area of town. In her capacity as president of the Save the Children Fund, the princess wanted to see the pioneering work carried out in this area over the previous ten years by Anne Klapper, an English nurse who was awarded the MBE for her achievement. In very difficult conditions and with a tiny budget, which relied on donations, she had created a clean, efficient clinic, where she worked day and night on a health programme for women and children. However, all too often she was called on to assist men with machète or gunshot wounds. She alone was trusted by the whole community in an area of tremendous poverty and crime.

The princess's visit to the clinic caused great excitement in an area where few outsiders would choose to go and the resulting publicity raised awareness of the problems and put pressure on local authorities to do more to help.

I had not gone to the clinic as my next detail was to receive the princess at the Union Club. Our guests were gathered on the principal floor, which is approached by an imposing flight of stairs from the front door. I was to wait by the stairs and escort her up. She had especially requested that there be no guest line but that she be allowed to mingle and talk to some people before sitting down to lunch. But our guests were having none of this and duly formed up in two rows, all wanting to be presented. The princess had arranged for a room to be available by the door in the club so that she could quickly change her dress after arriving from the clinic and before entering the hall. She changed into a yellow, flowered dress remarkably quickly and caught me by surprise. I was chatting to Peter Gibbs when she suddenly appeared and bounded up the stairs with me in pursuit. The daunting line was now facing us.

My ability to instantly remember names is poor at the best of times, and I rely on Ceci to fill in the gaps. Today, I was on my own and, being somewhat tense with anxiety that all should go well, I was completely useless. I was confronted by a sea of 120 eager faces, all trying to catch my eye and I was in agony as I tried to match names to faces. But those whose names I recalled were presented. The princess would chat briefly to them, asking what they did and so forth, and move on to the next. Most people spoke English but I had to translate occasionally. Clemencia Tola, an elderly lady, was one example. I explained to the princess that she had been for many years the honorary consul general for Monaco. The princess replied: 'I wouldn't have thought Monaco had much need of a consulate here' and moved on. Clemencia wanted to know what she had said. As I did not want to upset her, my translation became 'She is very fond of visiting Monaco.'

Eventually, to my great relief, we headed towards the top table where the princess, the ambassador, Elsa Bucaram (the governor had opted out rather than sit at the same table as Elsa), the archbishop of Guayaquil (Monsignor Juan Larrea), Ceci and I were seated. I was placed between the princess and Elsa Bucaram. Now Elsa was a very controversial mayor of Guayaquil, sister of the populist former mayor and future president Abdala Bucaram (who was deposed after six months in office and went into exile in Panama). Her term in Guayaquil was plagued with corruption scandals and she brought the city almost to a standstill. A woman of the people, a rabble-rouser and taunter of oligarchs and the rich, today she was on her best behaviour and wearing a snappy grey suit.

The princess did not eat too much but kept up a very pleasant conversation. She talked of things that she enjoyed such as horses and her estate and farming, as well as world economic affairs. However, each time I raised my fork to my mouth, she addressed me and down it went again until the waiters removed both her plate and mine untouched. As I was almost always turned towards the princess, Elsa was growing fidgety and eventually asked me to ask the princess her impression of Guayaquil. The reply went through a most remarkable transformation and was translated as 'a most charming and interesting city'.

Lunch finished when the princess suddenly rose and went to study one of the paintings on the wall. It showed the famous railway up the Devil's Nose, which climbs a very steep place between Guayaquil and Quito. Then I just had time to present the consular guest book for her signature before the royal entourage swept out to visit a local university that was the recipient of British aid. While she was thus engaged, I drove Flight Captain Michael Herrington back to the airport and was allowed a peep inside the plane before she arrived.

Then there was a brief farewell and she flew away to Quito. The following day, there was a visit to Te Sangai, a British tea plantation run by our great friend Peter Wilson in the Amazon, and, after several events in Quito, she went on to Bolivia.

It was not my first meeting with the princess. It would not have been discreet to mention it but Ceci and I had been introduced to her in Quito by ambassador Peter Mennell on her return from her honeymoon in the Galapagos Islands. Now her marriage to Captain Mark Phillips was over and the press was full of the news, some suggesting that the Latin American tour was planned partly to keep her out of England at an awkward time. Be that as it may, her trip to Ecuador was a great success and the part I was involved in certainly did a lot for British-Ecuadorian relations as well as highlighting the terrific work of Anne Klapper and her helpers. The clinic also benefited from receiving medical equipment as a result of the money collected in the subscription lunch. Some time after the visit, Anne retired to England with her Ecuadorian dentist husband and children and I understand has been rather ill. Our thoughts are with her she is the nearest I have come to meeting a saint.

We later received a thank-you letter written by Mary Carew Pole on her royal highness's behalf. I was amused at the way she had been so pleased to be able to see such a contrasting district to Quito. That was putting it politely — poor old Guayaquil looked particularly down at heel at that time due largely to Elsa's maladministration which, apart from many other things, was totally lacking in rubbish collection.

MAPAN 1991 TODATE

MAPAN HAS GIVEN ME both pleasure and pain over the years. Many are the happy memories of building the house and improving the farm, of family events such as Alex's baptism and the queen's birthday parties held there, as well as the many friends who have enjoyed it over the years. Two of these come to mind.

Sam Duckworth visited Ecuador on several occasions for a month or two at a time and he would make a point of staying on the farm with me at weekends. Sam is a rather unusual chap who had made his home in Kettlewell in Yorkshire and made a living selling cups of tea and hamburgers to the many walkers and cyclists who visit Wharfedale every year. He operated from a caravan, parked illegally on a corner of the road outside Kettlewell and made enough during the summer months to be able to travel abroad in the winter. He managed to carry on this way of life for several years until the national park wardens caught up with him and that was the end of his business.

We had met Sam through Elaine and Charles and become friends. I think this was in one of the Kettlewell pubs, where he would do a turn on the piano from time to time. He is a natural, self-taught pianist. I believe that his mother intended him to be a Catholic priest but after a spell at a seminary, Sam found his vocation somewhat lacking. He had a very wide range of interests and we would walk the dogs around the farm on a Saturday evening, chatting about all sorts of things.

He travelled quite widely in Ecuador and had a fund of funny stories to draw upon, such as the time when he took the bus from Guayaquil to Cuenca and the driver went so fast that Sam kept telling him to slow down. The driver pretended not to understand what he wanted and raced on around hairpin bends, with rock on one side and a precipice on the other. Eventually a tyre burst and they ploughed into the rocky side of the road. Sam was so furious that he berated the driver and they almost came to blows while the other passengers cheered him on.

Once in Cuenca, he booked in to a cheap hotel and, as his boots were in need of cleaning, put them outside the door of his room. That was the last he saw of them. Not being able to face the bus again, he returned to Guayaquil by air. But he obviously developed a liking for Latin America as he has now made his home in Salta, Argentina, where he teaches English.

Richard Duffus spent a rather longer time in Ecuador. Richard's father is the tenant farmer of the National Trust property Braithwaite Hall, which marches with Tupgill. Once Richard had graduated from the Royal Agricultural

College at Cirencester, he approached me to see if he could join us in Ecuador for a year.

He worked at Agripac but his special interest was Mapan, where he spent many days working with the cowboys. He particularly enjoyed the thrice-yearly round-up when the cattle would be collected together, the calves branded, and the herd wormed and vaccinated against foot and mouth disease. It was also, of course, counted for that is the time we check that all are present and correct.

Richard's great love in life is shooting and, before coming out to Ecuador, he organised the pheasant and grouse shoot at Braithwaite. We did have some shooting at Mapan when the whistling ducks (called Maria locally) migrate there during the months of February and March. This was good sport but did involve getting up before dawn and driving to the marshes, where you have to wade into muddy water up to your waist and hide in the weeds until, with the light, the ducks circle around. There is no use of decoys so you take a chance on them coming within range. Having said that, Daniel Murillo, who was by then our head cowboy, had a way of whistling the ducks in and, as he is an excellent shot, he always ended with more than his fair share of the bag. Not that the ducks were in the bag as soon as they were downed for, if not killed outright, they dive underwater and stay submerged, defying you to find them. We did not have dogs to find them, but farm boys who would spot where they fell and then wade into the water and grapple about, trying to retrieve them. We would only recover, say, seventy per cent of those downed. While standing in the water, you were always very aware that it contained leeches, and there were also snakes in the weeds, which detracted from the fun somewhat.

Richard and I would spend the evenings in Mapan discussing shooting in England, where I too now had a shoot, which was managed by Ted Kettlewell, father of Steve, who trains at Tupgill. I could see that Richard would not stay for more than his year; the pheasants were calling him home. But he had a surprise in store for us as, a month or so before he was due to leave, he announced his engagement to Monica Carchi, a friend of ours with whom he had been going out for some while. This was quite unexpected but we were delighted for them and so they married in a civil ceremony in Ecuador and a month later had a church wedding in East Witton church near Braithwaite. They now live in Leyburn.

Richard works as a land agent but his heart (apart from Monica and their children, of course) is in shooting. Nick and I always have a day's shooting with him and he with us, and when we are in England, we are in and out of each other's houses all the time. Ceci and Monica take advantage of the opportunity to speak in Spanish together, as there are not too many opportunities for Monica to do this in Leyburn.

All this reminds me of buying my shooting suit some years ago. I had decided to have myself properly kitted out so that when the invitations to shoot grouse or pheasant poured in, I would be sartorially correct. I had fallen into the habit of buying a suit from Henry Poole in Saville Row every year, so this year's would be a shooting suit. Mr Cottrell, who usually attended me, showed me samples of cloth and I finally opted for a brown, which I thought was the closest to the colour of heather. Then he asked: 'Will that be plus two or plus four, sir?'. When the difference had been explained, we opted for plus four. While I was being measured, Mr Cottrell asked: 'Do you shoot much, sir?'. 'No', I said, 'I don't have too much opportunity with being abroad for most of the season.' Then, after a pause, he said: 'Do you ever hit anything sir?'. 'No, not a lot,' I replied. This has become a family joke.

To be fair to myself, I do have times when any bird within reach of my gun seems to come to grief. But sadly those moments are few. I have always been rather an erratic shot, even back in my Rossall days when shooting with a .303 rifle in the combined cadet force. On some days, I could not even hit the target while on others I was the top shot. I did, however, earn my marksman's badge. Nick is a much better rifle shot than I was and represented Sedbergh at Bisley. He and I used to have a bet on our individual scores of pheasants for each shoot. Of course, I always won when he was young. Lately, I have stopped betting as it is getting too expensive.

Mapan had grown by that time. Despite the legal battle with his father, Philippe Reiset offered to sell me another 500 hectares of Guarumal. It was not good land and was, in fact, the very marshes where we shoot duck, which was probably one of the attractions to me. But I was still land-hungry and it adjoined Mapan. It was a complete mess of water weed and what grass there was had been badly overgrazed by Don Louis's cattle, which ranged at will as there were no fences. So I negotiated a cheap price and we went ahead.

Daniel Murillo is a man of many parts. He is much too good for a head cowboy, although he enjoyed the work. He had trained as an assistant surveyor with the banana company Dole (Standard Fruit) and knew his way around a theodolite. He rented one and investigated the possibilities of draining the new area (which we had baptised Louisiana because it had belonged to Don Louis and, like the Louisiana purchase in the States, was vast and marshy). He found that it was possible so we hired diggers, dug canals and built dykes over the whole area, draining it to the far corner, where we built a sluice gate. From there, by deepening a natural watercourse, we connected it to the river two kilometres away.

It worked. Following the rainy season the next summer, we were able to drive tractors on to the land and spray the weeds, allowing the natural grasses to become established and making excellent pastures. This has allowed us to move the cattle on to this area during the dry months when the rest of the farm provides little grazing.

Rather pleased with my purchase, I was negotiating to buy an additional 150 hectares from Philippe Reiset, when I was stopped in my tracks by a labour problem.

I have already mentioned that when Don Louis sold Mapan to me, he never paid off his workers for their years of service, as required by law in Ecuador.

Alfredo Ledesma warned me to insist on this but I thought that I might lose the deal entirely if I did so. I risked it and that risk came back to plague me sixteen years later.

The problem began with a change of management when, after having run the farm hands-on since I had bought it, I decided that I was not doing a very good job. I had two foremen, Diego Cano and Julio Vera. (Here I must mention a lovely turn of phrase of Diego's. When something was clearly impossible to achieve, he would say it was 'el sueno del perro capon', which translates as 'the dream of a castrated dog.') Diego ran the banana operation and Julio, together with the then head cowboy, Daniel Murillo, ran the cattle side.

After talking to a Dole manager (with whom I had a contract for the purchase of the fruit), I brought in a consultant, Rafael Alvarez, to advise me on how to increase the banana production, which was consistently lower than my neighbours'. He told me that I had to change the way that I worked and employ a professional manager, who could then set about making the necessary improvements. However good and loyal Diego was, new ideas were called for. I accepted the consultant's advice and hired the expert he recommended, Marco Gutierrez.

Marco was a new broom and soon he had fired several workers who were not prepared to accept his management style. For the sake of peace and quiet over the years, I had put up with some inefficiency and changed hardly any staff, so the lads were somewhat upset by this change of affairs.

The first I knew of the trouble to come was when a group of sixty workers turned up at the office of the government labour inspector, Liliana Troya, in Babahoyo, accompanied by a lawyer. They announced that they were forming a union. This was bad news indeed as, under the laws of Ecuador, once a union was in formation, nobody could be fired without double compensation. Now some of them were claiming that they had been employed for sixteen years by Mapan and up to twenty years by Don Louis — a total of thirty-six years of uninterrupted service at the going rate of one and a quarter months per year. Now, I would have had to double the compensation if I fired anyone.

That would have meant practically selling the farm to pay off the hundred or so workers. What should I do? I had learned from bitter experience during the Don Louis court cases that negotiation is better than litigation so I set out on a charm offensive to sway the lads.

We had arranged to meet them after work finished at 12.30pm and, as I arrived at the farm early, I thought that I might as well have a ride and see the cattle. My horse, Sin Rival, had some bad habits. One of these was becoming upset if another horse passed him from behind; he was very much the leader. I had a guest with me whose horse ran away with him and as he was passing me, Sin Rival turned into his path. We all came down, two horses and two riders, and although we got up again, I had hurt my shoulder and was in some pain.

So when the lads turned up for the meeting, I was not quite as bushy-tailed as I might have been. They assembled on the lawn and I stood in front of them with the foremen and began by reminding them of the long time we had been together; of loans, presents and favours given to many of them; of help in building their houses and in times of sickness and so on. I even tried a joke or two, although I was not feeling very jovial (and it showed!). Then I promised that no more would be fired if they accepted Marco's changes. When I had finished speaking and asked for their response, they all looked at their boots and the leader said: 'You'll have to talk to our lawyer.'

That was that for the day and I returned to Guayaquil. Johnny Coloma, the Agripac credit manager, knew the lawyer in question and he sounded him out as to how we could come to an agreement. For the mere consideration of a case of Johnny Walker Black Label whisky, he agreed to arrange a meeting. We met and talked for hours but made no progress. They would not have Marco or any change of working practice. Clearly the lawyer had no interest in a quick finish to the case. The workers were paying him by the week and if we wanted to talk to him, we had to supply liquid refreshment just to keep the door open.

Work continued on the farm, however, because the men were all very aware that if it stopped, we could legally fire them for failing to do their jobs. But Marco had little authority and certainly no changes could be made. Sadly, at this time Diego Cano died of a heart attack and I lost a good friend and one of my few supporters on the farm.

What to do? Alfredo Ledesma, our lawyer, advised me to be patient and wait and see if the other side made a mistake. So we waited and they did indeed make a mistake.

The process of forming a union is long and complicated and there are deadlines for each stage. Perhaps thanks to the effects of the Johnny Walker, its lawyer missed one of these deadlines and immediately Alfredo appealed that the process be declared null and void. It was, and then we could act.

We approached the labour inspector and declared that we were going to fire all our workforce legally and pay them off with the full amount that they claimed, minus, of course, the doubling effect of union formation. She agreed that we could do this and so we appeared at Mapan the following day with the inspector, twenty private security guards and a great deal of cash in notes. We called the workers to the table one by one, negotiated their compensations and terminated their contracts with Mapan SA. But we sweetened the pill for most of them by taking them on again in another service company, which just employed labour and had a maximum of twenty-nine staff as thirty is the minimum needed to form a union. Of course, the ring leaders who had stood to gain most from the union were not offered more work.

Those affected were obviously not delighted with this and, with their chastened lawyer, went to court to try to better their terms. They claimed to have worked for Don Louis since they were toddlers, having never had a holiday in their lives nor been paid overtime and so on — a really extreme position. But the law states that in any labour dispute, the judge must rule in favour of the worker (a throwback to the socialist days of the sixties). They also cleverly sued both Mapan and myself in my personal capacity as its manager. This was irritating because during the course of the proceedings, and there were twelve cases, I could be called to appear in Babahoyo court on numerous occasions. They knew that I would soon get tired of the two-hour journey and the hours wasted while waiting at the court.

That made us decide to wind up Mapan as a company, with myself resigning as manager. Instead, we divided Mapan into two companies: Rodeo Grande, which is the cattle farm of 1,100 hectares, and Skipper, the banana farm of eighty hectares.

Eventually, the court cases were settled. I lost them all, of course, but saved some of the cost and inconvenience by this manoeuvre. And so ended the sequel of events which began in 1977 with the Don Louis purchase.

Now the farms, particularly Skipper, could be run more efficiently and, as a result, production increased well. We entered a good period for the banana industry when demand and prices were high, which enabled us to pay off the money borrowed to pay the workers out quite quickly.

It is said that farmers the world over live poor and die rich — that is to say that they immediately rush to re-invest any money which they make. We are no different and decided to plant a further thirty hectares of bananas. This is an expensive business. It involves digging huge ditches and building subterranean drains, an irrigation system and funiculars to transport the fruit, enlarging the packing station and buying the planting material. This was produced by a new Israeli system called meristem, which involves taking cuttings from a superior plant and propagating them, free of nematodes and diseases. It produces a better plant but is expensive when compared to the old way of taking the corm, or bulb, of an existing plant and cutting it in pieces before planting it again. This method was cheap and cheerful but you were propagating weaknesses along with the plant.

Following the great payout to the workers, for which we had had to borrow heavily, we lashed out again to plant this extra area. We thought that it would all be paid back by increased production. But Nature makes fools of us all, and no sooner were the thirty new hectares in production, than El Niño hit in 1997.

This was the second such weather phenomenon that I had experienced. But they were not the same, starting at different times of year and lasting different periods. In 1982, El Niño had begun in September and lasted for ten months. In 1997, it began as the main rainy season was finishing in May and we all said that the finish would coincide with the peak of the normal wet season and so there would be no great problem. In fact, it lasted fifteen months and the worst of it came during the rainy season so that we had month after month of with over 1,000mm of rain. We had built some defensive bunds around part of the farm and were managing to keep it dry quite well until one exceptional night. The neighbouring banana farm went under and water poured into our pastures. We hired an excavator and spent the next six weeks continually raising the bunds around the bananas. The pastures were lost and the cattle taken off to other farms but we saved the bananas. Well — almost saved them as they had been exposed to very high water tables and Dole was very severe in rejecting fruit for fear of premature ripening when the plants are waterlogged.

So the investment which we had meant to pay off in a couple of years took much longer. Finally, it was all paid off but in the final year, banana prices have fallen to their lowest level in living memory (or certainly in the years that I have been in the business). So there is still no payback from the investment. Perhaps one day both Nature and the market will work together to help us. There is hope for an improvement in trading conditions with the new European decision to allow banana imports from the dollar area on a 'first come, first served' basis. This favours Ecuador over Costa Rica and Colombia, which were previously given high quotas for the European market to the detriment of Ecuador. Of course, a much more glaring anomaly is the preference given to 'European' and ex-colonial bananas, which cost three times more to produce but have privileged access to the market. Ecuador produces bananas at lower cost than any other country and could do very well indeed in a free and fair market.

More recently, the farms have grown a new crop — tourists. This came about when I read in the British publication *Farming News* in 1994 that columnist Anthony Rosen was escorting a party of tourists to Ecuador in January of the following year. I contacted him and offered to provide lunch in Rodeo Grande (as it now is). They came, saw and were conquered by the farm. We showed them the cattle, buffaloes and bananas, then we had lunch together. They were kind enough to say that this was the highlight of their trip so far — even though they had already visited farms in the Sierra, and there are some very attractive farms there too.

Anthony has returned several times with tour operator Metropolitan Touring, which has asked us if it can bring other groups. It is somewhat lost for something to show people on the coast of Ecuador. The Sierra does not present a problem with Indian villages and lovely scenery as well as Quito and its colonial centre. Guayaquil does not have the same appeal and there is normally one day spare before the groups fly to the Galapagos Islands, so a trip to a typical farm fills the gap. We have now got into the rhythm of this and have hosted many groups numbering from one and two to up to 200 people once, who were on a cruise ship which put in to Guayaquil. We have even got around to making a leaflet to distribute to tourist agencies — shades of the Forbidden Corner!

Apart from the normal run of tourists visiting us over the years, some have had special interests which we have tried to accommodate. One most singular gentleman was Simon Starling, who first contacted us from Glasgow University. He had a project financed by the Melbourne museum in Australia, for which he had to go to Ecuador, find and photograph a balsa tree, then cut up some

Anthony Rosen's tour visit to Mapan 1998, looking at the Buffaloes.

balsa wood, make it into a model plane and send it to the museum. The most important consideration was authenticity. Balsa traditionally comes from Ecuador. He contacted me as consul to ask if I had any idea where a suitable tree could be located and I think I surprised him. Easy, I replied, on my farm. So he came out and duly did his thing.

While he was here, we talked of other projects he had undertaken with sponsorship by the Arts Council and a couple come to mind. One involved taking a mahogany chest of drawers, dismantling it and making a boat, with which he went fishing. He caught a fish then, returning to shore, burned the boat and cooked and ate the fish. The other project seemed to me even stranger. He took a metal chair, dismantled it and made a bicycle, then took a bicycle to pieces and made (wait for it) a chair. I am told that this is art but I am only a simple chap so have difficulty in understanding it.

Agripac has its uses for the farms too. Over the years, we have taken our new recruits there as part of their training process. We have carried out many product demonstrations, both in bananas and pastures, and held many a field day for customers. More recently, we have taken to holding the annual sales conference there in November. We started one year when it was a very bad time for business, so we looked around for a cheap venue for the event which had previously been held in a resort hotel. We hit on the idea of using the farms and it was a great success. We contacted the Civil Defence in Babahoyo and asked to borrow its tents to accommodate the 250 participants, which it was happy to lend us for the cost of a second-hand computer. The Agripac catering service of Bandurria provided food and we contracted a show. Our own divisions each set up a stand around the garden to illustrate a certain topic and we divided the participants into groups and circulated around the stands. This was the work aspect but there was time for organised games too, and in the two nights that we were there, apart from the show, there were talent contests and sketches about the company, which were hilarious. These get-togethers are also very useful for helping one to put names to faces as, with over 400 people and eighty shops scattered around the country, there are not many opportunities to meet each other.

So that is how the farms are today, twenty-three years after I began the Mapan project. Marco is running the banana side very efficiently under the supervision of Victor Hugo Quimi (as one of his many responsibilities). Rodeo Grande developed a dairy herd when Melvin Azofeifa (then the head of Agripac's animal health division) ran it some three years ago. Rodeo Grande is today run by Juan Carlos Gomez, whom Melvin brought in as farm manager. We even tried to farm ostriches but found the conditions too wet, although we do have two beautiful peacocks in the garden.

I have had a series of horses for my personal use over the years. Piolin was followed by Sin Rival and more recently by Granizo, who was bought at the Cattlemen's Association auction.

I had joined the association early in my farming career and had once been persuaded to become treasurer. However, I dislike committee work and was glad to give it up when my term ended. But I was not to escape from public office as Rafael Wong, a good friend, was standing for the presidency in 1997 and asked me to stand for vice-president. We won the election and then began the business of running the association.

A large cattle fair is held in the association's premises outside Guayaquil every year in October. For years, Agripac has had a stand there. Now that I was vice-president, we had to become more involved. Melvin Azofeifa was on the fair committee and Agripac adverts were everywhere. It looked as though we were sponsoring the event single-handedly. We showed cattle too (not very successfully) and the Rodeo Grande cowboys entered a rodeo team, which put on a fine show for the public.

At the end of the fair, which lasted eight days, there was an auction of cattle and horses. It was a light-hearted affair and, as we all know each other, quite a party. The whisky is served while the bidding is in progress, which occasionally leads to disputes as to whether the animal has actually been bought or not on the following day. To prevent this, we arranged for an assistant to go around and ask the top bidder to sign for the animal, but all the bids were still not honoured.

The Agipac sales force at the year 2000 convention ate Rodeo Grande. This shows 250 of the total 420 staff.

I would normally put up all the animals that I had taken to the fair for sale and buy some too, mainly dairy cows, just to help the auction along. So when Granizo came into the ring and was announced as a four-year-old gelding sired by an Apalaluchan stallion, I raised my hand. I was half interested in buying a horse but thought that there would be plenty of competition. There was not, and I was successful. The owner came over to shake my hand and give me an abrazo (hug). I thought that he looked very pleased with his sale, as well he might have been for the asking price was high enough, but I had to set an example and honour my deal.

Granizo was sent to Rodeo Grande and the following Saturday, I went excitedly to ride him. In the plain light of day and without the benefit of the whisky, he did look somewhat older than his declared four years. I asked Albino Franco, my oldest cowboy and faithful companion, to look in Granizo's mouth. 'He's at least twelve years old,' he said.

Once again, there was a family joke about Father being conned and, as he was a tall, thin horse, I was compared to Don Quixote. Nevertheless, Granizo and I have ridden the range together for several years.

AGRIPAC: RECENT TIMES

In 1992, Rohm and Haas Inc, a chemical company in the USA, announced that it was to close Laquinsa SA, which was its only remaining veterinary factory and which was situated in San Jose, Costa Rica. We had represented Laquinsa for many years and would have been sorry to see it go as we had a good market position with its products. Apparently, it had tried to interest other veterinary companies in the factory but, there being no takers, it was to close.

Quite by coincidence, I visited Costa Rica to buy cattle from Juan Heinsohn. Juan had been the original founder of Laquinsa before selling out to Rohm and Haas and becoming its regional manager for the Andean Pact countries, and so I knew him well. Now retired, he spent his time cattle farming and exporting.

As we drove from San Jose to his farm, La Pradera del Norte, on the Pacific coast, we talked about Laquinsa. I suggested that he should forget about retirement and we could join forces with other distributors of Laquinsa to see if we could buy it. He was enthusiastic and we agreed to contact Fritz Trinler, the owner of Trisan SA, and Oldemar Echandi, who has a large veterinary business, Echandi Hermanos. Following these meetings, we approached Rohm and Haas and, after some negotiation, we arrived at a sales price.

We were thrilled with our deal and set up the new board with Fritz as president, myself as vice-president, Juan as managing director and Oldemar as director. We bought existing stocks and immediately set to work to grow the company, which had been deliberately run down prior to closure. At this time, it had sales of only $1.5 million a year but they had been double this figure. We also had an ace up our sleeves. Rohm and Haas is big in the mancozeb fungicide business and had a plant at Laquinsa for making a flowable formulation, which had been developed there. The machinery was not worth much once dismantled so it was sold to us with the rest of the factory, on condition that we did not compete with Rohm and Haas for three years. We respected this time period but afterwards Juan contacted Carlos Roberts, the genius who had created the product but was now retired, and asked him to create an even better one. He did so and we began to sell this and other agrochemicals quite successfully.

Laquinsa had always exported from Costa Rica and we applied for free zone status, which we obtained. This allowed us to import all the materials which we later re-exported duty free. Then we went ahead with many other product registrations and today export to sixteen countries.

The sales increased well and in 1994, we all gathered at the plant, together with customers and government ministers, for the thirty-fifth anniversary of the company and the official opening of the new manufacturing area. This was a laboratory for making and packing injectable products in a totally sterile environment. It was built to such a high standard that we could make pharmaceuticals for use on humans there too.

Juan was very happy to be back in the saddle, especially as many of his old employees were still there and he threw himself into the work heart and soul. Sales reached more than $7,000,000 in 1999 but in July of that year, we were to gather all the employees on the lawn for a memorial service. Juan had died of a heart attack in June. There were several speeches about the many good things he had done during his life and tributes from his friends and employees to a truly magnificent man. Everyone agreed that his last years had been very fulfilled and happy. He was a very dynamic person with a direct, even irreverent, approach to business but he was popular with all.

But life went on for the rest of us. Alba, Juan's widow, decided to sell his shares in the company and Mario Chavarria, who was previously the finance director, has become the new managing director and has bought some of Juan's shares to join us on the board. Mario is a very competent and hard-working man and the company has gone from strength to strength. Agripac is limited to Ecuador in scope, but Laquinsa is truly international in outlook.

I have mentioned that John Greaves took over from John Robinson as the senior manager for ICI. Now ICI was being divided into two companies. Zeneca plc took over the agrochemical and pharmaceutical divisions, while ICI kept the rest. John was promoted to Zeneca Agrochemicals business director for Europe and Latin America. He came up with several new ideas, one of which was to form a Partners Club for distributors and Zeneca companies around Latin America. Their meetings have been very successful and very enjoyable over the years, beginning in 1991 when the first one was held in Venezuela. There were some twenty delegates who came from Mexico, Central America and as far south as Argentina and Chile. There were outside speakers as well as Zeneca heavyweights and each of us had to give a paper on the topic of Zeneca products in our markets.

Quite apart from learning about what was going on at head office and new inventions that were on the way, we were able to discover what our colleagues' companies were doing to launch products. Informally, we could find out much more from each other as to the way forward, not only with Zeneca products, but any others, including generics, in the world of pesticides. There was also time for excursions, fishing, watching polo, trips to the theatre, ruins and art galleries, sightseeing, wine tasting and shopping (for our wives) as the group met over several years in Caracas, London, Merida, Buenos Aires, Madrid, Bariloche, Cartagena and San Francisco. This was the last of the series for now John, who was awarded the CMG in 1998 for services to British exports, has retired and Zeneca Agrochemicals fused with Novartis to become Syngenta.

But the friendships formed within the group will stay, and notable among them are Bob McIntosh from Panama, Jose Antonio Vargas and Luis Enrique

THE FORBIDDEN CORNER

The Zeneca Partnership Club at Cartagena, Columbia, 1995 which brings together the Zeneca Regional Managers and Distributors. Those mentioned in the text are: *Back row:* Luis Enrique Fraga (Venezuela), Bob McIntosh (Panama), Victor Hugo Quimi (Agripac), Valdemar Fischer (Agripac/Zeneca), Luis Villa (Mexico). *Third row:* Duilio Baltodano (Nicaragua), Jose Antonio Vargas (Venezuela), Jeff Pullen (Zeneca), Bertrand du Lassus (Bolivia), Des Hodnett (Zeneca). *Second row:* Raul Nogeira (Chile), Colin (Agripac),Vladimir Wagner (Zeneca), Gordon Farrell (Zeneca). *Front row:* Flavio Prezzi (Zeneca), Luis Guillerno Parra (Columbia), Nelson Echevarria (Columbia), John Greaves (Zeneca).

Fraga from Venezuela, Raul Nogeira from Chile, Bertrand de Lassus from Bolivia and Duilio Baltodano from Nicaragua.

We will also miss John for his very kind invitations to Ceci and I to join Peggy and he at Wimbledon on two occasions: once when we saw plenty of tennis, the other time being a series of interruptions by rain. But both were enjoyable for the atmosphere that surrounds the place. After the second visit, I mentioned to John that I had a growing interest in opera and he suggested that we change venue the following year to Glyndebourne. We did so and enjoyed three successive visits there, all with lovely weather. Weather for opera? Oh yes, Glyndebourne needs a fine day as part of the fun is to have champagne and sandwiches on the huge lawns which surround the house at four o'clock, before going into the opera at five. Then there is a break for a full dinner served in the Wallops and the opera finishes at about ten o'clock.

One can stay at a nearby hotel or there is a train that takes and carries one from London Victoria. It is altogether a very civilised experience. For me, the best of the three visits was to *Le Comte Ory*, which was very funny and has lovely music. The most challenging was *Rodelinda*, which was written by Handel to be sung by castrati. As they are hard to come by today, the parts are sung by counter-tenors, who in this case were very masculine but with high-pitched voices, which took some getting used to. After dinner that night, one lady in the restaurant announced in a loud voice: 'I am not going back in there for all the tea in China.' Each to his (or her) taste.

We did manage to repay John and Peggy once or twice for their hospitality. John enjoys shooting and joined us several times at Ferngill. We even had a crack at the grouse one year on Richard's moor on the Glorious Twelfth.

On another year, we managed too a visit to the Galapagos Islands, when John was to visit us in Ecuador and brought Peggy with him. We took a tour on the *Isobel 2*, which was very comfortable and we saw half the islands in three days. One can take a full week's trip but it tends to be more of the same. Ceci and I had been before, taking Nick and Diana when they were small, and too young to have really enjoyed it. Charles and Elaine Lister had gone with us. Now, fifteen years later, we were anxious to see if the islands had deteriorated, as some had said. But no, they were as good as, or better than, before. It is a part of Ecuador that is well looked after.

After flying from Guayaquil to Baltra for an hour and a half, one is collected and taken to the ship. This sails from island to island and one lands in a small panga (inflatable boat) and is taken along marked paths by expert guides to see the birds, iguanas, penguins and sea lions which abound there and which have no fear of humans. We walked through a colony of 8,000 albatrosses, which were nesting and they hardly gave us a second glance. We swam in the sea with the sea lions and went snorkelling to see the varied fish in the clear water. Actually, the others did because I have never been able to use the masks without getting water in them. Without a mask, you see nothing.

The accommodation on board the ship was excellent and in the evening there were lectures about what we would see the next day. After these came dinner and socialising with the fifty other passengers on board. Most were American but there was a party of British people too. In the nature of cruises, we gradually got around to talking to each group and on the last night the British group asked us for a drink. I remember the names of only one couple but they were clearly the leaders of the little group of six. They were Sir Reasby Sitwell and his lady. We enjoyed our chat with them but one thing that Lady Sitwell asked has stuck in my mind ever since: 'Do you know anyone in Ecuador?' Rather surprised by the question, as I had already told them that I had lived there for twenty-five years, I replied: 'Oh yes, loads of people of all nationalities.' 'Yes,' she said, 'but I mean ANYONE?' Then I realised that she meant anyone important. There was no answer to that. Who is important and who is not is a matter of personal opinion.

In 1993, Agripac changed its policy of selling almost exclusively through dealers and began to open retail shops. There were several reasons for this. We began in the little town of Pedro Carbo, which had once been famous for cotton growing and where we could then sell to the cotton growers' federation. But now that cotton had virtually disappeared from Ecuador the customers had become more dispersed. There were hundreds of small maize growers, who bought their inputs from two or three dealers. We and our competitors had to work through these men who were, to say the least, cavalier in their business practices. We would sell to them in December and collect, if we were lucky, the following September. Any pressure to make them pay sooner would result in loads of returned products, which could not be sold until the next season. As they were the only available outlets, there was not much that we could do about it because, with the farmers being smallholders, we could not reach them individually.

Or was there? Why not open our own shop to replace the dealers? We debated the idea for some time. It was attractive in principle but had its drawbacks. The dealers knew many of their customers and would give them a few days' credit. We obviously could not do this as we were going in fresh. Then there was the question of whether we could trust someone to look after the stock and invoice correctly, out of sight of the managers. Finally, and perhaps most importantly, we did not know how other dealers would react when they saw that we were trading directly.

We went ahead and it was a great success. But we limited our one shop to this area although we had warehouses all over Ecuador that could quickly be transformed for retail sales. We had been instrumental in setting up many of the dealers around the country and they were loyal to us in their way. I say 'in their way' because they were equally loyal to our competitors. We had traditionally had a great advantage because we handled Gramoxone, a non-selective herbicide, which was the biggest-selling agrochemical on the market. But now this was out of patent protection and generic products were coming on to the market at lower prices.

Victor Hugo and I had spent weeks touring the country and talking to the dealers, to try and make them to sign a clause with us whereby they undertook not to handle a competing product to Gramoxone. We thought that we had been quite successful but later there were reports that the agreement was not holding. The dealers, who hated to lose any business at all, were buying competitive paraquat and hiding it under the counter or in another warehouse. As the margins on it were better than those on Gramoxone, they were pushing it. So we reckoned that we had not as much to lose as we thought and we went ahead with the plans for opening the shops, beginning with our fifteen warehouses and spreading out from there.

By the end of 1994, we had forty-eight shops but we did lose a great deal of momentum in the short term. The dealers in one town after another boycotted us for competing with them and the great beneficiaries were Ecuaquimica, number two in the market, which chiefly represented Ciba at this time, and Febres Cordero, which handled the most important generic paraquat (quaintly called Killer). But plenty of other smaller competitors gained at our expense and Gramoxone was opened up to a great deal of competition from which it has never quite recovered. Were we wrong to go down this route? We do not think so. The dealers were increasingly calling the shots, demanding ever more credit and better margins, so sooner or later we would have had to do something.

But now we were halfway through rolling out the new policy. We did not have sufficient points of sale to cover the country and the competition was having great fun, telling all the dealers that we would open a shop next to theirs in the near future and that it would be better not to promote Agripac products. There was no way that we could cover all the country at once. We did not have the personnel, or the sites to rent, or the cash to equip so many shops. Fortunately, the tenacity of the dealers came to our rescue. They hated to lose a sale and if they did not sell our well-known products, someone else would. So we existed for now with our mixed system.

Cash sales, which had traditionally been about ten per cent through our offices now rose to over twenty per cent of total sales. Of course, the shops also provided supply points for servicing the dealers nearby and also enabled us to invoice large direct accounts.

We had previously recruited new graduate agronomists to manage the shops on an ad hoc basis and they went straight into the job. This, of course, led to untold problems of inexperience, particularly as we were by now supplying the shops with PCs and invoicing through them. So we hit on the idea of what we call the 'Escuelita' or little school. We have just finished the eighth course this year.

We ask the universities to provide us with the details of about 100 of their best students who have graduated in agronomy or veterinary science and, from that list, we choose twenty who start the course. This takes six weeks and, using our own senior professionals, we train the students in all the technical and commercial aspects of our business as well as our computer systems. Those who prove the most apt are finally selected and twelve from each group are offered jobs in the company, although all who start the course are paid during this time. The new intake is then dispersed around the country as trainee shop managers or put into an extension job in, say, bananas or maize for six months or a year, when they finally become fully fledged shop managers.

We have trained over 100 students in this way and the best of those from the earlier courses are now in more senior positions as supervisors and managers. But this, of course, is all in-house training and in the early days, we were no experts in retailing ourselves although we are learning fast

Some years ago, in an attempt to kick-start the retail venture, we contacted a British organisation called British Executive Service Overseas or BESO (although 'beso' means kiss in Spanish, which is rather more fun!). It put me in touch with Ken Hemsworth, who had retired as general manager of the

Agripac shops. Today there are 80 of these.

The Agripac big truck.

Yorkshire Cooperative Society. He and his wife Treena came to Ecuador and spent six weeks with us, during which time we travelled around all our shops and Ken gave me ideas about shop layout and inventory. He had many good ideas which helped us but on one point we were both wrong. His experience had been in general retailing so he said that our shops were rather boring and needed a better selection of products to attract customers.

We thought about all the ancillary lines we might carry and went for it with a vengeance. We bought saddles and bridles, machètes, hammers and nails, picks and hoes, barbed wire, torches, boots, shoes and God knows what else. But these lines were not a success and we were still getting rid of the last ones years later. Customers had not looked for these products in our shops and, when they did find them, saw that we were too expensive. We had just bought from local suppliers without any market research and could not compete with the traditional small stores, which had years of experience in these lines and worked on very small margins.

We had been wrong for several reasons but had learned from the experience. In other parts of the world, especially New Zealand, I have seen small-town agrochemical dealers handling all of these things and more, even clothing, but these tended to be the only store in town for the farmer.

One line that I also saw in New Zealand has worked for us too and that is dog food. Until, say, ten years ago, the concept of manufactured dog food did not exist in Ecuador. The animal ate what was left over from the table. Then a local manufacturer tried making a product called Guau (woof, in English). It flopped because it gave dogs diarrhoea. But it was followed by an invasion of products, mainly from the States and Colombia. We contacted Ralston Purina, one of the world's largest producers of pet food, and obtained its line. As well as selling Purina through our normal shops, we opened four pet shops, two in Quito and two in Guayaquil, which are the largest markets. We also took on people with experience in the canine world to sell to independent pet shops. The line started very well indeed and Melvin Azofeifa, a Costa Rican who managed our veterinary line, took a great deal of interest in it as he is also a dog breeder himself. We sponsored all sorts of dog shows and the sales increased no end.

But as the dog food business, which had started from nothing, increased in value to over $10,000,000 per year (for the whole industry, sadly not for us alone), there was more and more competition. Of the latecomers, Pedigree (Mars) and Alpo (Nestlé) pushed in and more than fifteen national brands were established. Then came the great meltdown of 1999 and the market collapsed. Our sales were badly hit as, with 250% devaluation during the year, prices were constantly changing and rose much faster than wages, so that the housewife had to make economies and the family mutt went back to its leftover meals. To add to the problems, one of the pet shops which we had bought in a fit of enthusiasm, instead of renting as usual, was closed when the brand-new Puntilla Mall in Guayaquil collapsed with heavy debts. We also closed one of the two Quito shops so we just had two exclusive pet shops.

Over the years, we have been serviced by a series of ICI/Zeneca managers, who normally work in the area for two to three years before being sent to another part of the world as part of their career path. Jeff Pullen, Chris Richards, Nelson Echevarria, Flavio Prezzi and Sergio Dedominici have followed each other in sequence. Jeff retired this year; Chris has become the European marketing manager for Syngenta; Nelson joined BASF and is now its Mexican manager; Flavio is the Syngenta manager for Central America and Sergio the marketing manager for the same area. All have done well but we pride ourselves on helping the career of one very special friend, Valdemar Fischer.

In 1994, John Greaves and Flavio thought that Agripac could do with some fine-tuning (to put it mildly) in marketing. Flavio gave us several courses on the art of market segmentation and product differentiation. But he felt that we needed more permanent tuition so John decided that he would make Valdemar Fischer, one of his rising executives in Zeneca Brazil, available. Of German parentage, Valdemar comes from the south of Brazil near the Argentinian border, where they think of themselves as gauchos and need their daily infusion of maté. This is a tea-like plant and its effusion is drunk through a metal straw. The gaucho cannot function without it. So Valdemar, his wife Josi and their two little girls came to Ecuador on a three-year contract. He was not exactly

Tomas Guerrero, Chris Richards, John Greaves, Chris Bailey and Colin in front of Mapan House, 1995.

an Agripac employee so we created a position for him as marketing director, and Victor Hugo was to be his understudy. Valdemar is a tremendously hard worker and wasted no time in coming to grips with the local market and setting out plans for increasing Zeneca's sales.

We had lots of product launches including those of Bankit and Amistar (new-generation fungicides and the latest Zeneca discoveries), together with the relaunch of Karate, a rather more dated insecticide. There were plenty of field days and demonstrations and he had the idea of holding an annual conference for all sales personnel. Previously we had brought them together in groups. We first went to the Hotel Punta Carnero (site of the first Agripac meeting in 1972), then a beach resort in Esmeraldas, on the northern coast of Ecuador, and another time to Manta, on the west coast. These were all memorable occasions and valuable for staff morale.

At the same time, Zeneca was sponsoring Valdemar to take an MBA through a correspondence course with Lancaster University. His evenings and weekends were taken up with homework, quite apart from the modules which were completed in various places around the world, especially France, Montreal and Tokyo.

Valdemar had been one of several product managers in Brazil and, had he remained there, his career might have taken a very different course. But as he was approaching the end of his very successful time with us, he had a stroke of luck. The Zeneca general manager in Mexico left suddenly and John thought of Valdemar. He rang me for my opinion. 'He is excellent', I said, 'the best I have ever seen.' And that was very true. I have had several ICI young men through Agripac over the years and each one was returned to sender with low grades, because they lacked either brain or energy. Here was someone who was really going up. He was given the job of running the US$90,000,000 business and neither John nor I were mistaken, because it was later announced that Valdemar had been appointed the new general manager of Syngenta Mexico, which had a turnover in excess of US$150,000,000. He will go higher yet.

Back in 1993, I decided to seek some advice on the structure of the company and asked Juan Heinsohn for his opinion. He recommended that I talk to Mario Chavarria who, apart from being the Laquinsa finance manager, had a consultancy business. Mario agreed to come to Ecuador for a week and have a look at us. When he presented his report, he had made an organogram in which several lines of command radiated down from me. 'But where does Mario Ramos come in?' I asked. 'He doesn't', he said, 'as currently everyone is reporting to you.' This made me think. Mario Ramos and I had been partners for twenty years and it was generally understood that he handled the administration, finance and personnel while I was responsible for the sales

But I saw what Mario Chavarria was implying. We had always worked in harmony but recently there had been one or two divergences of ideas. While I was in favour of expansion, he felt that we could be less aggressive. There was also some polarisation in the office between Colin's men and Mario's men. This is not healthy because it leads to irrational decisions. Over the years, I had stood up for people long past the point at which they were defensible simply because he was attacking them, and he did the same. Then we had a row over the new personnel manager, Cecil Villacres. Mario did not think that we needed a manager in this position as he handled personnel very well himself. But I had heard a fair amount of comment about favouritism in promotion and salaries from several people in the company. It was an area that I did not want to become too involved in, so I felt that we needed a professional personnel manager, particularly now that we had some 400 people in the group.

These and other considerations made me decide to suggest to Mario that we go our separate ways. He was very reluctant as he clearly enjoyed his job and status as the Agripac general manager and he continued to perform this role well and faithfully. But I still thought of buying him out until the idea dominated everything else and finally he agreed to talks on the value of the shares. We had some difficulty in valuing these as they were not quoted on the stock market, his estimates obviously being very high and mine somewhat lower. Eventually we agreed on an honest broker, Pedro Filipe Riveira, the vice-president of Citibank in Guayaquil, who was a friend of both of us. He made his calculations, discounted cash flow, produced residual values and so forth and came up with a number which was accepted by both sides. Then Alfredo drew up the necessary documents, which were somewhat complicated as there were several companies involved. We signed in front of a notary public, shook hands and that was that.

I had to borrow quite heavily to buy Mario out and, although this took some time to pay off, I have never regretted my decision to do it. Curiously, as Guayaquil is not a very big place, I have not bumped into Mario since that day six years ago. But I do hear of him as my one remaining partner, Ivan Noboa, is related to Mario through his wife and they meet occasionally at Mario's grandmother's house. He has investments both inside and outside of Ecuador and is doing well. He also asks after the company and takes an interest in how we are doing.

After Mario left, I was faced with the prospect of looking after those sides of the business which had been his domain. I did not fancy the idea so I asked Price Waterhouse to advertise for a financial manager. And that was when Elena de Portes came into my life. It was not the first time that we had met, as I had known her as the assistant manager of Lloyds Bank in Guayaquil ten years previously. Since then, she had worked for Abbott Laboratories in Guayaquil and now that they were moving their operations to Quito, she was looking for a new position.

Elena is a large woman in every sense of the word. She has a great deal of personality and, after the first interview, I had no hesitation in selecting her from the three candidates shortlisted. She had been brought up in New York and spoke perfect English, had exactly the right curriculum vitae and I was keen to employ her. She bargained hard as to her salary but we finally reached an agreement, although, if I remember correctly, she negotiated again before finally arriving at her desk. She came in like a whirlwind and before too long changes were being made. Cecil Villacres (who was actually a woman, although the name sounds like that of a man) was shown the door. All the departments under her command were reorganised, but she was obviously very competent and things improved. She instituted a format of balances in dollars which, although we had had dollar balances for several years, was a great improvement. We had adopted dollar balances as the only way to compare one year with another as, by this time, we were in a period of increasing inflation and devaluation of up to fifty per cent per year. This meant that to make comparisons one had to remember what the dollar rate had been at any given moment in the past.

Elena joined the company in February 1995 and, although it was a year of growth, we did not make much money at all. But there was one niggle — we did seem to be looking after ourselves too well. Elena introduced a car purchase plan which, she assured me, was used by all large companies. This meant that executives were allowed to buy cars of their choice within a certain, fairly generous price range. This was financed by a loan from the company to the executive and paid off at so much a mile rent. After four years, the car belonged to the executive. The company paid for the insurance, petrol and a set of tyres every year. Of course, the snag was that it paid the executive to have the biggest car possible. The larger it was, the more it held its value and the more they would make when selling it at the end of four years, so the company car park became full of expensive autos. As Agripac paid for the petrol, we ended up paying much more to have the same job done. I could never understand the benefits for the company but I had every faith in her judgement and went along with it. Then there was the question of changing the furniture and carpets. It seemed that it was very important for the wellbeing of our staff that their working environment should be perfect.

The year 1996 was better and we did make reasonable profits. As these were forecast to double in 1997, I was carried away and, when she asked to be made general manager in February of that year, I agreed. Since Mario had left, I had taken the title of both president and general manager. She argued that she had an ambition of being a general manager before she was forty which, by coincidence, was that year. So I agreed and, from then on, she really took the bull by the horns.

Agripac's twenty-fifth anniversary was also in 1997. It began with a pleasant surprise. The rather noble Spanish-style house, which had stood empty next to us for seven years, was finally for sale and Gerado Pena, a lawyer whom I knew, called me in January to offer it for sale. We offered $350,000 and, after some bargaining, bought it for $400,000. It was perhaps no bargain but we really wanted it and had done for some years. We went to look at it excitedly and, despite having been empty for so long, it was not in too bad a condition although it was very dusty and contained the odd dead rat. It is quite large, about 700 square metres on two floors with a flat roof terrace. It has very high ceilings and an open courtyard in the centre with a fountain — altogether oozing with potential for renovation. We immediately decided that this house would not be used for offices but for a staff dining room, guest dining room, bar, two conference rooms and six bedrooms for our out-of-town staff and visitors. All in all, it would be Agripac's social centre and, with the twenty-fifth anniversary celebrations to come, the challenge was to have it renovated by November. Actually, we claim May as our anniversary date but we could stretch a point there.

I called my old architect friend, Nelson Farah, and we made plans to make an atrium by putting a glass roof over the open patio, which would allow us to install central air-conditioning. We would keep everything that we could in its original state including the floors and doors, which were in good condition. However, the bathrooms had all to be renovated and each bedroom made en suite. We started with only five bedrooms but gained one more and a conference room by roofing over the balconies in which the house abounded. The kitchen was far too small for our needs and we built on to the house at one end to double the space. Then, as the house had been built on a platform some four feet above the ground, we found that, by excavating earth from beneath it, we could create several cellars. One of these was made into a larder, another into an extra dining room for outside staff and a third into a wine cellar under the bar. Then we converted the odd rooms on the flat roof of the house into a laundry and the chapel into a bar. The latter caused some eyebrows to be raised but, as I explained, the use was the same and only the spirit had changed!

Then we had to join the new house to Agripac. There was only a wall separating the garden from our car park and, taking this down, we discovered that the ground levels differed by about two feet. We set about correcting this and removing an old swimming pool and restoring the garden, which was totally overgrown. This had a lovely fountain, which we managed to repair, and finally we extended our car park behind the building and we had a seamless join to Agripac.

Next came the furniture and fittings and Ceci and I had lots of fun deciding on these and buying a job lot of paintings. The paintings were taken on approval, as we were rushing to be finished for our twenty-fifth anniversary but, in the end, we kept them all. So now we have the Agripac social centre where every day over 100 of us meet for lunch, where meetings are held, where our out-of-town staff and overseas visitors stay and where we hold parties to celebrate birthdays and other social occasions. But, of course, a guest house cannot function without people.

Elena knew of Maria Dolores Molinas, who was running a catering service in a nearby convention centre. She introduced us and it was agreed that she would start at the beginning of 1998, bringing all of her ten staff with her. So we had a complete team who could work well together. The kitchen equipment took some collecting but in February 1998, we finally had our first lunch there

The 25 year celebrations. Photo shows *from left to right* – A distributor, Javier Lavayen, Chris Bailey, Antonio Zambrano (the first employee), Colin, Lourdes Rodrigues and Valdemar Fischer.

and everyone agreed that it was excellent. The standard has been maintained to this day.

There are many advantages of eating together, one being that we can relate with each other much more. With more than 100 people in the office and another 300 in other parts of Ecuador, we obviously cannot see each other all the time. But with regular meetings held at head office bringing people in from the provinces, there is a good chance that we will meet over lunch. It is even difficult to contact the office staff at Guayaquil when one needs them. Telephones are busy, they are travelling or in meetings but, luckily, they all eat lunch and I can generally tick off several pending points in my diary at lunch time.

The building was all kitted out but we had no name for it. We toyed with Villa Agripac or Cecilia House but this was not what we wanted. At this time, Ceci and I went to the Zeneca Partnership meeting at Barilochi in Argentina, where we stayed at a magnificent hotel called the Llao-llao. In the gardens were a type of hornbill, the size of chickens, which were called Bandurria. That was it — we would call the new house Villa Bandurria. And so it was. To reinforce the message, we bought a wooden carving of the bird and it now stands proudly on a table. At first, people had trouble remembering the name but now it is well known both inside and outside the company because, during the El Niño period, we held two queen's birthday celebrations for 250 people

Agripac head office 1997. Bottom left Villa Bandurria. Bottom right the original Agripac house.

there. Now that we hold the party at Rodeo Grande again, our Bandurria staff still do the catering. Moreover, all company entertaining in Guayaquil has to be done at Bandurria which saves us a great deal, and which is positively disliked by the local restaurants. An institution has been born.

So we began 1997 with a large purchase and that set the tone for the year. We went on to buy a large plot of land outside the town of Machala, to the south of the country, which had been a tractor distribution centre and which had some buildings and workshops on it. We then proceeded to build on to these to make a base of offices, shop and warehouse. We had needed a base in the south for years as we were using a series of rented warehousing and a shop.

The next offer which we could not refuse came from the other end of the country, where we rented a large warehouse and shop in the middle of Santo Domingo. It belonged to a bus cooperative and it had offered to sell it to us the previous year. But, at the last moment, it backed out of the deal and sold to a bank which, we suspected, was collecting a debt from it under duress. We were rather worried that we would have to move and there was no other suitable place for us nearby so we would lose our clientele. But the bank offered to sell us the site, albeit at a considerable premium to the sum that we had been negotiating. Having found few satisfactory options in the meantime, we went for it.

This purchase was followed by a similar one in Pedernales. The problem is that there is no such thing as a binding lease for a fixed period of years in Ecuador. One rents a property for a year or two at a time. Even so, the rental contract is terminated if the property is sold. So it was in Pedernales: we had to either buy the property or leave. Pedernales is on the west coast and at the time was very much on the up and up, with the shrimp industry booming. Once again, there was little alternative to the good location we already had, so we went ahead and bought it. We then bought a pet shop in a new shopping mall called Puntilla Mall. This was one of my poorer decisions, as the mall opened at the same time as three other malls in Guayaquil and failed to find an anchor company. It had tried to attract Sears Roebuck of the USA which went elsewhere; the two big supermarket chains had their own malls; and the company which it found, Santa Isabel of Chile, had only recently set up in Ecuador and failed to attract customers. After a year the mall closed, taking our shop with it.

But the biggest purchase was yet to come. Travelling to Quevedo, which is in the centre of the country and its most important agricultural area by far, I had noticed a battery of grain silos for sale. We thought long and hard about this and decided that they would fit well in with our business, as they would allow us to receive grain from the farmers as payment for our credits. We would dry it and store it until we could sell it to feed mills and thus get our money back. The easiest way to collect these credits is to approach the farmer before he sells his crop, as we have found from bitter experience that, once he has the cash, he can find an awful lot of uses for it besides paying his debts! So we negotiated this for several weeks and before we had completed the deal, I went to England on holiday, leaving Elena with a maximum price that we were prepared to pay. She did not contact me before closing the deal and I found, to my annoyance, that we had paid somewhat more than I had wanted.

This was also the year of the new software, although the deal had been signed in 1996. Elena and Bolivar Vallejo, our long-time computer expert, had been telling me that the original in-house system, which Bolivar had developed very successfully over many years and which was his own invention, no longer allowed us to do all that we needed to do. A brand new software system was called for.

I have since heard many horror stories of other companies buying and installing software but at that time it did not seem such a big deal. As I am an absolute dunce on the subject, I opted out of the preliminary meetings as being beyond my ken. So Elena took the project on. The contract was signed with a Venezuelan company for $230,000. I was staggered by the amount but, on asking around, was told that it was par for the course. The system would be installed and up and running in eighteen months. Those eighteeen months had passed by early 1998 and I kept asking when we were to see the wonders that were to come. Soon, I was told, just another month. But the months came and went with nothing to show for them. A group of technical people from the supplier seemed to live with us for months on end, using the facilities of Bandurria. They had a very tranquil air about them and I often saw them wandering across the patio on their way to lunch or back. But the contract had a fixed price and it was in their interest to finished it as soon as they could, so I imagined that these high-powered programmers were using all available energy for their brains and leaving little over for fast walking.

Towards the end of 1998, I was becoming somewhat irritable about the endless excuses for not finishing the plan but was told that the last, the very last, date for completion was the end of December of that year. I was not too happy with this either, as we were in the middle of our big season and changing computer systems then did not seem the wisest move. But we had to do it sooner or later.

By early February 1999, work was still in progress and I began to look into the reason for all the delays and, I suspected, costs too. Manuel Suco, our controller, carried out an audit and, lo and behold, the system had already cost $460,000, ninety-five percent of which had been paid already, and it was still not functioning properly.

The technical people were being paid on an hourly basis at an extraordinarily high rate, with travel expenses back and forth to Venezuela, and neither they nor their employer had any incentive to finish the contract. There were no penalty clauses. This led to a short, sharp meeting with Elena. Why had I not been told of the escalating cost, why did she accept the work on a time plus basis and why had so much been paid before we had proved that the system worked? This and other matters led to Elena's resignation.

So now, for the first time since 1973, I had to face running both the administration and sales of the company. I was no longer prepared to look for another general manager. Mario had been excellent but eventually we had disagreed, and Elena had been a powerhouse but had taken too many decisions which I considered mine. What should I do now? My first reaction was to call my old friend Fred Brown, a partner in Deloitte and Touche. We discussed my predicament and talked of carrying out an analysis of our management structure. But we never did this, as the solution was fairly obvious.

We had a top layer of management in Ivan Noboa (administration of the Sierra region), Chris Bailey (purchase, plant and distribution), Victor Hugo Quimi (agrochemical and seeds sales) and Manuel Suco (controller). Johnny Coloma had left shortly after Mario did. But we had a new recruit in Ivan's son, Eduardo, who had just returned from doing an MBA in Spain and had been taken on to carry out a marketing project, but who now was promoted to personnel manager. The solution was simply to close ranks. Each was given part of Elena's role and I took on the financial aspect, together with Manuel Suco and Liz Sevilla, our treasurer.

We had started 1999 in a most promising manner, with record sales in January and February. We were looking forward to a record year. The best year so far had been 1998, with sales of over $52,000,000 (although with precious little profit, thanks to the finance charges on all our spending) and we were budgeting for $60,000,000 for this year. We had seventy-five shops and all was well. Or was it?

A crisis was about to hit of proportions never yet seen in Ecuador. It is difficult to pinpoint the precise cause of this, although it has been widely debated. It stemmed from political difficulties going back some time. We had also expected an excellent year in 1995. Sixto Duran Ballen was the president and Alberto Dahik vice-president. The year before had finished well, with plans for modernisation of the economy and privatisation of the electricity and telecommunications industries. After years of dithering, Ecuador was about to make a leap forward into the brave new world.

How Satan must have laughed! He had other plans for Ecuador. These began with a war with Peru in January — an explosion in the simmering border dispute between the two countries, which had been an open sore since Peru had invaded and taken a large area of Ecuador's Amazon basin in 1941. Both sides rushed to arms, although the fighting lasted only a month or so with relatively few casualties, including thirty-five deaths on the Ecuadorian side (mainly caused by mines). However, the cost to the economy in weapon purchases was estimated at $500,000,000, thus skewing the budget, which was already in deficit. Then, in June of that year, Dahik was accused, rightly or wrongly, of misusing public funds and impeached. He fled to Costa Rica to avoid remand in gaol.

After that, the resolve went out of Sixto's government and no more was heard of privatisation. Inflation began to rise. His government was followed by that of Abdala Bucaram, who lived up to his nickname of Loco (crazy) with performances of singing and dancing around the country, while his eighteen-year-old son Jacobo held a widely reported celebration of his first 1,000,000 dollars. He lasted six months until, in a huge demonstration of public disapproval, millions of people took to the streets and he fled to Panama, later being deposed by Congress as mentally unfit to rule.

Things grew little better under his successor, Fabian Alarcon, who was elected as president of the country by congress instead of Rosalia Arteaga who, as vice-president, should have taken over, according to the constitution. Alacon had achieved his position in congress by wheeling and dealing and showed the same form as president of the country, bending over backwards to accommodate every pressure group. Public sector salaries increased and the budget deficit grew worse. Mercifully, his term of office was only eighteen months and Jamil Mahaud won the new elections in July 1998. But these were close-run as Alvaro Noboa, Ecuador's richest man (although his fortune was inherited from his father) stood for Abdala's party, the PRE, and nearly made it. He made allegations of fraud and thereby undermined the legitimacy of Mahaud's presidency. The year was characterised by strikes and civil disorder as both Alvaro Noboa and Abdala Bucaram (having meanwhile fallen out) organised street protests. The situation was made worse when the Guayaquil chambers of commerce and industry went into permanent opposition to the elected government and Humberto Mata, a new player to politics, began a campaign for autonomy for Guayas.

Despite all the protests, the new president started well. He obtained a final peace agreement with Peru and reaped the peace dividend by reducing the military budget. But he neglected the economy. The time bomb of the budget deficit was ticking away and urgent measures were not taken. Inflation increased alarmingly, as did devaluation, so that, by early 1999, the sucre was rapidly losing value. It began the year at 6,000 to the dollar. By February, it was 8,000, by March 10,000, then 14,000, then 18,000. Clearly things were out of control.

Then banks began to collapse through lack of liquidity. Several had gone down in previous months but each one appeared to be an isolated case and could be explained away. Now the effect was across the board. In alarm, the government closed all the banks for a week and froze fifty per cent of all deposits as well as bank loans for a year.

The banks reopened and the dollar stabilised at around 9,000 sucres, before beginning to run again from June onwards. But the damage was done and fourteen banks, representing seventy per cent of total bank capital, were taken into government receivership. The sucre continued to run until January 2000 when Mahaud, in desperation, decreed that the dollar should be adopted as the national currency at a parity of 25,000 sucres. Too late to save his political life, he was ejected from office ten days later by an unholy alliance of dissident colonels, Indians and left-wing factions. However, everything ended happily as, with pressure from the USA, the vice-president Gustavo Noboa (no relation to Alvaro) took over the presidency. He has proved to be an excellent president and has steered the economy towards recovery.

But now back to February 1999 and Agripac. I took the reins of the company back into my own hands and was appalled at the problem facing me. Cash just did not flow. We had had an excellent January and February, which means that we had extended large amounts of credit to our distributors and farmers, in the latter case until harvest in June. When the cash came in, it simply would not buy the required amount of dollars with which to pay our suppliers. It was a classic case of the danger of buying and selling in different currencies.

We had, of course, always lived with this problem but now the sucre was falling so fast that it was impossible to keep up. In March, we met with all our competitors and decided to sell only in dollars so we were covered from then on. But what about our outstanding collections? There was no way that we could negotiate them again: we just had to wait and see what the dollar rate would be at collection time. In fact, the government's action in freezing deposits and thereby stablising the sucre gave us a breathing space to collect sucres, buy dollars and pay suppliers. It was not as bad as it might have been but it was certainly bad enough.

We talked to Zeneca and all our suppliers, explaining the situation and asking for extra time to pay. At one point, we were running ninety days and more behind with payments. Chris Bailey and I spent all day long fielding calls from both national and foreign suppliers, who were obviously worried about their exposure to the meltdown in Ecuador. Some were more generous than others, who went for their pound of flesh and charged interest on the late payments. Some, to their great credit, extended payments free of charge and talked of many years of good business before and more to come in the future.

We planned to sell little and expensively while we were in this difficult position of being behind with payments and having trouble making some suppliers ship to us at all. The plan worked and gradually we caught up with payments until, in February 2000, we were finally up to date with everyone.

But that was only half of our problem as we had bank debt too, which had begun to increase since I had bought out Mario. This was compounded by our buying spree of the previous year and Elena's cavalier approach to cost control. In 1997, money had been cheap and it was easy to make a case for borrowing ever more. But in 1998, with El Niño affecting the country, political problems and inflation, the interest rates shot up — to ninety per cent for sucres and even to eighteen per cent for dollars, at a time when we were greatly exposed to debt. We had then to decide whether to pay the suppliers or the banks first. They were both pushing us very hard. The friendly banker of yore, who asked what more he could do to help us, had vanished, to be replaced by the ogre who demanded that we fulfil our obligations to repay, which had been contracted in another world. In the end, we paid some to one and some to another, but were very careful to pay bank interest up to date so that we did not drop our prized credit rating. Once we had the suppliers up to date, we attacked the bank loans and have done so well that we are almost debt-free by now, for the first time in the history of Agripac.

How? In part this was possible because most of our debt was in sucres and, as the sucre devalued by 250 per cent, the debt melted like snow in summer. It was partly down to good planning but also partly to good luck as the government's decision to freeze most bank loans for a year gave us a respite.

But there are always winners and losers and the hapless loser was the owner of the sucre savings account who, when he finally recovered his savings, found that they too had melted like snow.

Apart from reducing what we owed as quickly as we possibly could, we took a hard look at expenses and cut out all advertising and any expense that was not strictly necessary. We reduced our workforce, more or less by natural wastage and freezing recruitment by about eight per cent, from 470 to 416, although it later began to rise again. But rather than concentrate on total numbers, we looked closely at the largest salaries.

Elena, the most well paid, had already left. Now we offered Caupo Manriques a deal whereby he took the small household fumigation business that he ran in exchange for leaving our payroll. Then John Greenwood, who ran the seeds line, was laid off and returned to England, later taking a job in Brazil. Daniel Loor, who was already the manager for short cycle (as opposed to plantation) crops, took on this extra responsibility. Finally, Juan Fernando Gutierrez, who ran the consumer products line (dog food and household insecticides), was replaced by a long-term insider, Ricardo Ochoa. Our three directors, Ivan, Chris and Victor Hugo, accepted a deal whereby their salaries were reduced in exchange for profit sharing. I cut my salary by fifty per cent, which reflected the average reduction in everyone's pay due to the huge devaluation. So we were all on half pay in dollar terms, but this was not as bad as it sounds as prices had also fallen.

All in all, the cost of running the company had been reduced by forty per cent and, with little debt, we were now lean and mean and ready to face the future. In the dreadful year of 1999, our sales were reduced by over twenty-five per cent and 2000 would be only a little better. But we were gearing up for a tremendous 2001 when, with more shops, more salespeople and particularly better prices, we aimed to beat the last record and take the company sales figures into new realms.

THE FORBIDDEN CORNER

I HAVE MENTIONED the origins of the Forbidden Corner from time to time. Now is the moment to tell the tale in more or less chronological order.

In 1974, just before marrying Ceci, I had talked to Aunt Do about the possibility of buying Tupgill. She had agreed to the idea and Tupgill had become ours later that year. It was a labour of love to restore the stables and while doing so, I had noticed, or remembered as I was well aware of it before, that the wind howled down the yard from the west, scattering straw everywhere. It was difficult to keep clean. So I decided to plant a windbreak to the west of the yard in a small, triangular field containing Nissen huts left behind by the army after the war. Aunt Do had kept chickens in those huts for many years but now the chickens had long gone and they were in a sorry state. We had them removed and, during the winter of 1979, planted hundreds of fir trees in this field.

The wind howled down the yard.

As anyone who plants little trees knows, the first years are ones of great deception when the only things that appear to grow are weeds. So it was in was our case. The field had been a bed of nettles and they came back with a vengeance to smother my trees. Brian Morris (the father of my almost adoptive son, Leo) undertook most of the planting with Doug Weatherill. Then each summer was a battle with the weeds. We bought two strimmers and would go round and round, trying to keep our charges alive.

The winters would lead to beating up, the practice of replacing each dead tree with a new one. But after three years, the trees finally start to grow properly. Weed control continues but it is easier to see the heads of the trees and one avoids strimming so many to death.

The years went by and gradually Ceci and I produced our family of three. Nick was born in 1976, Diana in 1978 and Alex in 1981. They grew with the trees, but a little faster.

Then as now, summers were spent at Tupgill but we stayed longer, even eight or ten weeks, as we visited only once a year. So I had plenty of time to help in the tree field. The children would come and see me there until they found something more exciting to do and, in an effort to keep them with me longer, I began to invent a game of hide and seek. By this time, the trees would be about five feet high and, as they were quite densely planted, they provided good cover. With the strimmers, Doug and I (Brian having died) made paths and a rudimentary maze which the children, Ceci and I could play in. It was all good fun.

The years passed by and the children grew up but I still spent a lot of time during summer in my little wood, which we had named the Nicholas Wood. At the far corner, I discovered that there was a most lovely view right down Coverdale and across the Vale of York to the Hambleton Hills beyond. On a clear day, you could see the White Horse carved on the hillside near Sutton Bank, all of thirty miles away.

I decided to make a little bower here with a rustic seat where one could sit and stare. But bowers require seclusion and my selected site was at the corner of a field with small, crumbling farm walls and, as it was at the western corner of the site, it was perennially draughty too.

In 1989, I shared my ideas with Malcolm Tempest, with whom I had now worked for nearly twelve years, beginning with the reconstruction of Ferngill House and working our way through the rebuilding of the stables. Malcolm and I got on well and shared a love of good building as well as a sense of humour. But it must be said that Malcolm generally took an idea of mine and magnified it. If I had achieved anything left to myself, it would have been small, probably insignificant and, more than likely, not have given me or anyone else the pleasure which everyone has gained from his creation. As the family knows well, I do like to look after the pennies but lasting monuments are not built on the cheap. During the building of the Forbidden Corner, there were many times when I came close to despair with the cost but each time this happened, it could not be avoided for one reason or another. So I soldiered on, vowing that we would just finish the piece we were doing and no more. But then I so enjoyed the effect that my enthusiasm returned and we went on with the next piece of the jigsaw, until finally it was all coming together and developed a life of its own. I read somewhere the phrase that 'the quality remains long after you have forgotten the cost' and think that this is a fitting epigram here.

Malcolm and I walked the course together in the summer of 1989. We looked at where the bower was to be and agreed that the first job was to build a high wall around Nicholas Wood to give the effect of a walled garden and to shelter it from the wind.

Malcolm generally took an idea of mine and magnified it.

A large 25 foot hole had been dug.

Denis Fawcett had been working at Tupgill as a waller since 1985 and it was to him that we entrusted the work. It was quite a project as it was some 400 yards long and initially the walls were seven feet high. To the south of the wood, the ground fell away quickly into a field and we decided to terrace this, which involved building an especially strong wall to withstand the pressure of the infilled earth behind it. Denis started at the south-west corner in September 1990 and walled uphill along our boundary with Sally Hall's Brecongill estate.

I had just bought two small pieces of land adjoining the Nicholas Wood from Sally, as the original field tapered to a point on the west side and was rather an awkward shape. Sally kindly let me square it off.

While Denis was starting the wall, which was to take him some three years to finish as he insisted on working alone, Malcolm and I were already talking about a grotto. This is a perfect example of how one word can mean very different things to different people. When I talked about a grotto, I had visions of a little cave made of piled rocks in which a little 'green-eyed yellow monster' might be found — all very diminutive. In Ecuador, the word translates as 'gruta' and they are often found by the roadside with the statue of a saint within a mock-rock, shallow cave. To Malcolm, the word suggested the duke of Portland and Welbeck Abbey, where that eccentric fellow tunnelled for miles

Denis Fawcett on part of his 15 year walling programme with Dairy cottages in the background.

under his park. Malcolm and I recently went to see it and managed, with special dispensation, to enter, as it is now part of a military academy. The tunnelling is now largely blocked off and weeds abound at the several entrances but it was still worth seeing, as was his underground ballroom. But this was years after building our grotto.

I cannot remember now why there was no plan at the beginning. Malcolm always draws what the final result of any project will look like beforehand, but in this case the drawings came afterwards. Perhaps we had agreed on an exploratory dig to see what the subsoil was like. In those days, we still communicated by mail which is a very slow procedure, with letters taking ten days each way from England to Ecuador, if indeed they ever do arrive. As an aside, I once received a book from the Good Book Guide, which had been posted seven years previously.

Ceci and I had returned to Ecuador in November 1990 after spending half term with Nick and Diana. In December, Elaine called me to say that she was very worried that Malcolm had gone over the top on the grotto project. He had a huge digger on the site and a large twenty-five-foot deep hole had been dug, with spoil being carted away in dumper trucks down to the old Coverham Dairy site, which we had bought a couple of years ago and which was now our builders' yard. She asked me to talk to Malcolm and see what it was all going to cost because, as so many times since, she was worried about all the bills that were coming in and our overdraft with Barclays.

There were many other work sites on the estate at the time including the renovation of the dairy cottages from derelict, white-painted brick to beautiful stone houses; the widening of the road to Birdridding Farm; the building of the new Tupgill gates and the widening of the drive.

The gates project led to my second brush with the Yorkshire Dales National Park Authority planning committee. The first of these had been a plan to convert the Tupgill garages into offices, which was refused permission as not being in keeping with the area. Now the authority ordered a halt to the building of the gates as being out of keeping and 'pretentious'. We clearly had to fight this. The offices plan was just an idea for the future but the gate pillars were already built and huge wrought-iron gates had been ordered. The gates are a work of art and Malcolm has incorporated birds and animals from Ecuador in the design. Clearly, they were somewhat larger than those they had replaced but we argued that they were the entrance to four racing stables, which could not be viewed in the same light as a farm, and that there were already many gates of this sort within the national park. We finally won this one by a small majority of votes from the committee.

I called Malcolm and, as always, he convinced me that I should have faith and I would like the result. I next saw it at April, when we were again in England to return the children to school after the Easter holidays. It still looked pretty awful. Very heavy rains had filled the hole with water and, to drain it away, a channel had been dug southwards. But that meant even more digging

The dairy cottages get a face lift.

and more spoil to be moved. We found the subsoil to be boulder clay and the huge, rounded boulders were taken out and stockpiled for future use in the rock-walled canyon approach to the Temple. But we also discovered that there were many underground springs, which was why the hole was constantly flooding. Drainage would need a great deal of care or the grotto would be permanently damp.

We did drain it well and, moreover, collected the water in underground tanks, which today stand us in good stead for irrigation and filling the Griffin Pond. But at the time, everything looked very sad, with the rain causing the sides of the hole to cave in continually and even threatening to undermine the foundations of Denis's wall, which ran close by on two sides.

That was one of the moments when I wondered if we should stop. But I would have had only a muddy hole to show for a great deal of expense and could not face the prospect of filling it in. It would also have meant collecting up all the spoil and carting it back. Soon I returned to Ecuador, not exactly thrilled with what I had started. But I had meanwhile bought a book called *The Art Of The Maze*, by Fisher and Garster and reading this rekindled my enthusiasm.

The New Tupgill gates.

Detail of the Tupgill gates showing a humming bird.

The summer of 1991 was better. By now, the hole was stabilised and a vast wire cage was being built in it, which had been recommended by the structural engineer to withstand the weight of the ground to go back on top of it. It was in the shape of a bottle and the neck was to become the ventilation point. There were three entrances to the bottle at its base. The wire cage took ages to construct and then came the great day when we poured in the first concrete. One after another, the concrete lorries came over the field (which was fortunately dry) and pumped their loads into the shuttering around the wire. With each pouring, the level was raised only a couple of feet as the concrete had to be very dense and all the air removed so as to be completely waterproof. Slowly, painfully and expensively, the bottle took shape. Nick even worked on it at this time as his week's work experience after his GCSEs.

That summer, looking for ideas, I went to see Skipton Castle, where it was reported that there was a shell grotto. I went into the booth at the entrance to the castle, paid my entrance charge and asked for the location of the grotto that I had come especially to see. 'You're in it,' said the bored cashier. I looked around me and, sure enough, there were shells on the walls but it was quite small and not very impressive. The rest of the castle was better, though. Later, Ceci and I drove to Wales and saw Portmeirion. Now that is worth seeing and, although not a grotto, it is a most delightful place, an Italianate village planted in a cove on the Welsh coast. It is truly lovely with its gardens, piazzas and cobbled streets, and I hope that we have created some of this effect in the Forbidden Corner. That night, we stayed at Bodysgallen Hall Hotel on the north coast of Wales, which once again provided inspiration because of its huge gardens and use of terraces.

Aunt Do died in 1992. She was blind by that time so there was no way that she could ever have seen the grotto being built. But each evening, as I sat with her for an hour or so and we sipped a gin and tonic, I would tell her of all the work going on. She had lost her sight ten years ago and whenever anyone asked her if she missed the lovely views from Tupgill windows, she would reply that she had the view in her memory and could see it every day. In the same way, she could visualise all that I told her of the work as it progressed. We did not talk of the cost at all; we had a sort of pact and never discussed unpleasant things. In a way, this made our conversations somewhat superficial but we both preferred it that way. She was ninety-four when she died and is buried next to Father in Coverham churchyard.

That year Allan Bell joined us from the Bolton Estate, which was retrenching somewhat. Allan is a forester and the original idea was that he spend his time exclusively on the new plantings on the estate. By then, we had planted some twenty acres of trees and went on to plant lots more. In 1992, we turned our attention to the park when, with Malcolm helping with the design, we set about converting the twelve acres of grassland into woodland and glades — just as Coverdale was in the fifteenth century, when it was a hunting chase belonging to Middleham Castle. Richard III would have hunted here, as would

The building of the main chamber.

his elder brother, Edward IV, who was a prisoner at Middleham during the Wars of the Roses, although given liberty to hunt in the surrounding area.

The grotto was taking shape and Malcolm and I were looking for new ideas and materials to use. He knew of the company Haddonstone of Northampton, which made garden ornaments from reconstituted stone. Its local agent was Tulip Bemrose, who lived in a lovely old house with a large garden in the village of Wath near Bedale. We went to see her and immediately decided we liked the look of the things they produced, which were displayed in the garden. Later, Malcolm and I went to Northampton and bought a couple of lorry loads of ornaments, including statues, vases, pillars and capitals. Tulip moved house soon afterwards and gave up her agency but became the artist behind the gardens we have made. She continues to look after them, together with Allan Bell and Allan Morris, Harry's son, who transferred from the farm to the estate when his father retired as farm manager. After Harry, David Findlay (a graduate of Harper Adams) took over as farm manager and, in turn, has Graham Heseltine to assist him.

By the end of 1992, the concrete bottle had been finished and Albert Calvert, the building contractor, began to form the entrance tunnels. We decided that we could avoid the huge expense of the cast and reinforced concrete model used in the bottle by building these in double layers of concrete blocks with reinforcing bars and concrete fillings. We thought that this would be strong enough for the entrances as their volume was much less. The whole structure had to be wrapped in plastic sheeting and gravel before the soil was put back on top to ensure that the water drained away and did not make it damp.

Up to this stage, the project was entirely private and I was receiving a certain amount of criticism from the family for pouring their inheritance into a hole in the ground. It was difficult to explain why I was doing this, even to myself. It was not that I had so much money that I was looking for ways to waste it.

It is said that if you seriously want to spend your cash, you either buy a yacht, keep racehorses or have a mistress. I am a poor sailor, have had a racehorse and Ceci jibs at the third option. I was doing this because it gave me a lot of fun. During troubled times in Ecuador, I relaxed by thinking of the grotto and planning new additions. Malcolm expressed these ideas in pictorial form and we went on.

Now, we had our first chance to enjoy it together at Hallowe'en. We planned a fireworks party and decorated the inside of the grotto with candles. Then, in fancy dress, we drank our mulled wine and ate a stew made of black beans and pork with rice, a great Ecuadorian dish which is served at Mapan every Saturday night when we are there. Malcolm rose to the occasion and made a very impressive Viking; even more so when, around a bonfire on the frosty evening, he darted to and fro, letting off the fireworks he had provided. Malcolm being Malcolm, these were not the normal Brocks fireworks but outsized Chinese ones, which made an impressive show. As he is, shall we say, a little portly, he looked quite the real thing when wrapped in sheepskins with leggings and helmet. So finally the family was realising that the grotto would be a perfect place for parties. 'But it's all done now, Dad, so finish there.' 'Ah no, me dears, there is a lot more to come.'

At the time of the party, the entrance to the grotto was just a concrete passageway at the bottom of an earth ramp. We had several ideas about how to finish it. Malcolm favoured a cave effect, with an approach up a canyon of boulders which would be a stream bed with stepping stones. I preferred something rather more classical so we hit on the idea of using the largest Haddonstone pillars to make a temple-like entrance. These pillars are some six metres high and had Corinthian capitals on top, which raised them another metre — altogether very imposing. Then they were crossed by lintels so they really stood out.

It did cross our minds that the planners might at last begin to notice us although we could not understand how they had failed to so far. Some thirty of Albert's men had been working for two years, together with all sorts of machinery. We were obviously invisible to mortal men. There was never any question of asking for planning permission. For one thing, we had no idea where we were going when we started. Then again, the planners who had

Building the boulder canyon.

The Temple.

objected to a quite conventional office conversion and new gates were hardly likely to approve a Greek temple in Coverdale. To decorate the temple, Malcolm asked an artistic girl from his office to paint a frieze on the theme of Orpheus going into the underworld, which we thought appropriate.

At the same time, we were working on the exits from the bottle. We decided that one would come out on the southern side through a large skull into a little chamber with seven doors, all exactly the same. The trick was that the doors would open only one at a time and one had to work out which led to the open air. To add to the fun, there was a revolving floor in this chamber which complicates things a lot — especially as one is tempted to look up to the light above, which comes in through a pyramid of molten glass.

This was another Malcolm original. He had heard of a fire in a glass factory and asked if he could buy a load of molten glass blocks. We had them for a year or so before he thought of this use. From the garden, it is a pyramid of glass stuck together with glazing seal. From underneath, it is hollow and throws a lovely light into the seven-door chamber. But while you look at this, the floor turns and confuses you as to which door you came in by and which you should leave by. One of them leads to a passage, which imitates the old lead mines in the area and is lit by authentic old lanterns. This, in turn, leads to the open air and will one day go on to the cat and mouse feature. This has been in the

The glass pyramid.

building for some time and will now be finished given the planners' recent approval.

We decided that the third door of the bottle would lead to stairs, which would take you up to the light at the top of the hill. We had already put some stairs against the boundary wall so that we could look over if we wanted to. Now it was decided to incorporate these stairs into a tower, so that one would come up to ground level and then go higher in the tower, finally having a stunning view from the top. Although this was not my original bower, it turned out to have the best view of all.

Of course, having built the tower, the walls of the boundary looked too low at seven feet. We went back to Denis, who had moved on elsewhere on the estate. Could he perhaps come back to the wall and raise it, say, three more feet? He said that he still had enough width to be able to do it so, with the help of Albert's men who brought him stone and erected scaffolding for him, he manfully plodded on, raising all of the wall except for the terrace at the front.

Malcolm had yet another bright idea for the stairs leading up to the tower. Why not do something completely unexpected and make the stairs in wood with panelling and portraits on the wall, and even a red carpet. Well why not? The final touch was to transform famous portraits into personalised ones by substituting the heads of Ceci and myself for the original ones. So we have our very own gallery of ancestors.

The main chamber inside the bottle needed a grotto effect as, until then, it had just been covered in concrete. To be authentic in practice as well as in spirit, Malcolm and Albert went to Sicily and bought — wait for it — two forty-foot containers of genuine lava from Mount Etna. These were used to line the chamber and are very effective, especially as there are flickering red lights behind some cracks.

We now had to construct the way into the grotto. We had the Temple and, working backwards, made the Canyon with our spare boulders. But the path would cross this and we built the Thatched Bridge. Below the bridge is the Griffin Pond and this serves as the reservoir for the water that is pumped around to create the stream in the Canyon. Malcolm's sense of humour came into play here and the water spout was made. This spout, triggered as the visitor approaches the Temple, is designed to give him or her a soaking before reaching the safety of the Temple. Beyond the Thatched Bridge, the path goes into the Eye of the Needle, where a clever optical illusion leads you to a tiny door. Then the path winds over the top of the grotto through the gardens to see the Glass Pyramid and the Horse's Head, and so one reaches the Griffin Pond and the Canyon.

In the summer of 1993, we had our first visitors. Malcolm was contacted by Hull University, which had somehow heard of our grotto. It had a party of mature students, who were studying gardens in Yorkshire and would like a peep at what were doing. We thought about this for a while, then decided that we would be amused to see other people's reaction to what we had done. The

The thatched bridge.

date was fixed for July of that year. I planned to arrive in Tupgill on the previous day and go around with Malcolm to see that everything was as good as it could be made, in its unfinished state, before we received our guests. Malcolm and I were on our way around when Doug Weatherill said that there was a bus outside with the Hull students. We had the wrong day and there was nothing for it but to let them in. They really enjoyed it and so did we. How satisfying for the artist when one's work is admired.

Perhaps that was the moment when we decided that we would open to the public. Until then, the garden had been for family and friends. Now we had an urge to let the world in. We were vindicated in what we had achieved — a great joy.

But Malcolm was in no state to enjoy it as, sadly, Alison Tempest, who had been poorly for some time, died. Malcolm was very upset and spent a month or so travelling on his own but eventually returned once more with enthusiasm for the future, having collected lots of new ideas.

It was at this time that he introduced me to the Folly Fellowship, a small group of people with an interest in follies both in Britain and abroad. There used to be many more follies than there are today 200 years ago, when wealthy landed gentry decorated their parks with towers, ruins, obelisks and statuary. To be classed as a folly a construction must have no use and be built for fun.

The castle.

Many have disappeared because of urbanisation; many more still exist in forgotten corners of fields but are ruined and covered with vegetation. The mission of the fellowship is to visit, catalogue and, if possible, restore them. It meets at least once a year and that year, the event was at Hawkstone Park in Shropshire. I had something to do in the area so Ceci and I went to Hawkstone. For some reason, we were late in getting there and missed the reunion but we walked the paths and saw the many follies of the park, which was fascinating. It provided more ideas for what we now aspired to do.

Once we had decided that we intended to open to the public, we bore this in mind for each new piece that we made. The grotto was not at all damp but if we were to decorate it inside with scenery painting, we would need to maintain

The stepping stones.

the correct ambient temperature so we thought about central heating. Malcolm suggested that we use underfloor heating and, as we had not yet laid the final floor, this was still possible. Phil Machin, the plumber, did this very well indeed, putting coils of pipes around the central pond in the main chamber, and then Albert laid concrete on top of it. This has worked excellently as the grotto has no draughts and functions as a giant storage heater. We had to use radiators in the outlying passages but these are well hidden. We did not want it to look

The eye of the needle.

domestic in any way. We had created both a lavatory and a kitchen area so that we were equipped for holding parties down there. The boiler went into the kitchen and we laid the diesel pipe all the way across the garden, later hiding the tank in the new Face Tower.

The builders were finally backing out of the grotto area and towards the entrance of the garden, taking up the temporary road that they had put down behind them. That meant that we could start gardening. Tulip completed her design and we created the Rose Garden, the Lavender Garden, the Long Garden, which had climbing roses and a lawn, and the Ivy Garden. We had already planted yew hedging along the terrace at the front to form a maze and this was progressing well, although it takes ages to grow. We had long since established the paths through the wood, which were essentially the same ones we had created for playing with the children.

While the grotto was being built, we had made more paths and improved the existing ones, with increased planting to thicken the hedge effect. Now that they had to withstand more feet, we had to improve the surfaces. These had originally been of grass but, because of wear and shading, they were now just earth. This was a job for the two Allans and it took hours of back-breaking work to cut out the topsoil, then lay quarry waste below and stone chippings on top. There was no space to use tractors and everything was brought in and taken out in wheelbarrows.

To give the garden a feeling of age, Malcolm came up with the Ancestor Grave. We put this in a small clearing with a mock inscription in Malcolm's

Denis building the face tower.

best doggerel about the death of poor John Armstrong in a hunting accident back in the seventeenth century. It might seem somewhat gloomy to come across a gravestone there but the rhyme soon cheers one up. Meanwhile, having raised the boundary wall, Denis was backing out of the garden, forming small garden areas as he went by walling across the former roadway but leaving doorways into each. Some opened, some did not. When he reached the garden entrance, he built the Face Tower and a small matching tower to the north as I fancied having my own secret entrance. In this tower, we put a door which led to a path through a small plantation towards Ashgill and then turned right to lead to Ferngill. I thought that I could then slip in and out of the garden without joining the crowd who might be looking around. I had visions of people saying that they had seen a mysterious, tall man who had just vanished into thin air. Then the ghost of Tupgill would be invented.

It did not quite work out like that as the path in question so intrigued me with its possibilities that we soon changed our minds and walled along one side of the little plantation, planted it more thickly and finally created St Cuthbert's Well at the end of it. Why Saint Cuthbert? I had just read *Credo* by Melvyn Bragg, in which he appeared as the hermit saint of the old Celtic Church, which was replaced by the Roman Church after the Synod of Whitby. But there was no changing Saint Cuthbert. His big rival, Saint Wilfrid of Ripon, was much more worldly, seeing which side to join in time. So we have our old Saint Cuthbert spending his last years by his well, outcast of the new faith but still beloved and revered by his followers.

Before we were ready to receive the public, Malcolm had a few more tricks to install: the Peeing Boy, Caliban and the water spout. Caliban came about because we had a place for a devil to rise up from the waters. So we decided to make a play on words and called him Caliban from the Shakespeare play *The Tempest*, as in Malcolm Tempest. We also installed a sound-and-light show within the main chamber and a soundtrack in the seven doors and Horse's Head.

Apart from the Hull students, who were really a one-off, we date our opening to the public from 23rd July, 1994. Eileen Harrison-Topham, our neighbour, had heard about the grotto and called Elaine to see if there was any possibility that we might open it for a charity event that she was holding at her house, Cotescue Park. The idea was that Ceci and I would join the guests and then lead them back to the grotto, which was by now named The Forbidden Corner. Everything went to plan and about 100 people came, saw and were fascinated by the experience. We had not completely finished work at that time but had rushed ahead, making a great effort to have it as pleasant as possible on the day. As Malcolm is fond of saying, were it not for deadlines, nothing would get done at all.

We had customers immediately following the opening day but not enough to justify someone sitting about all day to sell tickets. So we printed some black and white leaflets giving Margaret Weatherill's telephone number for

The peeing boy.

booking and, as she and Doug live in West House, just a few yards from the Forbidden Corner, she would give the visitors the key and charge an entrance fee. This saw us through the rest of the season and indeed the following one, until it became a bit too much to ask of Margaret and she handed over gratefully to her daughter Wendy in 1996. There was also the vexing issue of lavatories. There was one in the central chamber but it was not easy to find in a hurry. At first, any emergency was handled by Margaret, who kindly offered the use of her cloakroom but that was clearly not very satisfactory. We also needed somewhere to sell tickets. Both Margaret and Wendy had spent hours sitting in a pick-up near the entrance on cold days attending to this.

The answer we arrived at was the Clock Tower. This had been an old horse box garage, and we had replaced it with a new smart one with a clock on top in 1985. It had been meant to go with Tupgill stables but I was reluctant to part with it and we retained it as an estate store. It nearly became a stable when Micky Hammond, who had taken Tupgill stables in 1990, needed more boxes but in the end we were able to accommodate him without using it. So it was available at the right moment. There was not too much in it. The old estate tractor stood there and there were posts and rails and some road salt. We found a home elsewhere for these and Malcolm set to to make it into a ticket office, café and gift shop with, of course, the lavatories. The latter was a relatively simple operation as we had installed an outsized septic tank to allow for growth some years previously and we just ran a drain connecting this to the Clock Tower. The rest was really hardboard partitioning to make a tiny kitchen and gift shop but it was very effective and sufficed us for two seasons.

Even so, it was a rush to be ready for the Easter opening. At that time, we opened on Sundays and bank holidays but, as the summer holidays approached in 1996, we decided to open every day while the children were on vacation. One of the joys of the Forbidden Corner is that it is a pastime for all ages. The children come for the scary bits, the adults for the gardens and the scary bits. One group of primary schoolchildren made drawings of what they had seen on their visit. We were very amused at how several of them thought that the best bit was when the devil (which is really supposed to be Pluto as in Orpheus, and stands in the little pond in the main chamber) turned his head to follow them as they walked past. This was excellent but not the case. He is quite rigid. What counts is what you think you see.

We began to attract some publicity at this time. The Folly Fellowship was invited by Malcolm to hold a northern meeting at the Forbidden Corner. This was organised by Susan Kellerman, who wrote about us in the society's magazine. In fact, members were quite lucky to survive this as Malcolm had prepared a surprise: folly cake with a firework inside it! There were short articles in both the *Northern Echo* and the *Yorkshire Post*, and these were followed up by Yorkshire TV, which did not show the film until after we were closed at the end of the season. But it stood us in good stead for the following one.

Then we had an illustrious visitor. Ceci and I had been invited to a cocktail party by Sheila and Tommy Pitman to meet our new MP, William Hague. We were introduced as the owners of the Forbidden Corner and William said that he would love to see it, so that was arranged for the next day. There were a few visitors looking around and, of course, he was recognised. 'Here, that's Will Hague, our next prime minister,' said one lady. He was not yet leader of the opposition so she was clearly clairvoyant. He enjoyed the look around too and asked if he could bring some friends the next day. That was no problem.

One day, we decided to have a small party for friends when we were closed to the public and invited twenty guests. We set up drinks in the central chamber and waited for them to arrive. In Ecuador, you expect guests to be up to two hours late for an invitation. Not so in England and, when no one arrived for half an hour or so, I thought that I had better go and look for them. They were all in the garden, some becoming rather annoyed, as they could not find the way in to the grotto. That was supposed to be the fun of it but when you put a maze between good English folk and their expected cocktail it can become traumatic.

Although we were open to the public, improvement work did not stop entirely. We constructed the Green Man and were raising the Fawcett Tower (named after Denis) a few feet to set it off. This was because the tower had initially been higher than the adjacent wall, but when we raised the wall, it had

258 THE FORBIDDEN CORNER

The green man.

looked too low. Finally we were getting it right. At the same time, we built over the footpath below the tower to provide an escape route for those who would not return to the dark depths of the grotto once they had seen the light. That season, two ladies had jumped from the tower rather than return down the steps. Luckily, it was not too high and the only damage was to the flowerbed below but, after raising the tower, this was no longer a (safe) option so we needed another way down. We built a walkway along the top of the wall south of the tower and made steps down into what we called the Prison, from which there was a tiny door out. This door was an exit only as we did not want people spoiling the effect by going in that way. We called it the Chicken Door — for those too chicken to run the whole course.

Two ladies had jumped from the tower!

Farther down the garden path, we had the same problem of those who found themselves faced with having to repeat the underground part and being reluctant to do so. So there appeared a second Chicken Door and, just to make it more fun, we put a combination lock on it with the code to be found on the door behind — if, that is, you remembered where you had come from. As you will have guessed by now, the object of the Forbidden Corner was to confuse, amaze and amuse. Some people took two hours or more to emerge from it; others seemed to be there all day (because they wanted to or not) but they all seemed to have enjoyed it.

Since we have been open, we have filled many books with happy comments and have had very few complaints. As often as not, one comes across a crying child, who is scared by the dark and the surprises but, on leaving, is begging for a second turn.

In 1997, we were really on the map. We opened again at Easter and had a good start to the season as the Middleham trainers organise a collective open day on Good Friday, which attracts some 15,000 people to look around the stables. These are obviously a specialist crowd and have come to see the horses, not the Forbidden Corner, but some did come in while they were waiting for the shuttle bus to take them to the next stable. If they did not do the tour, they took a leaflet and came back another day.

We had some new leaflets printed in colour including Malcolm's drawings of the features and I press-ganged my children in to helping me distribute these to local pubs, hotels, caravan sites and other visitor attractions in the area, because each gives out the others' leaflets as mutual support. Obviously, we could not cover more than the immediate area without taking months to do so but we all felt that we were doing our bit to help the new enterprise. The children, having been dead against the project, had warmed to it when the party aspect became apparent. Now, when they saw that it could earn money, they were positively enthusiastic.

In June, a book called *Hidden Yorkshire* was published by Sue Gillman. It featured the Forbidden Corner and she asked whether the launch could be held there. Elaine helped to organise and the resulting press coverage did us no harm at all.

Shortly afterwards, I received a call from Patricia Cleveland Peck, who wanted to come from Surrey and see the place with a view to writing an article about it, as she specialised in interesting gardens. She came up, we toured the garden and grotto together and she went away to write. There was a delay in publication but her article eventually appeared in the *Daily Telegraph* under the heading 'A Rich Man's Folly-Filled Wonderland'. She apologised for the title, which she said she had no control over. But the article was excellent. It was followed by filming by a Channel Four crew, which brought even more people in.

We were more successful than ever in 1998, with over 80,000 visitors, three times more than the year before. However, it was then that the planners finally caught up with us. By now, Wendy needed more help to run the show. Her husband Johnny had been helping out at weekends for all of the previous year but now he left his other job to manage full-time. Once again, the Clock Tower was altered, this time by Allan Tunstall. It was constructed much more solidly in stone; an improved servery was made, which was much larger than before; another floor was added to make use of all the vacant height of the barn; and tables were set out upstairs. We installed heating and automatic glass doors. It was altogether much smarter.

The results of the press and television were now being felt, and the media kept coming back. There was a programme called the *Famous Five*, in which five children were taken to all of Yorkshire's main amusement places and had to vote on which they liked best. We came first ahead of such attractions as Lightwater Valley and Flamingo Land. That settled it. No self-respecting child could hold his or her head up at school again until he or she had been to the Forbidden Corner.

Johnny had seen an article about a shaggy dog needing a good home. It turned out that this particular mutt was made of wooden slats covered with evergreen foliage. It was a sculpture made by Robert Bradford and had been on exhibition at Hebden Bridge. Now it had to go and he was able to attract a good deal of publicity this way. I called Robert and we agreed that the dog would take up residence at Tupgill, where we had a sculpture trail in a field next to the car park. He told the press about the move and the cameras followed the dog (it was really only a dog's head but was ten feet tall) as it came down the A1 to Tupgill on a lorry, where we unloaded it with a JCB and put it on its prepared site. Then I had a light-hearted interview about whether it would settle in its new home.

We could not escape the notice of the planners for much longer with ever more television coverage, press articles and Middleham coming close to traffic jams. Nor did we and the dreaded moment came on the 9th July, when Johnny came to Ferngill to tell me that two planning officers from the Yorkshire Dales National Park were asking to speak to me. One of these was Walt Foreman, who had the impressive title of enforcement officer. I took them around the Forbidden Corner and he admitted that their children had already seen it and loved it but, by some oversight, we had failed to apply for planning permission. However, he said that we should try to put things right by applying for retrospective permission. I was not too downcast by this. It seemed quite reasonable and so many people had already enjoyed a visit that surely we would obtain the required permission.

When I talked to Malcolm, he was not half as confident. He said that he would contact a leading planning barrister, Harry Wolton, just in case. This threw me somewhat. I could not see the need for a barrister when the officers had appeared so reasonable but I was guided by Malcolm, the veteran of countless planning battles. We were advised to apply for retrospective planning permission once the planners had made clear that their objection was not to the building of the structures, most of which had been erected more than four

Closed by the planners.

years previously and could not be removed on legal grounds. However, they were objecting to the change of use of a private garden to one open to the public and on this count the power of the law extends back for ten years. We submitted our application in September but it was not considered until February 1999. Meanwhile, Middleham town council wrote to the national park authority expressing concern about the traffic that had been generated. Then some of the Middleham trainers wrote to complain that they had difficulty taking their horses from Middleham to the moor because of the volume of extra traffic.

Worse was to come. At a dinner party held by Neil Corner, a neighbour, in October, everyone present signed a letter calling on me to close the Forbidden Corner to the public as it was intrusive and spoiled their quiet enjoyment of the dale. I knew them all and really did not want to fall out with my neighbours. But I also could not accept that we should close down. What should I do? The letter was followed by an invitation to a meeting at Adrian Thornton-Berry's home, Swinithwaite Hall, in October. It was, to be fair, sweetened by an invitation to shoot with him a day or two previously. The appointed evening came and, feeling rather like Daniel going into the lions' den, I arrived exactly on time to find that I was the first person there. Bridget Thornton-Berry let me in and, very decently I thought, wished me good luck, as I was outnumbered six to one. Then Adrian arrived home, followed by Pat Haslam, Dick and Roger Harrison-Topham, Nigel Corner (Neil's son) and David Brown. They were all usually very friendly but did I detect some reserve in them tonight? I thought that I might have been offered a drink and I certainly needed one, but this was not forthcoming. They started making the perfectly reasonable point that their enjoyment of the dale had been curtailed by our activity. We should cease forthwith.

I, too, tried to be reasonable and argued that in my youth the dale had had double its present population. Farm expansion and the closure of the cheese factory meant that few jobs were available, except for racehorse training and I, along with my contemporaries, had had to leave to find work elsewhere. Now I was providing employment for dozens of people, who either helped to build or run the Forbidden Corner. I offered to restrict the opening hours to accommodate the horses and to erect signs to prevent customers getting lost and stopping to ask the way. But my powers of rhetoric were obviously lacking and we were not going to come to a solution. On the way out, Nigel said: 'We are going to stop you', to which I replied 'Maybe.'

Despite the build-up of opposition, we had plenty of supporters. These included the local branch of the Conservative party, which wanted a venue for a Hallowe'en party at which William and Ffion Hague were to be the guests of honour. This seemed a good idea, the only problem being that we had to put in lighting especially for the event which, I was told, would cost £3,000 but in the end cost twice as much.

The party went well. The night was clear and frosty and the guests, in appropriate fancy dress, walked the course down to the grotto and back before settling in the café of the Clock Tower, where food and drink were served. William was dressed as Batman and Ffion as a fair maid, which she is indeed. I was a wizard and there was the usual collection of monks, nuns and crusaders. Several Ecuadorians were present including Monica Duffus and Marta de la Mata and her daughter, so before too long the music changed to salsa and the South Americans showed them the way.

While we were waiting to hear our fate at the national park authority meeting, there was quite a lot of shuffling going on on both sides. The authority had asked Keith Wilson, the highways officer, to give his opinion as to the traffic problem. His first report was quite bleak: the roads just could not cope with the extra traffic, the exit from Tupgill was dangerous and the Forbidden Corner was simply in the wrong place. This led Malcolm to compile a list of National Trust houses, their attendance figures and locations, showing that they were often sited on small roads. Such arguments, while very satisfying, do not win battles of this sort. For this, we needed a traffic expert and brought in Chris Dallas from the firm of Bryan G Hall while both sides settled down to take road and traffic measurements.

Walt Foreman now disappeared from the case and Peter Watson, the senior planning officer, and his assistants, Mark Williams and Wendy Thompson, took it up for the park authority. They came and took photographs of the work which had been done so far and warned us not to do any more pending the outcome of the planning decision. They also brought along David Sykes of the footpaths department, who walked all of our many paths and noted that one which crossed the St Cuthbert's path was blocked and should be reinstated at once. Curiously, the public is encouraged to come to the countryside and walk or ride paths on private land, but the moment that the landlord is perceived to be making anything in return, the majesty of the law descends on him.

We also had to overcome obstacles from Richmondshire District Council's planning department. Malcolm and I went along to the hearing in Richmond in November and were successful as the potential for trade, employment and tourism was taken into account. We were helped by councillor John Blackie, who was very much in favour and who swayed the rest.

At this time, Dick Harrison-Topham became chairman of the Coverham-with-Agglethorpe parish meeting, and I suspect that he had the express purpose of using that office to oppose my venture. He wrote several letters to the park authority expressing his point of view and his concern that racehorse training might be forced out of the dale by the activities of the Forbidden Corner. I met Dick and his brother Roger, and said that this claim could not be justified as I had built or rebuilt more than 100 stables over the years and was building thirty new ones at Ashgill. Dick agreed not to push that point and, indeed, both softened their opposition.

The park authority meeting on the 9th February decided only on holding a site visit, which was to take place on the 24th. This was a cold and miserable day and the committee members shuffled around and then were kept in the cold while Malcolm defended us for perhaps too long. There was no meeting of hearts and minds on that occasion and, when our case was scheduled for the following park authority meeting on the 9th March, we were advised by our friends to withdraw our application and avoid certain defeat. We did so but the authority still decided to proceed with an order requiring us to cease activity at once.

Harry Wolton replied to this in no uncertain terms: that to do so would leave the authority open to a claim from us for loss of income. In the end, it decided on an enforcement order but did not serve it on us until the 22nd September. During this interval, we tried desperately to come to some agreement with it. It appeared that the main objection was the road issue and Peter Watson and Keith Wilson were seen looking at the alternative road over Middleham moor, which they declared to be preferable. In April 1999, Malcolm and I visited the YDNPA office in Bainbridge and met Peter, Mark and Wendy. The gist of the conversation was that if we used the moor road, there might be a way to come to an agreement. Peter even offered to contact the county council in Northallerton to obtain the necessary road signs to direct traffic that way. We had agreed to opening at twelve o'clock, rather than ten o'clock on weekdays, to let the horses go back home. We would also have an advance booking system during the school holidays, with people either telephoning us direct or through the tourist information centre at Leyburn. Pam Whittaker, the tourism officer, was very supportive. We looked to be moving towards an agreement. I contacted all my neighbours on that stretch of road to see whether there were any objections but no one minded. So on the 13th July, road signs were erected directing the traffic this way.

Two days later, all hell broke loose in the form of an irate phone call from the mayoress of Middleham, Dr Anne Williamson. What right had I to direct traffic over a road belonging to the town of Middleham? I was certain that I had rights to the road as my family had been using it since my grandfather first bought Ashgill in 1924. Moreover, together with Sally Hall, as the users of the road, we had maintained it for years and Middleham council had not done so within living memory. Now, as soon as it saw that we were filling in the potholes and directing traffic along it, it was affronted. The following day, we received a letter from a solicitor, telling us to cease using the road immediately as we had no rights on it whatsoever.

The advantage of working with the same solicitor for generations now came into play. Michael Hutchinson's father had worked with my grandfather and files of past correspondence were searched to prove the rights and wrongs of the issue. So we had a good defence for our use of the road but whether that extended to the Forbidden Corner was another matter. While the two legal firms were arguing the toss, Middleham's solicitors asked the court for an injunction to stop my use immediately. This would have been quite a blow as all our advertising indicated that the moor road was the way in and changing it abruptly would have led to chaos. Luckily, the judge thought the same way and ruled in our favour (for the moment), saying that nothing could be done until after the school holiday trial period. He awarded us costs as he considered the other side was being unreasonable, which was satisfactory to us but galling to Middleham town council.

However, it was only a pause in the battle which continued. The enforcement notice was finally served, giving us three months to close. We appealed at once and the hearing was set for a date in March 2000 but subsequently changed to the 17th July, to be heard by a government inspector over three days in Middleham Key Centre. We had sent out a letter to thousands of people who had indicated that they would back us and we received over 2,000 letters of support in addition to the 10,000 signatures we had collected at the gate. We used these as evidence.

Before the appeal date, we tried once more to have our planning application passed in the normal way. This was heard in June after another, and much more successful, site meeting on a sunny day when the members of the committee could see the happy customers and our bevy of young girls who were parking cars, making sandwiches and ensuring that all went well.

'Forbidden' folly forced to close

THE owner of a unique folly garden near Leyburn, which drew 84,000 sightseers in a year, is fighting a move to put it out of bounds.

The fantasy land of statues, labyrinths, towers and gargoyles at the Forbidden Corner has grown over the past two years on Colin Armstrong's Yorkshire Dales estate.

But he never got permission to open the folly at Tupgill Park in turesque Coverdale to p... now National P... him with ...

ready and would have been with the park authority in a week or so."

Mr Armstrong said claims of traffic congestion caused by Forbidden Corner were exaggerated. Restrictions imposed this year had reduced vis... numbers dramatically.

Peter Watson the Y...

Fantasy land 'out of character' in park

A FANTASY park opened in the ... without permission against all the ood for, a plan- ard.

... into the future ...orbidden Cor- eham, was told ... undermined ...we with disabilities.

A spokeswoman for the Folly Fellowship charity said: "The creation of an entirely new folly is a rare event these ays. One of such quality, like Forbid- n Corner, is a matter of pride and ebration.

...he added: "It probably ranks as one .he most impressive family sites in ain and is perhaps a modern ...alent of some of our most famous ... ardens.

...ould be accessible to the public ... hope it gets the required per- ... to be so."

to the public three years ago without permission came to light when complaints were made about traffic volumes.

The garden drew 70,000 visitors last year, riving by private tran... the narrow lanes to were unsuitable for ...es which ...un day out for

"While it may provide a visitor destination and a form of recreation, this is unrelated to the core qualities of the national park. The Forbidden Corner does not rely on the intrinsic ...ral beauty of the park for ...tion. Its appeal is in its ...ure, it is a folly and,

Theme park on brink of closure

A FANTASY theme park which attracted more than 80,000 visitors last year could be forced to shut down after a lengthy battle with National P... officials.

The Forbi... Middl...

By STUART MACKINTOSH

The authority also ... leading to the sit... of dealing ...

Corner's unique experience

From: Tony Carter, Portland Avenue, Pontefract.

Sir, – For some time now, the Yorkshire Post has been printing details of the antics of the North York Moors National Park and its attempt to close down "Forbidden Corner" at Middleham.

In order to find out what all the fuss is about I went to have a look on Sunday afternoon. I can reliably inform readers that the place is absolutely wonderful. I have ...tely ...thing like it

Inquiry to settle folly issue

THE future of the Forbidden Corner near Middleham is to be settled at a public inquiry after retrospective planning permission for change of use to public gardens was refused.

Members of the Yorkshire Dales National Park Authority's planning committee voted this week to refuse the application after the unique gardens opened to the public without permission three years ago.

Since then they have attracted 80,000 visitors a year, which planning officers said resulted in a significant intrusion into Coverdale due to extra traffic.

In September an enforcement notice was issued by the park's planning committee requiring the attraction to be closed to the public from October, and insisting on the ceasing of the use of the land as public gardens.

Mr Colin Armstrong, who owns the Tupgill Park attraction, is appealing against the enforcement notice at a public inquiry next month and applied for retrospective planning permission for change of use to public gardens.

Included in the application was a visitor management system to keep numbers down, as well as road improvements.

But members were still concerned about the visitor numbers, and would have preferred an annual limit or restricted opening times, rather than limits on visitor numbers allowed into the attraction each hour as proposed by the applicant.

During a long debate some members felt planning permission should be granted with conditions attached, because the attraction provided employment for locals, it boosted the local economy, offered children an insight into the national park, and would not detract from the park.

But others felt the attraction did not belong in the national park.

Mrs Deborah Millward said: "Do we have a leg to stand on when we turn down an application for a sun room or porch or something of that size when we allow something like this?"

However, Mr Mike Childs said: "The big issue is that it is a major departure from policy, but we have to accept it is there and really we have no control over it at all unless we approve it.

"If we don't make a decision there is one planning inspector who will and then it's out of our hands. If we approve it we can have the tightest possible controls."

However, members refused the application, which is expected to go to appeal and be heard at the inquiry into the enforcement order on July 18.

THE FORBIDDEN CORNER

New hope for 'forbidden folly'

THE operators of the Forbidden Corner tourist attraction are submitting what they hope will be a peace-making application.

The Yorks... park authori... at Tupgill Park Middleham, from October ... with an enforce... quiring it to stop... public.

The modern "fo... statues, undergr... gardens and tower... ed by Mr Colin Ar... private use 2½ years...

It was used occas... charity visits, but a... much interest that... opened to the public... out planning permissio...

Last year the park au... concluded that its 80,0C... tors a year was a significa... trusion into Coverdale, ...

turbing local ... ness...

Businesses back Forbidden Corner

By Felix Stewart

MIDDLEHAM businesses united in their support ... threatened visitor att... which draws in 80,000 ... year to Coverdale. They have rubbi... that businesses a... about the numbe... the Forbidden C... folly garden a... Armstrong... retrospec... folly, ... is a r... N...

site visit last week and will make a decision on June 13. ... recommendation to ... ee members is to refuse ...ion.

...l businesses say ...iver a body ...my... an ... meeting of businesses in ...ddleham because one pub ...rded up, a butchers was ... and so was this ...ham seemed to

local economy is built around it.

One of the signatories, Derek Jarvill, who owns Castle Antiques in the town, said: "It really instills a lot to help us by having this traffic going through here.

"Six years ago there was a

was crucial in bringing regular income to the town.

"People go up there and see this unique folly and by doing so go through Middleham, see what a nice place it is and come back and stay in the B&Bs and hotels, and come into the shops."

But planners will have to grapple with planning policy as well as commercial interests and concerns among the cluster of local racing stables about the volume of traffic in Coverdale brought by the attraction. Mr Armstrong has also appealed an enforcement notice compelling the site to close. ... will be heard in July

Trainers and traders offer support

...e very ...ch a

Town lines up to back threatened tourist attraction

BY PIP LAND

ALL the local business in Middleham, and... ty of the race... came out ... Colin ... Co...

he area each year is extremely ...lcome and can make the dif... ...nce to local businesses sur... ...g.

...ess to the Forbidden ... should also be allowed ... Middleham. One local

public statement this week to refute any suggestion th... large majority of them... objections to th... Corner. Th... were f...

Thousands sign Corner petition

PUBLIC backing continues to grow for a Yorkshire dales fantasy park threatened with closure.

Richmondshire district council received a 10,000-name petition ... and 1,670 individual letters of support for a retrospective ... the Forbidden Corner,

'A victory for common sense'

BY MIKE CHIPCHASE

SUPPORTERS of the controversial Forbidden Corner in the Yorkshire dales have hailed the decision to allow it to remain open "a victory for common sense".

The tourist attraction at Tupgill Park, Coverham, near Middleham, originally had its retrospective application for planning permission refused by the national park.

But following an appeal by its millionaire owner, Mr Colin Armstrong, last month's three-day public inquiry has overturned the authority's decision.

County Coun Mike Childs this week described the planning Inspector's decision as great news for local people and businesses.

He added: "This is good news for everyone – for the 25 people who could have lost their jobs, for local businesses which will continue to benefit from visitor spending power, for the thousands of visitors from all over the country who enjoy the experience, and for the local objectors, who can now be confident that numbers will be controlled and managed properly.

"In addition, we will all benefit

"My overall impression was that the road was not busy."

Mr Peter Watson, head of planning at the park, said the decision was a disappointment, but the inspector had accepted a number of conditions which would go some way to regulating the Forbidden Corner's impact on Coverdale.

These included opening hours of noon-6pm on weekdays and 10am-6pm on Sundays and bank holidays. Entries must be prebooked, with a maximum of 120 tickets issued for any one hour.

Coach parties, other than schools or special interest groups, will not be admitted without prior arrangement and will be limited to two per day.

Mrs Elaine Lister, agent for the Tupgill estate, said: "We are delighted with the decision, which confirms what we and thousands of others have always said – that the Forbidden Corner is in no way damaging to the area environmentally. Also that the national park blatantly ignored the creation of local employment and the benefits to local traders

We were hopeful that we had sufficient votes to win but were beaten eleven to nine despite sterling support from Mike Childs and John Blackie. It was particularly galling that one or two known supporters had been absent that day and the opposition was led by Robert Heseltine, who was under a cloud for expenses fraud and who resigned the following week. So did the YDNPA chief executive Heather Hancock, who was not a supporter of ours either.

But we had lost and now there was one last throw of the dice. The secretary of state for the environment appoints a single inspector, who decides an appeal. In our case, it was David C Pinner, who had been a planning officer and was therefore well qualified to judge the case on its merits. We were allowed representation by a barrister and asked Harry Wolton to fight our corner. Harry is a very successful barrister and a great performer to watch so that, apart from being nervous about the outcome, I enjoyed my three days in court.

As the Duke of Wellington is reported to have said, time spent in reconnaissance is seldom wasted. Harry was leaving nothing to chance. Apart from Chris Dallas, the roads expert, he called on Richard Wood of Wood Frampton as a planning expert. Both brought stacks of files into the meeting room. Harry would put his expert witnesses in the stand and question them to obtain the answers he wanted. The lady barrister for the park authority, Nicola Allen, would try to shake their testimony in cross-examination but would get nowhere. They were expert at this and had been in similar situations many times before while working with Harry.

Some thirteen people had put their names down to speak but nine were in favour and only four against. We received some lovely plaudits about the fun that the Forbidden Corner gave to people and its spin-off for local trades. I am very grateful to these people for their help. They were Mike Childs, Richard Duffus, Chris Thornton, Derek Jarvill, Peter Whitehead, Mrs Joyce Ellwood and Miss Susanna Cox. Of those against, one was a Mrs Sheila Webster, who complained that her house had been devalued by the extra traffic but this was very difficult to substantiate.

Pat Haslam, the trainer, complained about traffic affecting his horses but, as we had had a letter from twelve other trainers supporting us, his case was weak. He said that many others in Middleham were against us but asked forlornly 'Where are they today?' Clearly they did not want to come out into the open and be counted.

Nigel Corner and his tenant farmer, Mark Suttill, made their case about there being too much traffic up the dale. But, as they had been in and out of the room during the hearing, they had missed the part when Harry had estimated, to great effect, what the traffic flow of one car a minute really meant, and so weakened their case. A Mrs Rigby and Mr Halstead from the British Horse Society argued for greater freedom for riders on bridleways and were accommodated by the stipulation that the Tupgill road should not be fenced to allow horses to move on to the verge to avoid traffic.

Follies magazine proclaiming "business as usual".

The park authority had agreed the road figures out of court so Chris Dallas's testimony was not needed. Andrew Plumridge, director of the Garden History Society and of the Folly Fellowship, very kindly came all the way from Newbury and testified as an expert witness that the Forbidden Corner was among the best European follies of this century. And Peter Sylvester of the nearby village of Carlton, a staunch supporter, spoke magnificently on our behalf.

Peter Watson did not appear in person but delegated the task to Mark Williams, who had to take the grilling that Harry handed out. He was finally forced to admit that there was a number of people and vehicles that would be acceptable to the authority. So we had finally moved from the Forbidden Corner being completely unacceptable as a matter of principle to a question of numbers. From then on, it was easy. The park authority was prepared to allow fifty people an hour while we stuck to our previous offer of 120 an hour. The inspector summed up and closed the session, saying that he would then visit the Forbidden Corner for another look (he had visited once before as a member of the public) and would announce his decision in due course.

Our team was very happy with how the hearing had gone and we had a celebratory dinner at Ferngill. 'If we don't get the decision, it will be a miscarriage of justice,' said Harry.

And we duly obtained it. On the 14th August, Elaine rang us in Ecuador with the great news. We could continue our business subject to our agreed plan with a new car park and some minor road widening.

COURT AND SOCIAL

THIS SEEMS TO BE a good title for a chapter which contains all sorts of things which have happened over the last few years and which do not fall easily into other chapters.

In 1992, I was contacted by Ted Armstrong of the Armstrong Clan Centre with the news that Gilnockie Tower was once again for sale. It had changed hands twice since a Mr Armstrong-Wilson had acquired it from the Buccleuch Estate and made it habitable again after centuries of being open to the elements. The Duke of Buccleuch, whose family name is Scott, had presumably acquired the tower from the Maxwells, who had been awarded the Armstrong lands after Carlenrig. It has appeared in many paintings and photographs in its ruined state over the years. But now it was for sale in its new and habitable form and Ted was desperate to buy it for the clan to make into a clan centre home.

The asking price was £160,000, which was clearly impossible for the clan to raise. Some years previously, when it had last been for sale, Ted had tried to raise cash by selling the stones in its walls one by one to members so that each would own part of it. This had not been a success and a total of only £5,000 was pledged. This time, Ted asked me to do the job. It was a strange thing to buy as it was not close to Tupgill, standing five miles over the Scottish border. On the other hand, history is not for sale every day and, as he pointed out, it was Johnnie Armstrong's tower and the only remaining building which could claim to be the clan centre. So I bought it and leased it to the clan for twenty-one years.

Ted was thrilled and he showed me around with pride. It is indeed quite imposing. There are five floors, with one room per floor and a circular stair within the width of the wall. The battlements provide a most spectacular view over Eskdale, although only a few square metres of land, where a wooden garage stands, went with the tower. I contacted the Buccleuch Estate to see if it would sell the cottage standing next to the tower, but it refused. This is a pity as it would have completed the clan centre.

So the descendant of old Will, who had ridden to that fateful meeting at Carlenrig in 1530, had bought back the property taken from the Armstrongs by the treachery of a graceless monarch.

The previous year, I had received my coat of arms and now had a flag made which flies over the tower on high days and holidays. One of the conditions of sale of the tower was that is should be opened to the public and Ted does this on behalf of the clan. It stands five miles over the border at a village called Hollows, to the right of the A7 from Carlisle to Edinburgh, is easy to find and is worth a visit.

Gilnockie tower roofless, circa 1800.

At about the same time, I decided to have a family portrait painted and contacted Gordon Butler, who lived in Middleham and who specialised in pictures of horses. Diana had a pony called William, and I thought that we might ask him to paint us and represent each of the children's hobbies: Nick with his shotgun, Diana with William and Alex with her bike. As usual, they were not in favour of my idea and it was difficult to persuade them to participate, as they all had to be elsewhere at any one time suggested for the sitting. But

The Armorial Bearings
of
COLIN ROBERT ARMSTRONG

Coat of arms.

The Armstrong family painted by Gordon Butler.

Gordon overcame this by taking lots of photographs of us individually and putting us together in the painting. It came out very well indeed and I had two copies made from the original: one for the house in Guayaquil and one for my office while the original hangs in Ferngill. The family is in the foreground and behind is the Ferngill lake, the Fishing Temple and the Clock Tower. It is painted in summer and there is plenty of foliage. It is a lovely picture, with Ceci and I looking very proud of our brood.

Richard Lavers was the British ambassador to Ecuador in 1995 and Ceci and I became very good friends with Brigitte and he. He is a year younger than I am — young to be an ambassador. That year saw my fiftieth birthday, which we celebrated with a wonderful dinner with our closest friends in the Union Club in Guayaquil. Nick was the only one of our children who could be there as Diana and Alex were at school in England. Richard Lavers made a very flattering speech in my honour and, to keep the party amused, I replied by reading out some of the more suggestive birthday cards I had received and mortifying the senders.

Towards the end of that year, Richard telephoned me to ask if an OBE would be acceptable as he had thought of forwarding my name for the new year's honours list. But he said that it should be kept a secret until after the official announcement. Of course, I was delighted and kept it entirely to myself.

So in December, when all four of us were having dinner and he said to Ceci: 'Isn't Colin's award thrilling?', she was very surprised. But I said that I was told to keep quiet and so I had done. 'I didn't mean from Ceci,' he said, but then we could all talk about it.

Curiously, the first written indication of the award was a cutting from *The Times*, which was faxed to me by Elaine. I had to look down the list starting with the knighthoods, then the CBEs and on to the OBEs 'Armstrong C R for services to British interests in Ecuador'. I will admit to being very pleased with my honour and rushed to the ancient copy of *Whitaker's Almanack* in the consulate to check where I now came in the English pecking order. The list is headed, as one might expect, by her majesty and royalty then runs through dukes, marquesses, earls, barons and knights. Then, way down the list, I found the OBEs and was very happy to know that my new rank was somewhere below judges of county courts but certainly above 'eldest sons of younger sons of peers'.

Some time later, I did receive the official documents from the palace informing me of the OBE and giving a list of possible dates to attend an investiture. The most convenient for us was the 17th July, 1996. We all looked forward to going but one is restricted to taking a spouse and two children. As it turned out, Alex was going to be staying with a friend in Portugal at the time, so we did not have to draw lots for it. The day before the great event, we all went down to London by train and booked in at the Berkeley Hotel in Knightsbridge. Then I went to Moss Bros in Covent Garden and was kitted out in a morning suit with a black top hat.

The next day, we took a taxi to Buckingham Palace and all looked very smart, Ceci and Diana in new outfits and Nick in a suit (a rare event in those days). There was a lot of traffic, and security guards with guard dogs and policemen looking under the cars with mirrors. The taxi was waved straight through and a very large policeman, seeing that I was looking somewhat stressed, put his head in the window and said: 'Cheer up, sir, it's the happiest day of your life.' This did indeed make me smile.

The taxi left us at the main entrance and we walked across the inner courtyard to where a queue of people was waiting, all elegantly attired and the ladies wearing hats. Here there were officials to sort us out. 'Candidates for investiture to the left, companions to the right.' We went our different ways and I was guided to a large saloon where an elegant colonel told us what to do. There were about 100 investitures and we were grouped by rank. I did not know anyone but we made small talk while we waited. The colonel finally reached the OBEs and said: 'Tongues get tied on these occasions but you should begin with "your majesty" and then just "ma'am".'

He told us the procedure of how many steps to take along the red carpet from the door; when to turn and face the dais; what to do there and when to retire backwards, bowing. After our turn, we were to join our family in the rows of chairs and wait for the ceremony to end. Then we formed a single line and waited in the antechamber. Officials checked our names several times to see if we were in the right order as the queen is primed with information about each candidate and it must be the right person. My turn came at last and, for all that I was trying to keep cool, I was frightfully nervous.

I watched the man in front of me carefully and thought that I had got it right. Then it was my turn. The correct number of steps, a turn to the left and three more steps brought me face to face with the queen. She was on the dais but I was still somewhat taller than she was. She asked me how long I had been in Ecuador and one or two other questions, and I forgot to say 'your majesty' and managed only 'ma'am'. Then, as we had been prepared in the antechamber with a hook pinned on to the lapel of our coats, she took the decoration from a helper and hung it on the hook. My turn was over, she shook my hand and I made the regulation three steps backwards, bowed, turned to the right and quick marched away. In the next antechamber, a lady removed the decoration, put it into its box, which she gave me, took off the hook and showed me to a door which led to the back of the audience. I took my seat with my family and watched the rest of the proceedings.

When it was all over, the national anthem was played and the queen left, escorted by beefeaters and Gurkhas. Then we all trooped out into the inner courtyard, where there were official photographers to record the happy event. Then we walked out of the palace gates and took a taxi back to the Berkeley for a celebratory lunch.

After this, the children had other things to do so Ceci and I went to Garrards the jewellers, where I bought a miniature copy of the OBE for myself and a brooch of the OBE for Ceci. Both happy with this, we went on to St Paul's Cathedral, intending to see the British Empire Chapel. When we arrived, we found that it was closed to the public for an event. But we persuaded the man at the door that, having just received the decoration, it was a rather special occasion. He relented and showed us the chapel, which is in the basement and somewhat gloomy.

The celebrations continued that evening with a trip to the theatre to see *Les Misérables*. We had seen this before, but the children had not, and I was very much in to the music, playing the CD over and over on my car player. We had very good seats in the second row of the stalls. When we arrived, I thought that we might be too close but it was great and, being an emotional fellow, I was in tears when the would-be girlfriend died. The family has now grown used to this sort of thing as I sit in the theatre, blowing my nose loudly. It was a great evening and finished with supper.

This was my third visit to the palace. The first I have recounted, and the second was as a tourist. Some two years previously, with Diana in tow, we paid our fee and followed the route from hall to hall, admiring the lovely furniture and paintings on display. At least I did, as I remember Diana urging me to get on so that she could get back to the hotel where *Neighbours* was on television.

There was a fourth visit in the summer of 2000, when we were invited to a garden party to honour the honorary consuls from all over the world. The last time I had been to such an event, I had been on my own. Ceci was pregnant with Alex and the other two children were too small. Now four of us could go together as, once again, Alex was busy elsewhere. This time she was in Tanzania, where she was working with Health Projects Abroad for three months, building a school in a rural area near Tabora.

The previous evening, we were all invited to a reception at the Foreign Office as part of the same programme. Richard Lavers had shown me around it the year before and it is quite a palace inside with gracious stairs, huge paintings, the Locarno room and the Durbar Court. The reception was held in the Durbar Court and we were all given labels showing the country that we lived in and wandered around looking at everyone else's badges until we found a neighbouring country or, indeed, a friendly face to talk to and compare notes with. In the end, we all discovered that we had very similar work, which consisted mainly of replacing stolen passports, visiting prisoners, authorising documents and occasionally burying the dead. It came as a surprise to learn that some of us had been consuls for twenty years or more and that this was the first official invitation to the Foreign Office or, indeed, to any gathering of consuls. It was to celebrate the millennium, so we might have a lengthy wait until the next one.

This time, we were staying in the Goring Hotel, which is right behind Buckingham Palace. As the clock struck three, Ceci, Nick, Diana and I emerged from the hotel to walk across the road and into the palace gardens by the back gate. First, we paused on the hotel steps and asked the doorman to take our photograph, showing Ceci and Diana in their smart outfits and hats and Nick and I in morning suits and grey top hats. Then we joined about 7,000 of her majesty's closest friends for the day. The palace garden is huge and it was a pleasant walk down paths lined with shrubs to the vast extent of lawn where the marquees were and the band was playing. It had been nineteen years since my last visit and what struck me was the change in dress. Before, the vast majority had been in morning suit or uniform; now Nick and I were in a very small minority and lounge suits were the order of the day. Then as now, the invitation had given the option but the world had grown more informal. However, I was glad that we had made the effort to put on the real thing. It made more of the occasion; we wear suits in our everyday life but morning suits only very infrequently.

We mingled with the crowd until the beefeaters appeared at four o'clock and good-naturedly cleared the royal way from the palace steps to the royal tea tent, forming a wide thoroughfare. The crowd lined this some dozen deep. Officials then went down the line, selecting people to meet the queen, who were moved forward to await her. She appeared with Prince Philip and a bevy of top-hatted officials and slowly worked her way down the line, talking to the favoured few. It took her about an hour and a half to complete this but once

Garden party at Buckingham Palace. July 2000. Nick, Ceci, Diana and Colin.
Photo taken on the steps of the Goring hotel.

she had passed us, we wandered off for a cup of tea and a look at the garden. How much more pleasant it was to be there with the family, rather than alone as I had been on the previous occasion. We also caught up with some of our new consular friends of the night before so the afternoon passed all too quickly and it was time to withdraw.

Then we went back across the road, had a quick change into civvies, took a taxi to Kings Cross for the six o'clock train to Darlington, met Doug and went back to Ferngill.

We had been away from Ferngill for just five days but we had packed a lot into it. First we had been to Glyndebourne for a performance of *Cosi Fan Tutti*, then to our niece Penny's wedding at a hotel in Bournemouth and back to London for the events just mentioned. Penny was marrying for the second time to Leeham, who is also a second-timer, so it was a great opportunity to bring the family together. Penny's mother, my eldest sister Jane, her father Peter and brother Peter came over from Johannesburg. Kate, my other sister, was there and her daughter Emilie, who had come from Sydney together with her children, Daniel and Sophie, although her husband Mitch could not make it in time. Her children, together with Penny's Matthew and Amelia Jane and Leeham's offspring, were bridesmaids and pages.

The wedding was conducted in the hotel, then we went out on to the promenade for photographs and back to the hotel for a knees-up and to catch up with family gossip. We three siblings had not seen each other since the last event three years previously, when we met up at the house of Uncle Frank Wilson and Aunt Eleanor in Hungerford to celebrate his eightieth birthday. Frank was Mother's youngest brother and had been a market gardener for years after leaving Cambridge University, simply because that was what he wanted to do. Later, he had sold up very profitably for building land and had then taught at a prep school, where his pupils had included Prince Edward. Retiring from this, he had built a house at Hungerford with a stretch of trout stream, where he rented rods as a pleasurable little earner. He made this a family reunion as well as a birthday event and collected together many of my Wilson cousins, some of whom I had not seen since sister Jane's wedding in 1962.

We had not been a close family, the cousins at least, and I had difficulty recognising some of them. We had obviously all grown older, some more graciously than others, and now paraded our offspring proudly to the family. Ceci had not been able to attend on this occasion as she had just had an operation in Guayaquil, but I had my three children with me and very proud of them I was too. With their father's height and mother's colouring, they are very good-looking children. And this is not just a father's opinion: Diana has recently been working successfully as a model in Milan.

Following the queen's garden party, we all headed back to Yorkshire. All plus one, in fact, as Nick had his Spanish girlfriend with him, who was confusingly also called Diana. There we collected together our safari kit because we were on our way to see Alex in Tanzania.

This was the third and latest in our great Armstrong family holidays. We had had a wonderful tour to Yellowstone Park in the States and from there to San Francisco and Vancouver in 1991 when Rachael, Doug and Margaret's granddaughter had come with us. This was followed in 1995 by our trip to New Zealand, where Nick had been working in his gap year on David Davison's farm near Christchurch. Ceci and I flew out from Ecuador and the girls from the UK and we met Nick there. Then we spent two glorious weeks touring the South Island before flying to Australia to visit Emilie, Mitch and their children in Sydney, where we spent four days. Then we went on to Hong Kong and thence to Beijing where, of course, we walked the Great Wall and saw the Forbidden City, and so back to our respective bases, Nick returning with us.

Now we were about to embark on the third of the series. We flew to Amsterdam and from there to Kilimanjaro airport in Tanzania, where Alex was waiting for us. This was an organised tour and we were met at the airport, stayed overnight in a charming hotel outside Arusha, the Safari Spa, then flew over the Serengeti in a little plane. We landed at Seronera, where Karachi, our guide, met us with an extended Land-rover and drove us through the Serengeti to Lobo campsite. Here the tour operator had erected a camp just for us with six attendants to wait on us. We had lunch then spent the rest of the day viewing the huge number of animals present. We saw many species including lions, but those that we saw on the first day were just visible, lying in the long dry grass on their backs with paws in the air. As in the Stanley Holloway rhyme *Albert And The Lion*, seeing them lying there so quiet like just didn't seem right to the child. We suggested to the guide that we get out of the car and take a closer look but that was strictly against the rules.

We went back to the camp that night and after an excellent dinner to bed. Ceci and I had hardly climbed into bed when we heard the roar of a lion. I then had to get her down from the inside of the tent roof. 'It's probably a baboon,' I said, anxious for some sleep. 'That's a lion and tomorrow I am leaving for a proper hotel.' She calmed down eventually but then the lion roared again, at what sounded like five yards away. She shot up in tears this time — that was it. She was going to be eaten alive and it had been a bloody stupid idea of mine to camp where lions feed and so on. Eventually, we had some sleep. I said nothing about the disclaimer I had had to sign agreeing that if we were eaten, we would make no claim against the park.

The next day was again excellent and we were all very happy as we saw many more animals including a pride of lions hunting. They had killed a buffalo in the night and as we arrived, we watched as the pride was chased away by another bigger pride. When lions run, everything runs and we saw giraffes, warthogs, zebras, antelopes and wildebeest dashing away in every direction. Then we drew closer and saw the lions eating their kill.

Later, we saw a graceful cheetah loping along and large numbers of elephants. On our third and last day of camping, we caught up with the great migration and had a glimpse of the 1,500,000 wildebeest and thousands of zebras, which travel the 200 or so miles each year following the rains.

On the last night at camp, we once again had an excellent dinner in the mess tent and the waiter collected up the plates to take them to the kitchen. He went outside and we heard a crash of broken crockery and a shout of SIMBA! He had almost walked on a lioness, which was following her cubs into the camp. Karachi was quite up to the situation and, grabbing his torch, he ran out of the tent and flashed it in the lioness's eyes. She turned and quietly walked away. Then he followed her a little distance in the Land-rover until she was well away from the camp. The waiter was paralysed with fear. One more step and he could have been badly mauled. This set Ceci off again about the dangers I had exposed the family to. But we all soon went to bed and a good night's sleep.

The following day we struck camp, said goodbye to our excellent staff and were driven by Karachi to see the Leakey Museum, where Dr Richard Leakey discovered Lucy, an early hominid. Then we went on to a Masai village, where the villagers danced for us (and insisted that we join in), and finally to the Ngorongoro Crater, where we stayed at what must rank as one of the most splendid hotels in the world, the Ngorongoro Crater Lodge. It is perched on the rim of the crater with a magnificent view down into it. The rooms are luxurious cabins, where your bath is run for you and the water strewn with rose petals. This was followed by drinks and dinner in the central building.

The following day, we drove into the crater and, apart from seeing more of the same, there were rhinos and flamingos. As the day ended and we were returning for a second night at the hotel, something magical happened. A huge bull elephant came out of the bush to cross the road and Karachi stopped the Land-rover right in its path. Closer and closer came the elephant until we were urging that we drive on, but Karachi waited and the elephant stopped just a couple of yards from the car and stood looking at us. Then he walked around the car and away. Nick, who had been filming the whole safari, captured some very impressive close-up footage.

We had seen all the larger animals except for the leopard and it had been the most wonderful experience. We left the game park the next day and drove to a landing strip, where we flew to Arusha and spent some time buying souvenirs before flying on to Zanzibar, where we stayed at the Serena Inn. The hotel was excellent but Zanzibar, or Stonetown at least, is rather rundown and dirty.

We ate our last dinner of the holiday at Mtonis, a beach restaurant nearby, which was really good and Ceci and I were toasted by the young for providing a really memorable holiday. Nick, the family joker, had us in tears of laughter with his description of the sacrificial wildebeest which, it appears, have been put on earth for the sole purpose of feeding lions. They can neither run fast enough nor fight so there they go, as he suggested, calling for volunteers to provide each day's lion dinner.

Returning to Ferngill on a Sunday, we had the forty-third annual Armstrong Cup at Ripon the following day. Sixty people were invited for lunch in a box

Ceci presenting the Armstrong Cup at Ripon to the winning owner Noel Hetherton. Colin, Nick, Diana and their cousin Louise Henderson 1986.

on the course and to see the cup presented to the winning owner by Ceci. We had each invited some friends and had a lovely day catching up with everybody. Cousin Sue Piggott was there, as always. She and her brother Robert sponsor the race jointly with us and she had hosted it on the previous year when we did not get over. I made some £50 from the Tote too, which is a very rare event for me.

As consul in Guayaquil, I am a member of the Consular Corps which holds events during the year to honour countries on their national days and to keep us in touch with government ministers, who we need to know when we have visiting dignitaries from our own countries. There is also a Ladies of the Consular Corps for our wives and consuls who happen to be ladies. They run two charity clinics in poor parts of Guayaquil and have done a terrific job over the years, Ceci being very involved in this work.

Recently, the Consular Corps held a dinner to mark the millennium and recognition was given to the consulates which had been established longest in Guayaquil. It was rather like watching the results of the Oscars. The dean of the corps began by naming those who had been in existence for more than fifty years. A parchment was given to each with polite applause. Then he went on to those that had been present for sixty years and so on up to 150 years. There was no sign of Great Britain. Then, with a flourish, he announced: 'The longest-established Consulate is...Great Britain.' Our consulate had been set up way back in 1825, soon after independence from Spain in 1822. I stood up and proudly walked to the front to receive our parchment, which is now framed in the consulate.

EPILOGUE

NUMBER FIFTY-FIVE Los Lagos is a tall, white house built in the American plantation style with a flat roof and terrace above and tall pillars at the front. We bought the plot of land ten years ago and on my birthday, the 9th September, 1996, began to build the house. Giselle Saporitti designed it to fit in to the rather unusual wedge-shaped plot and she supervised the construction and decoration over the two and a quarter years that it took to build. We finally moved in in December 1998 and, after some disorientation because it is twice the size of our old flat, we have now adapted to it and it serves us very well. Ceci is an enthusiastic hostess and we entertain on more nights than we spend alone, normally inviting only comfortable friends like Trevor and Roci Harding, Peter Calstrom (Sueco), Martha Cevallos, Javier Pino and Amelia Pinoagote, who play cards with Ceci while I have my nose in a book. But at least two or three times a month, we hold a more formal dinner party in the dining room decorated with the Indian mural painted so expertly by Sebastian Wakefield. He painted it on canvas in his studio in Kettlewell in the Yorkshire Dales and then brought it out to Ecuador and spent the New Year with us with Ann Lister, his partner, while putting it on the wall. The girls at last have a room of their own instead of having to share, and I have a library to store my hundreds of books and, of course, the booze cabinet from where the necessary 'crafty one' comes as I stagger in from work. Ceci has her garden which, although quite small, is beautifully kept.

We now have three dogs to go with the house. These are dear old Charlie and Phoebe, the beagles, and Shushi, a Japanese mongrel, which we inherited when its owner's yacht capsized in the Pacific. Derek Hitchings, his daughter Harriet and Shushi were rescued by a passing vessel and brought to Guayaquil. After a week with us, Derek and Harriet left for England but Shushi would have required quarantine and so remained with us. She is a fluffy little hound and is fast working her way into Ceci's affections, being allowed on the sofas when the others are not.

Los Lagos is a walled enclosure of some sixty houses surrounding a lake in the new area of Guayaquil, being developed on a stretch of land over the bridge from the city. Almost all of the development is of this type, which allows security at the gate of each enclosure. Robbery is an increasing problem as the population of Guayaquil grows to over 2,500,000.

Today, 10th November 2000, as always, I drive out of Los Lagos at about half past seven, over the bridge and towards the cemetery, admiring the Agripac advert on the hoarding 'Number one in farmers' supplies'. I like that — a bit of one-upmanship. The competition has to pass it too, which probably spoils its day.

EPILOGUE

Diana, Nick and Alex with Sushi (The shipwrecked hound) Christmas 1999 in Los Logos.

Colin and Ceci 2000.

So, by twists and turns, I arrive at Agripac. As you pass the Ministry of Agriculture building, you can see the yellow and green Agripac building at the end of the street some ten blocks away. Driving past the security guards and into the patio in the middle of the several buildings that are our offices, I park and head into the oldest building and up the stairs to my office. This is where I have sat and worked for some twenty-three years and it is more or less the same as when we originally furnished it. Sueco has just finished smartly reupholstering my chair. He is an expert in restoring furniture.

I sit down and switch on the laptop. Five years ago, I would not have known what to do with one. Now, although no expert, I turn it on in the morning and gaze at it all day, obtaining statistics from the mainframe with which to run the company and e-mails from many sources. My children all communicate in this way: Nick from his job with Zeneca in Madrid; Diana from Leeds University, where she is reading languages and Alex from Newcastle University, where she is studying philosophy.

Roci comes in to say good morning. My sister-in-law and secretary for seventeen years manages to juggle Agripac work, the consulate and her husband and four children's lives and still keep sane. She is really the face of the consulate, fielding the problems and helping all who come to us, only referring to me

EPILOGUE

when she cannot fix it alone. Today, she started with bad news. 'We have another British man arrested for drug smuggling.' Damn! We have had a respite since the last one, a girl of eighteen, was arrested a year ago. She is still on remand and if not tried soon, will be freed under the new law.

On to Agripac business. Sales of knapsack sprayers are much better than we projected. Where is the next import? Chris's office is next to mine and we have a joke about the number of times I put my head in there each day. Well, it is easy, I guess, and we often chat about other things too. The sales conference at Rodeo is in the offing and I want to know how many of our suppliers are invited so I call Victor Hugo. Liz, our treasurer, calls to see where to allocate the free cash to overseas payments. I call Antonio Zambrano, our first employee, now twenty-eight years with the company and the manager for the province of Manabi. He has a cattle farm too so, after talking about sales, we turn to our hobby, cattle. Then Maria comes in with a cup of tea. There is a fax from Elaine regarding the cost of the new Forbidden Corner car park.

The morning passes and Ceci turns up for lunch. We go to Bandurria together, where there is cheery chatter from the fifty people eating. The company is in good form. We are prepared for a really good season, we have taken on more staff and are searching for new shop locations. Moreover, rumour has it that the Old Man is considering a pay rise.

This afternoon, I must finish the book as I leave for England in a few days and have an appointment with my publisher. I have been working on it for over two years now, although the original idea goes back much further to when I began to research history to write the background for the early times. I am an avid reader of biography and enjoy reading the lives of others. I hope that you have found my story interesting.